J. J. Abrams: Interviews

Conversations with Filmmakers Series
Gerald Peary, General Editor

J. J. Abrams
INTERVIEWS

Edited by Brent Dunham

University Press of Mississippi / Jackson

www.upress.state.ms.us

The University Press of Mississippi is a member of the Association of University Presses.

First printing 2019
∞

Library of Congress Cataloging-in-Publication Data

Names: Dunham, Brent, editor.
Title: J. J. Abrams : interviews / edited by Brent Dunham.
Description: Jackson : University Press of Mississippi, [2018] | Series:
Conversations with filmmakers series | Includes index. |
Identifiers: LCCN 2018017429 (print) | LCCN 2018019070 (ebook) |
ISBN 9781496820433 (epub single) | ISBN 9781496820440 (epub in-
stititional) | ISBN 9781496820457 (pdf single) | ISBN 9781496820464
(pdf institutional) | ISBN 9781496820419 (cloth : alk. paper) | ISBN
9781496820426 (pbk. : alk. paper)
Subjects: LCSH: Abrams, J. J. (Jeffrey Jacob), 1966-—Interviews. |
Motion picture producers and directors—United States—Inter-
views. | Screenwriters—United States—Interviews.
Classification: LCC PN1998.3.A27 (ebook) | LCC PN1998.3.A27 A5 2018
(print) | DDC 791.4302/33092—dc23
LC record available at https://lccn.loc.gov/2018017429

British Library Cataloging-in-Publication Data available

Contents

Introduction

Jeffrey Jacob Abrams has wanted to be J. J. Abrams since he was eight years old. During his formative years, Abrams obtained two items that had a major impact: a Super 8 camera and a mystery box from Tannen's Magic Store. With the camera, Abrams would enter a life of filmmaking, beginning with short films testing special effects make-up and car chases. With the mystery box, he would be forever drawn to the unknown, the allure of the secret and boundless imagination. Abrams still owns the mystery box and has yet to open it. Over the last twenty-seven years, Abrams has risen through the Hollywood ranks from a college senior with dreams of selling his first screenplay to a TV mogul and film director whose films have grossed billions around the world. His career was born out of an insatiable drive and exuberance for the work, with a dash of serendipity. "I've always wanted to be a director,"[1] proclaimed Abrams at fifteen, in the first of many interviews he would give during a career so dripping with destiny, it could only happen in Hollywood.

Despite Abrams's father being a TV producer, it was his grandfather, Harry Kelvin, who seemed to have the most influence on his future career in filmmaking. Kelvin was an electrician and would bring home gadgets to show young Jeffrey Jacob the inner workings, to see how a thing is made and to appreciate the craftsmanship. Abrams would later attribute these lessons to his own obsession with design and construction. Abrams pays homage to his late grandfather in many of his films and television shows: Kelvin Ridge is a location in *Star Wars: The Force Awakens*, the USS *Kelvin* was the starship captained by Kirk's father in *Star Trek*, and Kelvin was a character who once occupied the Hatch on *Lost*. As a kid, Abrams lived and breathed movies. Like his idol and future collaborator, Steven Spielberg, movie making was a lifestyle, not a hobby. It was a trip to Universal Studios when he was eight that Abrams recalls as being absolutely inspirational. "It galvanized the dream for me of writing and direction for film and television."[2] Later, when his father was working on the Paramount lot, he sat in on rehearsals for shows like *Happy Days* and *Mork and Mindy*. Like his grandfather showing him the inside of a radio, these behind-the-scenes experiences showed him how the cogs and gears of Hollywood turned.

In 1982, the *Los Angeles Times* printed an article that landed his first project with Steven Spielberg. "Beardless Wonders of Film Making" by Robert Young was a brief story about a local festival of amateur filmmaking called "The Best Teen Super 8 Films of '81," where Abrams's film *High Voltage* won the audience award. On the brink of releasing both *Poltergeist* and *E.T.: The Extra-Terrestrial*, Spielberg reached out through his then-assistant (and Abrams's future boss), Kathleen Kennedy. Spielberg asked Abrams and his friend, Matt Reeves, another future Hollywood director who also had a film in the festival, to repair his own early 8mm films. Abrams and Reeves completed the job and were paid $300. Coming full circle nearly thirty years later, Spielberg helped produce Abrams's *Super 8*, a heavily autobiographical love letter to his childhood filmmaking pastime.

Also in 1982, J. J. earned his first credit on a feature film, *Nightbeast*, for which he contributed sound effects and to the musical score. This low-budget horror film was written and directed by Baltimore filmmaker Don Dohler, who also published *Cinemagic*, a sci-fi/horror magazine. It was when young Abrams started writing letters to the magazine that Dohler responded and asked the sixteen-year-old to work on his movie. Said Abrams, "It was just a very exciting thing, to be involved in a movie on any level. And then to get a credit on a movie was literally the thing that all my life I had said, 'If I get my name on a movie, a credit on a film, I could die happy.'"[3]

Abrams did not attend film school. With his father's advice ("It's more important that you go off and learn what to make movies about than how to make movies."[4]), Abrams attended Sarah Lawrence College. Four years later, with graduation looming, Abrams was a bit panicked about his next step. It was a chance encounter with a friend that provided a solution. In 2017, Abrams delivered the commencement speech at Sarah Lawrence, and he shared this story with the graduates: "I was heading down an escalator in LA when someone called my name—heading up the escalator beside me was Jill Mazursky, whom I'd met freshman year through a friend at Sarah Lawrence. She was a writer, had sold scripts, and had an agent. In an act of self-preservation, I suggested we write something together. We did. And we sold it to Disney."[5] From there, Abrams has gone from project to project and has yet to slow down.

Talk show host Tavis Smiley once dubbed Abrams "Mr. Everything,"[6] a succinct and accurate moniker. He is a multitasker of the highest degree, not because he *has* to be but because he *wants* to be. Abrams is motivated more by the "coolness" of a project than the potential profit. He hasn't always been successful—he's had more TV shows fizzle out than he's had hits. Yet, he bounces right back. Has Abrams's passion for the work faded over the years, especially after hitting a milestone like directing a *Star Wars* film that became the highest-grossing film of all time? No, he is still the scrappy, hungry dreamer he was at fifteen.

What many interviewers point out is just how prolific Abrams is. His name has been attached to multiple projects at any given time, and he is visible and participatory, even those in which his role is minimal. For *Cloverfield* and its pseudosequel, *10 Cloverfield Lane*, Abrams still gives interviews, despite merely being the films' producer. He cocreated *Lost* and was only creatively involved for the first season, but he is asked about that show repeatedly. There is a tendency within these interviews to treat them as "his" projects, but, again, Abrams will make sure to name who actually did the heavy lifting.

Why, then, would he subject himself to press tours and junkets, what many actors and directors abhor? Perhaps after becoming such a household name, Abrams is leaned on by the studios for his celebrity. Perhaps, and more likely, he is just enthusiastic about the projects and wants to talk about them.

Despite working on major studio projects, with the inflated budgets and extensive resources available, Abrams is still in his heart a lo-fi filmmaker. Greg Grunberg, a childhood friend and roommate, recalls one of their earliest projects, a short film called *The Attic*, and notes Abrams's skill at creative problem-solving. "He shot it, then scratched in the monster, frame by frame. It was a bolt-of-lightning creature. He compensated ahead of time for where the monster would be," Grunberg says. "We were, like, eleven."[7] A more recent example of this ingenuity can be found during the production of *Star Trek*. In the space-drop sequence, when Kirk and Sulu are plummeting to the surface of Vulcan, Abrams and his crew found a simple, cheap, and elegant solution to filming the actors mid-drop. Instead of a wire rig suspending the actors in front of a green screen, where a digital sky would later be added, he filmed them outside, standing on a mirror, looking up. The sky was captured in the mirror, and Abrams himself manually shook the camera to simulate the motion of wind and falling. He is in charge of a $150 million film, and he's using the same old-school, poor man's techniques he would have used for *The Attic*. According to Abrams, the biggest misconception people have about him is "that what I do is work instead of fun."[8]

After resuscitating franchises like *Mission: Impossible*; *Star Trek*; *Star Wars*; and *Westworld*, Abrams has been dubbed "The Master of the Hollywood Sequel."[9] Despite the fact that these projects represent a fraction of his overall output, the reputation has stuck, and it's something Abrams has been trying (and failing) to shake. "The last thing anybody wants to be known as is 'The Rebooter,'"[10] Abrams tells John Hiscock.

While Hollywood seems less and less likely to invest in original properties, Abrams might be considered complicit in the industry's seemingly incurable sequel-itis. Abrams explains, "I do think that if you're telling a story that is not moving anything forward, that's not introducing anything that's relevant, that's not creating a new mythology or an extension of it, then a complete remake of something feels like a mistake."[11] An argument can be made that his approach to these new iterations is closer to a redesign than a copy. For *Mission: Impossible III*, it was his idea to focus on IMF Agent Ethan Hunt's personal life, something we hadn't seen in the first two films and something that would raise the emotional stakes for his character. For his next film, the reboot of the now-fifty-year-old *Star Trek* franchise, Abrams's radical approach avoided the trappings of a traditional remake. He used time travel to reset the entire timeline of the *Star Trek* cannon, which, naturally, angered some fans but then allowed the filmmakers to explore new avenues and possibilities with these well-worn characters. After the success of *Cloverfield*, a sequel took eight years to be released—and it was barely even a sequel. *10 Cloverfield Lane* is different in almost every way from the first film in style, scope, and genre. Instead of another giant monster movie, it is a taut and claustrophobic thriller heavily inspired by *The Twilight Zone*.

After *Star Trek: Into Darkness*, and counter to his wishes to create instead of re-create, he was offered a dream job. Kathleen Kennedy, head of Lucasfilm, approached Abrams about directing *Star Wars: The Force Awakens*, the first project since the company was acquired by Disney for a whopping $4 billion. His first impulse was to politely take himself out of the running—he wanted to distance himself from yet another sequel. In the end, his wife, Katie, was the voice of reason, "If you say, 'No,' you will regret it." Abrams said, "Yes" and continued his reign.

After *The Force Awakens*'s release, we find Abrams once again claiming that he was finished with sequel-making. On the red carpet of the 2017 Golden Globes, when asked if he would consider doing another reboot, Abrams related his stance in no uncertain terms, "I don't feel any desire to do that again. I feel like I've done enough of that, and I am more excited about working on things that are original ideas that, perhaps one day, someone else will have to reboot." His current roster of projects being produced by Bad Robot, however, includes new entries in the *Star Wars*, *Star Trek*, *Mission: Impossible*, and *Cloverfield* sagas; film adaptations of videogames like "Half-Life" and "Portal"; a new season of *Westworld*; and a newish take on the Stephen King universe with *Castle Rock*. With the recent announcement that Abrams is climbing back into the director's chair once again for *Star Wars: Episode IX*, it seems his wish to stop making sequels has been postponed once again.

Outside of film and television, J. J. Abrams has produced in a few other mediums. In 2009, Abrams was the guest editor of *WIRED* magazine and turned the issue into a giant puzzle. He even produced a novel, *S.*, in 2013, with author Doug Dorst. In his discussion with Peter Sciretta on *10 Cloverfield Lane*, Abrams provides his own modest definition of his role on these projects: "I was just trying to do what a producer does, which is help out."[12] In 2017, Abrams further expanded his repertoire by bringing *The Play That Goes Wrong* to Broadway.

Abrams is constantly recognizing and thanking his collaborators. Nearly every interview he gives makes mention of those working with him and just how essential those collaborations have been. This philosophy of sharing credit was inspired by another pivotal moment in his adolescence. In 1980, Abrams's father took him to a rough-cut screening of John Carpenter's *Escape from New York*. Along with Spielberg, Carpenter was one of his heroes. After the film, Carpenter asked questions of his audience, requesting feedback. The idea that this master filmmaker was soliciting advice and willing to listen to everyone in the room was illuminating for young Abrams. "It was an amazing thing to watch someone . . . be so open to the better idea, no matter where it came from. It was an inspiring thing to see."[13] Abrams hasn't lost this deep appreciation for collaboration—and it doesn't seem likely that he will. Reading an interview from 2006 alongside an interview after *The Force Awakens* broke records, one would find it very difficult to track any differences. What will become evident to readers of this collection is Abrams's humility and gratitude.

Abrams is a populist filmmaker. As Paul Byrne suggests in his interview collected here, Abrams is "more *Star Wars* than *La Strada*."[14] But Abrams has never tried or pretended to be anything else, as Clint Morris accurately sums it up, "J. J. Abrams is clearly a fan before he's a filmmaker."[15] Some artists will use their medium to communicate something internal, but that doesn't necessarily become accessible for a mass audience. Abrams uses his mediums to give people that same rollercoaster experience he gravitated to as a kid. His stories are big and loud, but without sacrificing the heart, and they, inevitably, contain a strong vein of mystery running throughout.

Mystery pervades Abrams's work, and this tendency is famously explained during his TED Talk in 2007 where he described the Magic Mystery Box he bought as a kid. The box has remained unopened for over forty years because, according to Abrams, "It represents infinite possibility. It represents hope. It represents potential."[16] Abrams goes further with a mantra that clearly defines his output in the last twenty years: "[M]ystery is the catalyst for imagination."[17] In films such as *Cloverfield* and *Super 8*, and television shows like *Lost* and *Fringe*, the secrecy behind the projects, especially during the marketing campaigns leading up to their release, reaches national security levels.

Richard Corliss, writing for *TIME*, calls Abrams's love of secrecy "the art of withholding."[18] Abrams is aware that, despite his good intentions, this cloak-and-dagger approach to his projects might have a downside. "There's a really positive side to keeping quiet. You can protect the audience from spoilers or certain moments that, in a way, obviate the movie experience. But, on the other hand, you risk being seen as coy or as a withholding shithead. That's never my intent."[19] In 2002, Abrams wrote a script called *Superman: Flyby*, an early attempt to reboot the Man of Steel. This script was leaked and reviewed (quite savagely) online. The outcry was enough for Warner Bros. to shelve the script completely. It made

Abrams paranoid[20] and has greatly influenced his subsequent projects, but that's not the only reason he keeps his cards close to the chest. It also comes from a more philosophical approach that seems antithetical to our times. "We're smack dab in the middle of the Age of Immediacy,"[21] Abrams writes in a piece for *WIRED* magazine in 2009. For all the benefits of the internet being able to answer any question immediately, our appreciation for knowledge and experience seems to be in decline. Abrams elaborates, "True understanding (or skill or effort) has become bothersome—an unnecessary headache that impedes our ability to get on with our lives (and most likely skip to something else)."[22] Abrams curated this issue of *WIRED* with puzzles and mysteries on every page in the hopes of keeping the sanctity of inquisitiveness alive. When an entire season of a TV show can be consumed instantly, Abrams's withholding, in some ways, is a gift. In other words, there are few surprises left in our world, especially entertainment, and Abrams wants to help prevent that atrophy. "Mystery demands that you stop and consider—or, at the very least, slow down and discover. It's a challenge to get there yourself, on its terms, not yours."[23]

Any profile of J. J. Abrams would be incomplete without mentioning the philanthropic work he's done with his wife, Katie. In 2012, they founded the Katie McGrath and J. J. Abrams Family Foundation, a nonprofit organization that donates to several causes including education, the environment, civil rights, and healthcare. Katie was a member of the board for Children's Defense Fund, whose mission is to "educate the nation about the needs of children and encourages preventive investments before they get sick, drop out of school, get into trouble or suffer family breakdown."[24] In 2014, Abrams teamed up with theory11 to create designer mystery boxes, the proceeds of which would go to 826 National, an organization cofounded by author Dave Eggers that provides creative writing classes and tutoring for underresourced children. In 2017, McGrath and Abrams were executive producers on a short, animated film titled *100 Years*, directed by Lena Dunham, chronicling the history of Planned Parenthood. Abrams is also a member of the Creative Council at Represent.us, a political action group focused on passing anticorruption legislation.

For *Star Trek: Into Darkness*, Abrams and Bad Robot got involved with the Mission Continues, founded by Eric Greitens, whose goal is to provide education, jobs, and support for returning military veterans. Abrams cast Greitens and other veterans as extras in a scene in *Into Darkness* and the film is "dedicated to our post-9/11 veterans with gratitude for their inspired service abroad and continued leadership at home."[25] Proceeds from Bad Robot Interactive's FX app were donated to the Mission Continues, and campaigns were coordinated within the marketing of the film to raise awareness and show support. Inspired by the success of this campaign, Abrams and Bad Robot partner Bryan Burk formed a division called Good Robot that continues these charitable projects. In conjunction with the Bad Robot–produced TV series, *Revolution*, in which Earth is devastated by a global blackout, Good Robot lead an initiative between the UN and NBC to educate people about the real-life circumstances where 1 in 5 people on Earth live without power. In 2014, UNICEF partnered with Disney and Lucasfilm for Force for Change, where fans who donated could win a chance to be an extra in *The Force Awakens*. That program successfully raised over $4 million. Abrams is also working actively to increase diversity, both in front of and behind the camera. After the Oscar nominations were announced in early 2016, and all twenty acting nominees were white, for the second year in a row, the #OscarsSoWhite hashtag became a cultural talking point. Abrams was inspired by this, what he calls "a wake-up call,"[26] and set a new standard for future Bad Robot productions. Bad Robot "teamed with its agency, CAA, and studio partners (Warner Bros. and Paramount) to require that women and minorities are submitted for writing, directing, and acting jobs for the company in proportion to their representation in the US population."[27]

Acknowledgments

Consistent with the standards set by the University Press of Mississippi and the Conversations with Filmmakers series, all interviews within are unabridged and unedited from their original source. A conscious effort was made to locate interviews from a variety of regions, sources, and mediums. Represented here are interviews from top news publications like the *Telegraph* and the *Los Angeles Times* as well as independent blogs and Q&A sessions. Some of the interviews have been transcribed to the best of my ability and are now printed for the first time. An attempt was also made to not favor any one film, show, or era, thus giving the less successful projects as much attention as the major hits.

I would like to thank the publication liaisons who were instrumental in assembling this collection: Erica Varela at the *LA Times*; Susan Quatresols at NPR; Rosie Guerin from *Charlie Rose*; Olivier Sherman at TED; Grant Ossler at the *Onion*; Brooke Hunter at Femail; Vincent Donnelly at Movies.ie; Dawn O'Driscoll at the *Telegraph*; Kyle Joe, Chris Kapalowski, Paul Sommer, and Risa Rosenfield at CTV; Brad Miska at Bloody Disgusting; June Williams at Buzzymag; Patrice Leymarie at Iamag.co; John Owens at UKTV; author Doug Dorst; Pamela Brown at Little, Brown and Company and Mulholland Books; and Stephen Pizzello at the American Society of Cinematographers.

I would also like to thank the writers whose contributions have made this a fantastic project to work on: Robert Young for the *LA Times*; Ed Gross for Voices from Krypton; David Bianculli for NPR; Peter Canavese for Groucho Reviews; Clint Morris for MovieHole; Noel Murray for the AV Club; Paul Fischer for Femail; Rob Carnevale for IndieLondon; Paul Byrne for Movies.ie; Peter Sciretta for /Film;

John Hiscock and Horatia Harrod for The *Telegraph*; Tyrone Warner for CTV; Chris Eggertsen for Bloody Disgusting; Mat Toomey for the Film Pie; Abbie Bernstein for Buzzymag; Andrew Fish for the *American Cinematographer* magazine; and Tara Salinas for Trippin' with Tara.

BD

Notes

1. Robert Young, "Beardless Wonders of Film Making." *Los Angeles Times*. 25 March 1982.

2. Steven Prig1ge, *Created By: Inside the Minds of TV's To1p Show Creators*. Silman-James Press, 2005.

3. Jen Chaney, "J. J. Abrams, Director of *Super 8* on How He Got His First Gig, Courtesy of *Nightbeast*." *The Washington Post*. 7 June 2011. www.washingtonpost.com/blogs/ celebritology/post/jj-abrams-director-of-super-8-on-how-he-got-his-first-film-gig -courtesy-of-nightbeast/2011/06/07/AGiCkHLH_blog.html?utm_term=.000fe100f7e3. Accessed 31 October 2017.

4. "J. J. Abrams: On Filmmaking." *BAFTA Guru*. 1 May 2013. guru.bafta.org/jj-abrams-filmmaking. Accessed 31 October 2017.

5. J. J. Abrams, Sarah Lawrence College Commencement Speech. 19 May 2017. www .sarahlawrence.edu/news-events/commencement/undergraduate/jj-abrams.html. Accessed 31 October 2017.

6. Tavis Smiley, "Writer-Director-Producer J. J. Abrams." *Tavis Smiley*. 24 September 2013. www .pbs.org/wnet/tavissmiley/interviews/j-j-abrams/. Accessed 31 October 2017.

7. Bill Keveney, "The Many Aliases of J. J. Abrams." *USA TODAY*. 4 January 2005. usatoday30 .usatoday.com/life/television/news/2005-01-04-abrams_x.htm. Accessed 31 October 2017.

8. Edward Lewine, "LA Confidential." *The New York Times Magazine*. 16 April 2006. nyti .ms/2iQ1vEd. Accessed 31 October 2017.

9. Tom Huddleston Jr., "Why J. J. Abrams Is the Master of the Hollywood Sequel." *Fortune*. 16 December 2015. fortune.com/2015/12/16/jj-abrams-star-wars-sequels/. Accessed 31 October 2017.

10. John Hiscock, "J. J. Abrams Interview for *Star Trek: Into Darkness*." *The Telegraph*. 8 May 2013. www.telegraph.co.uk/culture/film/starsandstories/10042180/J-J-Abrams-interview-for-Star -Trek-Into-Darkness.html. Accessed 31 October 2017.

11. Aurelie Corinthios, "J. J. Abrams Says He's Done with Reboots: 'I'm More Excited about Original Ideas.'" Interview with JD Heyman. 8 January 2017. people.com/awards/golden -globes-2017-jj-abrams-done-with-reboots/. Accessed 31 October 2017.

12. Peter Sciretta, "Interview: J. J. Abrams Talks *10 Cloverfield Lane*, The 'Clover-Verse', Cannibal Airlines, and More." 10 March 2016. www.slashfilm.com/jj-abrams-interview-10-cloverfield -lane/. Accessed 31 October 2017.

13. Jonathan Tropper, "J. J. Abrams and Doug Dorst." *Meet the Author*. 24 November 2013. itunes. apple.com/us/podcast/meet-the-author/id266215977?mt=2. Accessed 31 October 2017.

14. "J. J. Abrams—Director of *Star Trek: Into Darkness*, *Star Wars* & the *LOST* Finale." *Youtube*, uploaded by Movies Ireland, 4 May 2009. www.youtube.com/watch?v=Zv58vpYoCT8. Accessed 31 October 2017.

15. Clint Morris, "Interview: J. J. Abrams & Michelle Monaghan." *MovieHole*. m.webwombat.com .au/entertainment/movies/mi3-int.htm. Accessed 31 October 2017.

16. J. J. Abrams, "The Mystery Box." TED Talk. March. 2007. www.ted.com/talks/j_j_abrams_ mystery_box. Accessed 31 Oct. 2017.

17. Abrams, "The Mystery Box."

18. Richard Corliss, "'What the Hell Would Spielberg Do Here?: J. J. Abrams Talks *Super 8*.'" *Time*. 6 June 2011. entertainment.time.com/2011/06/06/super-8-director-jj-abrams-interview/. Accessed 31 October. 2017.

19. Scott Dadich, "Lucky VII: Superfan J. J. Abrams on Directing *The Force Awakens*." December 2015. www.wired.com/2015/11/star-wars-force-awakens-jj-abrams-interview/. Accessed 31 October 2017.

20. Charlie Rose, "J. J. Abrams." *Charlie Rose*. 15 June 2011. charlierose.com/videos/14269. Accessed 31 October 2017.

21. J. J. Abrams, "J. J. Abrams on the Magic of Mystery." 20 April 2009. www.wired.com/2009/04/ mf-jjessay/. Accessed 31 October 2017.

22. Abrams, "J. J. Abrams on the Magic of Mystery."

23. Abrams, "J. J. Abrams on the Magic of Mystery."

24. "About Us." Children's Defense Fund. www.childrensdefense.org/about/. Accessed 31 October 2017.

25. *Star Trek: Into Darkness*. Directed by J. J. Abrams. Paramount Studios, 2013.

26. Rebecca Ford, "How J. J. Abrams's Bad Robot Is Bringing More Diversity to Hollywood." *The Hollywood Reporter*. 2 March 2016. www.hollywoodreporter.com/news/how-jj-abrams-bad -robot-872119. Accessed 31 October 2017.

27. Ford.

Chronology

1966   Jeffrey Jacob born on June 27 in New York City to Gerald and Carol Abrams. He is joined by a sister, Tracy, two years later.

1971   The Abrams family moves to Los Angeles.

1973   A visit to Universal Studios sparks Abrams's interest in filmmaking. Begins making films on Super 8mm.

1980   Abrams's father takes him to a rough-cut screening of John Carpenter's *Escape from New York*.

1982   Participates in Best Teen Super 8mm Films of '81 festival and wins the audience award for his forty-five-minute horror/comedy, *High Voltage*. First interview is published in the *Los Angeles Times*. Earns his first feature film credit by contributing music and sound effects to a low-budget horror film called *Nightbeast*.

1984   Graduates from Palisades High School.

1988   Graduates from Sarah Lawrence College. Sells his first screenplay that would later be made as *Taking Care of Business*, starring Jim Belushi.

1989   Meets with Steven Spielberg to work on an outline for a sequel to *Who Framed Roger Rabbit?*

1990   *Taking Care of Business* is released.

1991   *Regarding Henry* is released. Abrams also has a small role in the film. Earns his first producer credit.

1992   *Forever Young* is released.

1993   Has a small role in *Six Degrees of Separation*.

1994   His group, Propellerheads meets with Jeffrey Katzenberg to work on initial animation tests for *Shrek*.

1996   *The Pallbearer* is released. Has a bit part in *Diabolique*. Marries Katie McGrath.

1997   *Gone Fishin,'* his second collaboration with Jill Mazursky, is released.

1998   *Armageddon* is released. *Felicity* begins airing. First son, Henry, is born.

1999   *The Suburbans* is released. Daughter, Gracie, is born.

2001   *Joy Ride* is released, *Alias* begins airing. Creates production company, Bad Robot, with partner, Bryan Burk.

2004   *Lost* begins airing. Has a small role in *Comic Book Movie*. Assists in the development of a video game based on *Alias*.

2005   Wins two Emmys for *Lost*: Outstanding Direction for a Drama Series and Outstanding Drama Series. Makes an appearance on *Dinner for Five* with Mark Hamill, Kevin Smith, Stan Lee, and Jason Lee.

2006   *Mission: Impossible III* is released. *What About Brian* and *Six Degrees* begin airing. Guest-directs an episode of *Jimmy Kimmel Live*.

2007   Directs an episode of *The Office*.

2008   *Cloverfield* is released. *Fringe* begins airing.

2009   *Star Trek* is released, and Bad Robot is involved in developing a video game based on the film.

2010   *Undercovers* begins airing. *Morning Glory* is released.

2011   *Super 8* and *Mission: Impossible—Ghost Protocol* are released. *Person of Interest* begins airing. Son, August, is born.

2012   *Revolution* and *Alcatraz* begin airing. J. J. and Katie form the Katie McGrath and J. J. Abrams Family Foundation.

2013   *Star Trek: Into Darkness* is released. *Almost Human* begins airing. Awarded the Norman Lear Achievement Award in Television at the Producer's Guild of America Awards. *S.*, a novel co-written with Doug Dorst, is published.

2014   *Believe* begins airing. *Infinitely Polar Bear* is released.

2015   *Star Wars: The Force Awakens* and *Mission: Impossible—Rogue Nation* are released.

2016   *11.22.63*, *Roadies*, *America Divided*, and *Westworld* begin airing. *10 Cloverfield Lane* and *Star Trek: Beyond* are released.

2017   Produces a Broadway run of *The Play That Goes Wrong*. Named Filmmaker of the Year by the American Cinema Editors. *Star Wars: The Last Jedi* is released.

Filmography

Short Films

2004
THE ANIMATED ALIAS: TRIBUNAL
Producers: John Bernstein, Breen Frazier, and David Lipson
Executive Producers: **J. J. Abrams** and Jesse Alexander
Director: David Lipson
Screenplay: Breen Frazier
Editing: Dave Gargani
Music: Brian Aumueller
Production Manager: Steffanie Edwards
Visual Effects: Luciano DiGeronimo
Clean-up Artist: Ben Price
Cast: Jennifer Garner (Sydney Bristow), Terry O'Quinn (FBI Asst. Director
Kendall), Steve Kramer (Rudolph Gaborno), Frank Lyon (Lucian Cezar)
Animation/Live Action, Color
7 minutes

2017
100 YEARS
Producers: Natalie Berkus and Lena Dunham
Executive Producers: **J. J. Abrams**, Andrew Lee, Kirsten Lepore, and Katie
McGrath
Directors: Lena Dunham and Kirsten Lepore
Screenplay: Alex Ronan
Animators: Kirsten Lepore, Rasmus Bak, Olivia Blanc, Kyle Strope, and Zachary
Zezima
Music: Jack Antonoff, **J. J. Abrams**
Sound Designer/Re-Recording Mixer: Matt Yocum
Archival Research: Amani Vance
Cast: America Ferrera (Narrator), Mindy Kaling (Narrator), Jennifer Lawrence
(Narrator), Meryl Streep (Narrator), Constance Wu (Narrator)

Animation, Color

7 minutes

Feature Films

1982

NIGHTBEAST

Production Company: Cinema Enterprises

Producer: Ted A. Bohus (uncredited)

Associate Producers: Don Dohler, Dave Ellis, Pete Garey, Richard Geiwitz, Tom Griffith, Tony Malanowski, Larry Reichman, and George Stover

Director: Don Dohler

Screenplay: Don Dohler

Cinematography: Richard Geiwitz

Editing: Don Dohler

Music: **J. J. Abrams** and Robert J. Walsh

Sound: **J. J. Abrams** (effects), Don Dohler (editor/effects), Greg Dohler (record-ist), Dave Ellis (editor/effects), and Jim Fox (mix engineer)

Cast: Tom Griffith (Sheriff Jack Cinder), Jamie Zemarel (Jamie Lambert), Karin Kardian (Lisa Kent), George Stover (Steven Price), Don Leifert (Drago), Anne Frith (Ruth Sherman), Eleanor Herman (Mary Jane), Richard Dyszel (Mayor Bert Wicker), Greg Dohler (Greg), Kim Pfeiffer (Kim), Monica Neff (Suzie)

16mm, Full Frame (1.37:1), Color

80 minutes

1990

TAKING CARE OF BUSINESS

Production Companies: Hollywood Pictures (presents), Silver Screen Partners IV

Producer: Geoffrey Taylor

Executive Producer: Paul Mazursky

Associate Producer: Elizabeth Sayre

Co-Producer: Duncan Henderson

Director: Arthur Hiller

Screenplay: Jill Mazursky and **J. J. Abrams**

Cinematography: David M. Walsh

Production Design: Jon Hutman

Set Direction: Donald Krafft and Linda Spheeris

Costumes: Marilyn Matthews

Editing: William Reynolds

Music: Stewart Copeland

Casting: Lynn Stalmaster
Cast: James Belushi (Jimmy Dworski), Charles Grodin (Spencer Barnes), Anne De Salvo (Debbie Lipton), Loryn Locklin (Jewel Bentley), Stephen Elliott (Walter Bentley), Hector Elizondo (Warden Toolman), Veronica Hamel (Elizabeth Barnes), Mako (Mr. Sakamoto), Gates McFadden (Diane Connors), John de Lancie (Ted Bradford Jr.), Thom Sharp (Mike Steward), Ken Foree (J.B.)
35mm, Spherical Widescreen (1.85:1), Color
108 minutes

1991
REGARDING HENRY
Production Company: Paramount Pictures
Producers: Mike Nichols and Scott Rudin
Executive Producer: Robert Greenhut
Associate Producer: Susan MacNair
Co-Producer: **J. J. Abrams**
Director: Mike Nichols
Screenplay: **J. J. Abrams**
Cinematography: Giuseppe Rotunno
Production Design: Tony Walton
Art Direction: Dan Davis and William A. Elliott
Costumes: Ann Roth
Editing: Sam O'Steen
Music: Hans Zimmer
Casting: Ellen Lewis and Juliet Taylor
Cast: Harrison Ford (Henry Turner), Annette Bening (Sarah Turner), Michael Haley (Court Clerk), Stanley Swerdlow (Mr. Matthews), Julie Follansbee (Mrs. Matthews), Rebecca Miller (Linda), Bruce Altman (Bruce), Elizabeth Wilson (Jessica), Donald Moffat (Charlie Cameron), Kamian Allen (Rachel Turner), Aida Linares (Rosella), John MacKay (George), Mary Gilbert (Julia), Peter Appel (Eddie the Doorman), Harsh Nayyar (Liquor Store Owner), John Leguizamo (Liquor Store Gunman), Harold House (Policeman), Robin Bartlett (Phyllis), Cynthia Martells (ICU Nurse), James Rebhorn (Dr. Sultan), Brian Smiar (Dr. Marx), May Quigley (Hillary), Bill Nunn (Bradley), Marjorie Monaghan (Julie), Emily Wachtel (Nurse Gloria), Kai Soremekun (Loretta), Suzanne O'Neill (Real Estate Broker), Glen Trotiner (Elevator Man), **J. J. Abrams** (Delivery Boy)
35mm, Spherical Widescreen (1.85:1), Color
108 minutes

1992
FOREVER YOUNG
Production Companies: Warner Bros. (presents), Icon Productions
Producer: Bruce Davey
Executive Producers: **J. J. Abrams** and Edward S. Feldman
Director: Steve Miner
Screenplay: **J. J. Abrams**
Cinematography: Russell Boyd
Production Design: Gregg Fonseca
Art Direction: Bruce Alan Miller
Costumes: Aggie Guerard Rodgers
Editing: Jon Poll
Music: Jerry Goldsmith
Casting: Marion Dougherty
Cast: Mel Gibson (Capt. Daniel McCormick), Jamie Lee Curtis (Claire Cooper),
Elijah Wood (Nat Cooper), Isabel Glasser (Helen), George Wendt (Harry Finley),
Joe Morton (Cameron), Nicholas Surovy (John), David Marshall Grant (Lt. Col.
Wilcox USAF), Robert Hy Gorman (Felix), Millie Slavin (Susan Finley), Michael
A. Goorjian (Steven), Veronica Lauren (Alice), Art La Fleur (Alice's Father), Eric
Pierpoint (Fred), Walton Goggins (Gate MP)
35mm, Spherical Widescreen (1.85:1), Color
102 minutes

1997
GONE FISHIN'
Production Companies: Caravan Pictures, Hollywood Pictures
Producers: Julie Bergman Sender and Roger Birnbaum
Executive Producer: Jill Mazursky
Co-Producers: Lou Arkoff and Richard H. Prince
Director: Christopher Cain
Screenplay: Jill Mazursky and **J. J. Abrams**
Cinematography: Dean Semler
Production Design: Lawrence Miller
Art Direction: Phil Dagort and Michael Rizzo
Costumes: Lizzy Gardiner
Editing: Jack Hofstra
Music: Randy Edelman
Casting: Rick Montgomery and Dan Parada
Cast: Joe Pesci (Joe Waters), Danny Glover (Gus Green), Rosanna Arquette
(Rita), Lynn Whitfield (Angie), Willie Nelson (Billy "Catch" Pooler), Nick Brimble

(Dekker Massey), Gary Grubbs (Phil Beasly), Carol Kane (Donna Waters), Edythe Davis (Cookie Green), Jenna Bari (Gena Waters), Samantha Brown (Tracy Green), Jeff DiLucca (Mack Waters), Jamil Akim O'Quinn (Gregory Green), Frank Nasso (Young Joe), Raynor Scheine (Glenn), Robyn Hackett (Nicky), James R. Greene (Bubba), Steve Wise (J.P.), Claudia Haro (Julie)
35mm, Spherical Widescreen (1.85:1), Color
94 minutes

1996
THE PALLBEARER
Production Companies: Miramax (presents), The Chess Club
Producers: **J. J. Abrams** and Paul Webster
Executive Producers: Meryl Poster, Bob Weinstein, and Harvey Weinstein
Co-Producer: Jason Katims
Line Producer: Nellie Nugiel
Director: Matt Reeves
Screenplay: Jason Katims and Matt Reeves
Cinematography: Robert Elswit
Production Design: Robin Standefer
Art Direction: Stephen Alesch
Costumes: Donna Zakowska
Editing: Stan Salfas
Music: Stewart Copeland
Casting: Kerry Barden, Billy Hopkins, and Suzanna Smith
Cast: David Schwimmer (Tom Thompson), Gwyneth Paltrow (Julie DeMarco), Michael Rapaport (Brad Schorr), Toni Collette (Cynthia), Carol Kane (Tom's Mother), Michael Vartan (Scott), Bitty Schram (Lauren), Jean De Baer (Suzanne DeMarco), Elizabeth Franz (Aunt Lucille), Mark Margolis (Philip DeMarco), Barbara Hershey (Ruth Abernathy), Edoardo Ballerini (The Job Interviewer), Mattew Faber (Jared), Robin Morse (Sylvie), Tony Machine (The Undertaker)
35mm, Spherical Widescreen (1.85:1), Color
98 minutes

1998
ARMAGEDDON
Production Company: Jerry Bruckheimer Films
Producers: Michael Bay, Jerry Bruckheimer, and Gale Anne Hurd
Executive Producers: Jonathan Hensleigh, Chad Oman, and Jim Van Wyck
Associate Producers: Kenny Bates and Pat Sandston
Director: Michael Bay

Screenplay: Jonathan Hensleigh (screenplay and story), **J. J. Abrams** and Tony Gilroy (adaptation), Shane Salerno (adaptation), and Robert Roy Pool (story)
Cinematography: John Schwartzman
Production Design: Michael White
Art Direction: Lawrence A. Hubbs and Bruton Jones
Costumes: Magali Guidasci and Michael Kaplan
Editing: Mark Goldblatt, Chris Lebenzon, and Glen Scantlebury
Music: Trevor Rabin
Casting: Bonnie Timmermann
Cast: Bruce Willis (Harry S. Stamper), Billy Bob Thornton (Dan Truman), Ben Affleck (A.J. Frost), Liv Tyler (Grace Stamper), Will Patton (Charles "Chick" Chapple), Steve Buscemi (Rockhound), William Fichtner (Col. Willie Sharp), Owen Wilson (Oscar Choice), Michael Clarke Duncan (J. Otis "Bear" Kurleen), Peter Stormare (Lev Andropov), Ken Hudson Campbell (Max Lennert), Jessica Steen (Co-Pilot Jennifer Watts), Keith David (Gen. Kimsey)
35mm, Widescreen (2.35:1), Color
151 minutes

1999
THE SUBURBANS
Production Companies: HSX Films, Ignite Entertainment, Motion Picture Corporation of America (MPCA), Suburbans LLC
Producers: **J. J. Abrams**, Michael Burns, Leanna Creel, and Brad Krevoy
Executive Producers: Marc Butan, Tim Foster, and George Linardos
Co-Producer: John Saviano
Director: Donal Lardner Ward
Screenplay: Donal Lardner Ward and Tony Guma
Cinematography: Michael Barrett
Production Design: Susan Bolles
Set Direction: Catherine Pierson
Costumes: Pamela Withers
Editing: Kathryn Himoff
Music: Robbie Kondor
Casting: Sheila Jaffe and Georgianne Walken
Cast: Donal Lardner Ward (Danny), Tony Guma (Rory), Craig Bierko (Mitch), Will Ferrell (Gil), Dick Clark (Himself), Amy Brenneman (Grace), Bridgette Wilson-Sampras (Lara), Brian Chlebowski (Kenny), Perrey Reeves (Amanda), Robert Loggia (Jules), Jennifer Love Hewitt (Cate), Jerry Stiller (Speedo Silverberg), Ben Stiller (Jay Rose), Lisa Gerstein (Leslie Gonzalez), Antonio Fargas (Magee), Cleo Adell (Square-Q Girl), Richard Scobie (Music Video

D.P.), Kurt Loder (Himself), Emily Kuroda (Mrs. Lee Lee), David LaChapelle
(Thorlakur), Karl A. D'Amico (MC), Matt Cedeño (Tito), Mary Jane Lardner
(Amelia), **J. J. Abrams** (Rock Journalist)
35mm, Widescreen (1.85:1), Color
81 minutes

2001
JOY RIDE
Production Companies: Regency Enterprises, Epsilon Motion Pictures (in as-
sociation with), New Regency Pictures, Bad Robot, and LivePlanet
Producers: **J. J. Abrams** and Chris Moore
Executive Producers: Bridget Johnson, Patrick Markey, and Arnon Milchan
Executive Producer (Additional Photography): Jeffrey Downer
Associate Producer: W. Mark McNair
Director: John Dahl
Screenplay: Clay Tarver and **J. J. Abrams**
Cinematography: Jeff Jur
Production Design: Robert Pearson
Art Direction: Michael Rizzo
Costumes: Terry Dresbach
Editing: Eric L. Beason, Scott Chestnut, Todd E. Miller, and Glen Scantlebury
Music: Marco Beltrami
Casting: Mali Finn and Emily Schweber
Cast: Steve Zahn (Fuller), Paul Walker (Lewis), Leelee Sobieski (Venna), Jessica
Bowman (Charlotte), Stuart Stone (Danny), Basil Wallace (Car Salesman), Brian
Leckner (Officer Keeney), Mary Wickliffe (Salt Lake City Police Desk Clerk),
Dell Yount (Gas Station Mechanic), Kenneth White (Ronald Ellinghouse), Luis
Cortés (Night Manager), Michael McCleery (Officer Akins), Jim Beaver (Sheriff
Ritter), Rachel Singer (Gas Station Manager), Satch Huizenga (Ice Truck Man)
35mm, Super 35 (2.35:1), Color
97 minutes

2006
MISSION: IMPOSSIBLE III
Production Companies: Cruise/Wagner Productions and Paramount Pictures
(presents)
Producers: Tom Cruise, Paula Wagner, and Haicheng Zhao (China)
Executive Producers: Sanping Han (China), Stratton Leopold, and Buting Yang
(China)
Associate Producer: Guichun Wang (China)

Co-Producers: Arthur Anderson and Doming Shi (China)
Director: **J. J. Abrams**
Screenplay: Alex Kurtzman, Roberto Orci, and **J. J. Abrams**
Cinematography: Dan Mindel
Production Design: Scott Chambliss
Art Direction: Dennis Bradford, Stephen Bream, Sean Haworth, Kevin
Kavanaugh, Gary Kosko, Brad Ricker, and Domenic Silvestri
Costumes: Colleen Atwood
Editing: Maryann Brandon and Mary Jo Markey
Music: Michael Giacchino
Casting: April Webster
Cast: Tom Cruise (Ethan Hunt), Philip Seymour Hoffman (Owen Davian), Ving
Rhames (Luther Stickell), Billy Crudup (John Musgrave), Michelle Monaghan
(Julia), Jonathan Rhys Meyers (Declan Gormley), Keri Russell (Lindsey Farris),
Maggie Q (Zhen Lei), Simon Pegg (Benji Dunn), Eddie Marsan (Brownway),
Laurence Fishburne (Theodore Brassel)
35mm, Widescreen (2.35:1), Color
126 minutes

2008
CLOVERFIELD
Production Companies: Paramount Pictures (presents), and Bad Robot
Producers: **J. J. Abrams** and Bryan Burk
Executive Producers: Sherryl Clark and Guy Riedel
Associate Producer: David Baronoff
Director: Matt Reeves
Screenplay: Drew Goddard
Cinematography: Michael Bonvillain
Production Design: Martin Whist
Art Direction: Doug J. Meerdink
Costumes: Ellen Mirojnick
Editing: Kevin Stitt
Casting: Alyssa Weisberg
Cast: Lizzy Caplan (Marlene Diamond), Jessica Lucas (Lily Ford), T.J. Miller
(Hudson 'Hud' Platt), Michael Stahl-David (Rob Hawkins), Mike Vogel (Jason
Hawkins), Odette Annable (Beth McIntyre), Anjul Nigam (Bodega Cashier),
Margot Farley (Jenn), Theo Rossi (Antonio), Brian Klugman (Charlie), Kelvin Yu
(Clark), Liza Lapira (Heather), Lili Mirojnick (Lei), Ben Feldman (Travis)
35mm, Widescreen (1.85:1), Color
85 minutes

2009
THE PEOPLE SPEAK
Production Companies: The People Speak, Act 4 Entertainment, and Artfire Films
Producers: Dan Abrams, Jodie Evans, David Johnson, Ara Katz, Carolyn Mugar, et al.
Executive Producers: Anthony Arnove, Josh Brolin, Matt Damon, Nancy Dubuc, Russell McCarroll, David McKillop, and Chris Moore
Associate Producer: Brenda Coughlin
Co-Producers: **J. J. Abrams**, Jon Berry, Dan Fireman, Isabel Freer, Lorne Lieb, Kathleen McGrath, Alan Pao, Ted Robertson, and Andrew Spellman
Directors: Anthony Arnove, Chris Moore, and Howard Zinn
Screenplay: Anthony Arnove (book) and Howard Zinn (book)
Cinematography: Keith Dunkerley, Alex Lehmann, Tony Sacco, and Gretchen Warthen
Production Design: Mark Gabriel and Mercedes Younger
Art Direction: Shauna Aronson, Kevin P. Lewis, and Shane Middleton
Editing: Jon Berry, Yesenia Higuera, and Dan Swietlik
Music: David Baerwald
Cast: Marisa Tomei (Herself), Matt Damon (Himself), Josh Brolin (Himself), Morgan Freeman (Himself), Rosario Dawson (Herself), Viggo Mortensen (Himself), Sean Penn (Himself), Kerry Washington (Herself), Benjamin Bratt (Himself), Sandra Oh (Herself), Q'orianka Kilcher (Herself), Harris Yulin (Himself), Michael Ealy (Himself), Don Cheadle (Himself), et al.
Color
113 minutes

2009
STAR TREK
Production Companies: Paramount Pictures (presents), Spyglass Entertainment (presents), Bad Robot, and Mavrocine
Producers: **J. J. Abrams** and Damon Lindelof
Executive Producers: Bryan Burk, Jeffrey Chernov, Alex Kurtzman, and Roberto Orci
Associate Producer: David Baronoff
Co-Producer: David Witz
Director: **J. J. Abrams**
Screenplay: Roberto Orci, Alex Kurtzman, and Gene Roddenberry (TV Series)
Cinematography: Daniel Mindel
Production Design: Scott Chambliss
Supervising Art Director: Keith P. Cunningham

Art Direction: Curt Beech, Dennis Bradford, Luke Freeborn, Beat Frutiger, and Gary Kosko
Costumes: Michael Kaplan
Editing: Maryann Brandon and Mary Jo Markey
Music: Michael Giacchino
Casting: April Webster and Alyssa Weisberg
Cast: Chris Pine (Kirk), Zachary Quinto (Spock), Leonard Nimoy (Spock Prime), Eric Bana (Nero), Bruce Greenwood (Pike), Karl Urban (Bones), Zoe Saldana (Uhura), Simon Pegg (Scotty), John Cho (Sulu), Anton Yelchin (Chekov), Ben Cross (Sarek), Winona Ryder (Amanda Grayson), Chris Hemsworth (George Kirk), Jennifer Morrison (Winona Kirk), Rachel Nichols (Gaila), Faran Tahir (Captain Robau), Clifton Collins Jr. (Ayel), Tony Elias (Officer Pitts)
35mm, Widescreen (2.35:1), Color
127 minutes

2010
MORNING GLORY
Production Companies: Bad Robot, Goldcrest Pictures (in association with)
Producers: **J. J. Abrams** and Bryan Burk
Executive Producers: Sherryl Clark and Guy Riedel
Associate Producers: Udi Nedivi and Lindsey Weber
Director: Roger Michell
Screenplay: Aline Brosh McKenna
Cinematography: Alwin H. Küchler
Production Design: Mark Friedberg
Art Direction: Alex DiGerlando and Kim Jennings
Costumes: Frank L. Fleming
Editing: Dan Farrell, Nick Moore, and Steven Weisberg
Music: David Arnold
Casting: Marcia DeBonis and Ellen Lewis
Cast: Rachel McAdams (Becky), Noah Bean (First Date), Jack Davidson
35mm, Widescreen (2.35:1), Color
107 minutes

2011
SUPER 8
Production Companies: Paramount Pictures (presents), Amblin Entertainment, Bad Robot, K/O Camera Toys
Producers: **J. J. Abrams**, Bryan Burk, and Steven Spielberg
Executive Producer: Guy Riedel

Associate Producers: Udi Nedivi, Michelle Rejwan, and Ben Rosenblatt
Co-Producer: Tommy Gormley
Director: **J. J. Abrams**
Screenplay: **J. J. Abrams**
Cinematography: Larry Fong
Production Design: Martin Whist
Art Direction: David Scott
Costumes: Ha Nguyen
Editing: Maryann Brandon and Mary Jo Markey
Music: Michael Giacchino
Casting: April Webster, Alyssa Weisberg
Cast: Joel Courtney (Joe Lamb), Ryan Lee (Cary), Zach Mills (Preston), Riley
Griffiths (Charles Kaznyk), Gabriel Basso (Martin), Kyle Chandler (Deputy
Jackson Lamb), Ron Eldard (Louis Dainard), AJ Michalka (Jen Kaznyk), Elle
Fanning (Alice Dainard), Glynn Turman (Dr. Woodward), Noah Emmerich
(Colonel Nelec)
35mm, Widescreen (2.35:1), Color
112 minutes

2011
MISSION: IMPOSSIBLE—GHOST PROTOCOL
Production Companies: Paramount Pictures (presents), Skydance Productions
(presents), TC Productions, Bad Robot
Producers: **J. J. Abrams**, Bryan Burk, and Tom Cruise
Executive Producers: Jeffrey Chernov, David Ellison, Dana Goldberg, and Paul
Schwake
Associate Producers: Ben Rosenblatt and Pravesh Sahni
Co-Producers: Josh Appelbaum, Tommy Harper, David Minkowski, André
Nemec, and Tom C. Peitzman
Line Producer: Tabrez Noorani
Consulting Producer: Luca Paracels
Local Producer: Yuriy Sapronov and Evgeny Savostiyanov
Facilitating Producer: Tim Smythe
Director: Brad Bird
Screenplay: Josh Appelbaum and André Nemec
Cinematography: Robert Elswit
Production Design: James D. Bissell
Art Direction: Michael Diner, Michael Turner, Martin Vackár, Grant Van Der
Slagt, and Mark Zuelzke
Supervising Art Director: Helen Jarvis and Christa Munro

Costumes: Michael Kaplan
Editing: Paul Hirsch
Music: Michael Giacchino
Casting: April Webster and Alyssa Weisberg
Cast: Tom Cruise (Ethan Hunt), Paula Patton (Jane), Simon Pegg (Benji), Jeremy Renner (Brandt), Michael Nyqvist (Hendricks), Vladimir Mashkov (Sidorov), Samuli Edelmann (Wistrom), Ivan Shvedoff (Leonid Lisenker), Anil Kapoor (Brij Nath), Léa Seydoux (Sabine Moreau), Josh Holloway (Hanaway)
35mm, Widescreen (2.35:1), Color
133 minutes

2013
STAR TREK: INTO DARKNESS
Production Companies: Paramount Pictures (presents), Skydance Productions (presents), Bad Robot
Producers: **J. J. Abrams**, Bryan Burk, Alex Kurtzman, Damon Lindelof, and Roberto Orci
Executive Producers: Jeffrey Chernov, David Ellison, Dana Goldberg, and Paul Schwake
Co-Producers: Tommy Gormley, Tommy Harper, Michelle Rejwan, and Ben Rosenblatt
Director: **J. J. Abrams**
Screenplay: Roberto Orci, Alex Kurtzman, Damon Lindelof, and Gene Roddenberry (TV series)
Cinematography: Daniel Mindel
Production Design: Scott Chambliss
Art Direction: Kasra Farahani, Michael E. Goldman, Andrew Murdock, and Harry E. Otto
Supervising Art Director: Ramsey Avery
Costumes: Michael Kaplan
Editing: Maryann Brandon and Mary Jo Markey
Music: Michael Giacchino
Casting: April Webster and Alyssa Weisberg
Cast: Chris Pine (Kirk), Zachary Quinto (Spock), Zoe Saldana (Uhura), Karl Urban (Bones), Simon Pegg (Scotty), John Cho (Sulu), Benedict Cumberbatch (Khan), Anton Yelchin (Chekov), Bruce Greenwood (Pike), Peter Weller (Marcus), Alice Eve (Carol)
35mm, Widescreen (2.35:1), Color
132 minutes

2014
INFINITELY POLAR BEAR
Production Companies: Paper Street Films, Park Pictures, Bad Robot (in association with), KGB Media (in association with)
Producers: Sam Bisbee, Bingo Gubelmann, Galt Niederhoffer, and Wallace Wolodarsky
Executive Producers: **J. J. Abrams**, Jackie Kelman Bisbee, Bryan Burk, et al.
Co-Executive Producers: Stewart Anderson Burkland, W. Elliott Burkland, et al.
Associate Producers: Theodora Dunlap and William Goldberg
Co-Producer: Erika Hampson
Director: Maya Forbes
Screenplay: Maya Forbes
Cinematography: Bobby Bukowski
Production Design: Carl Sprague
Costumes: Kasia Walicka-Maimone
Editing: Michael R. Miller
Music: Theodore Shapiro
Casting: Douglas Aibel
Cast: Mark Ruffalo (Cam Stuart), Zoe Saldana (Maggie Stuart), Imogene Wolodarsky (Amelia Stuart), Ashley Aufderheide (Faith Stuart), Nekhebet Kum Juch (Kim), Manoah Angelo (Thurgood), Muriel Gould (Gaga), Tod Randolph (Ruth-Ann), Beth Dixon (Pauline Stuart), Keir Dullea (Murray Stuart)
Widescreen (1.78:1), Color
90 minutes

2015
MISSION: IMPOSSIBLE—ROGUE NATION
Production Companies: Paramount Pictures (presents), Skydance Productions (presents), Bad Robot, China Movie Channel (in association with), Alibaba Pictures Group (in association with), Odin, TC Productions
Producers: **J. J. Abrams**, Bryan Burk, Tom Cruise, David Ellison, and Don Granger
Executive Producers: Dana Goldberg and Jake Myers
Associate Producers: Helen Medrano and Maricel Pagulayan
Line Producer: Zakaria Alaoui
Director: Christopher McQuarrie
Screenplay: Christopher McQuarrie
Story: Christopher McQuarrie, Drew Pearce, and Bruce Geller (TV series)
Cinematography: Robert Elswit
Production Design: James D. Bissell

Art Direction: Andrew Bennett, Steve Carter, Matthew Gray, Aziz Hamichi, Amanda Leggatt, Florian Reichmann, and Helen Xenopoulos
Supervising Art Director: Paul Inglis
Costumes: Joanna Johnston
Editing: Eddie Hamilton
Music: Joe Kraemer
Casting: Mindy Marin and Lucinda Syson
Cast: Tom Cruise (Ethan Hunt), Jeremy Renner (William Brandt), Simon Pegg (Benji Dunn), Rebecca Ferguson (Ilsa Faust), Ving Rhames (Luther Stickell), Sean Harris (Soloman Lane), Simon McBurney (Atlee), Jingchu Zhang (Lauren), Tom Hollander (Prime Minister), Jens Hultén (Janik Vinter), Alec Baldwin (Alan Hunley)
35mm, Widescreen (2.35:1), Color
131 minutes

2015
STAR WARS: EPISODE VII—THE FORCE AWAKENS
Production Companies: Lucasfilm, Bad Robot, Truenorth Productions
Producers: **J. J. Abrams**, Bryan Burk, and Kathleen Kennedy
Executive Producers: Tommy Harper and Jason D. McGatlin
Associate Producer: Michael Arndt
Co-Producers: Pippa Anderson, Tommy Gormley, Michelle Rejwan, Ben Rosenblatt, John Swartz, Susan Towner, and Lawrence Kasdan (uncredited)
Director: **J. J. Abrams**
Screenplay: Lawrence Kasdan, **J. J. Abrams**, and Michael Arndt
Cinematography: Daniel Mindel
Production Design: Rick Carter and Darren Gilford
Supervising Art Director: Neil Lamont
Senior Art Directors: Alastair Bullock and Gary Tomkins
Costumes: Michael Kaplan
Editing: Maryann Brandon and Mary Jo Markey
Music: John Williams
Casting: Nina Gold, April Webster, and Alyssa Weisberg
Cast: Harrison Ford (Han Solo), Mark Hamill (Luke Skywalker), Carrie Fisher (Princess Leia), Adam Driver (Kylo Ren), Daisy Ridley (Rey), John Boyega (Finn), Oscar Isaac (Poe Dameron), Lupita Nyong'o (Maz Kanata), Andy Serkis (Supreme Leader Snoke), Domhnall Gleeson (General Hux), Anthony Daniels (C-3PO), Max von Sydow (Lor San Tekka), Peter Mayhew (Chewbacca), Gwendoline Christie (Captain Phasma)
35mm, 65mm, Widescreen (2.35:1), IMAX (1.43:1), Color
136 minutes

2016
10 CLOVERFIELD LANE
Production Companies: Paramount Pictures, Bad Robot, Spectrum Effects
Producers: **J. J. Abrams** and Lindsey Weber
Executive Producers: Bryan Burk, Drew Goddard, and Matt Reeves
Co-Producers: Bob Dohrmann and Ben Rosenblatt
Director: Dan Trachtenberg
Screenplay: Josh Campbell, Matthew Stuecken, and Damien Chazelle
Cinematography: Jeff Cutter
Production Design: Ramsey Avery
Costumes: Meagan McLaughlin
Editing: Stefan Grube
Music: Bear McCreary
Casting: Monika Mikkelsen
Cast: John Goodman (Howard), Mary Elizabeth Winstead (Michelle), John
Gallagher Jr. (Emmett), Douglas M. Griffin (Driver), Suzanne Cryer (Leslie)
Digital, Widescreen (2.35:1), Color
103 minutes

2016
STAR TREK: BEYOND
Production Companies: Bad Robot, Paramount Productions, Skydance
Productions, Sneaky Shark
Producers: **J. J. Abrams**, Bryan Burk, and Roberto Orci
Executive Producers: Jeffrey Chernov, David Ellison, Dana Goldberg, Tommy
Harper, and Lindsey Weber
Director: Justin Lin
Screenplay: Simon Pegg, Doug Jung, Roberto Orci, John D. Payne, and Patrick
McKay
Cinematography: Stephen F. Windon
Production Design: Thomas E. Sanders
Supervising Art Director: Don Macaulay
Costumes: Sanja Milkovic Hays
Editing: Greg D'Auria, Dylan Highsmith, Kelly Matsumoto, and Steven Sprung
Music: Michael Giacchino
Casting: April Webster and Alyssa Weisberg
Cast: Chris Pine (Kirk), Zoe Saldana (Uhura), Simon Pegg (Scotty), Karl Urban
(Bones), Anton Yelchin (Chekov), Zachary Quinto (Spock), John Cho (Sulu),
Sofia Boutella (Jaylah), Idris Elba (Krall), Shohreh Aghdashloo (High Command
of the Federation)

Digital, Widescreen (2.35:1), Color

122 minutes

2017

STAR WARS: EPISODE VIII—THE LAST JEDI

Production Companies: Lucasfilm, Ram Bergman Productions, Walt Disney Pictures

Producers: Ram Bergman and Kathleen Kennedy

Executive Producers: **J. J. Abrams**, Tom Karnowski, and Jason D. McGatlin

Line Producers: Boris Dmitrovic (Croatia) and Finni Johannsson (Iceland)

Director: Rian Johnson

Screenplay: Rian Johnson

Cinematography: Steve Yedlin

Production Design: Rick Heinrichs

Art Direction: Andrew Bennett, Neal Callow, John Dexter, et al.

Costumes: Michael Kaplan

Editing: Bob Ducsay

Music: John Williams

Casting: Nina Gold, Milivoj Mestrovic, and Mary Vernieu

Cast: Daisy Ridley (Rey), John Boyega (Finn), Oscar Isaac (Poe Dameron), Adam Driver (Kylo Ren), Mark Hamill (Luke Skywalker), Carrie Fisher (Leia), Anthony Daniels (C-3PO), Kelly Marie Tran (Rose Tico), Benicio Del Toro (DJ), Andy Serkis (Supreme Leader Snoke), Domhnall Gleeson (General Hux), Gwendoline Christie (Captain Phasma), Laura Dern (Vice Admiral Amilyn Holdo)

35mm, Widescreen (2.35:1), Color

150 minutes

Television

1998–2002

FELICITY

Production Companies: Touchstone Television and Imagine Television

Creators: **J. J. Abrams** and Matt Reeves

Series Producers: Gerrit van der Meer (21 episodes), Mychelle Deschamps (19 episodes), et al.

Series Executive Producers: **J. J. Abrams** (84 episodes), Brian Grazer (84 episodes), Tony Krantz (84 episodes), et al.

Series Co-Producers: Tiffany Marie Rocquemore Delorme (62 episodes), Jennifer Levin (57 episodes), et al.

Series Directors: Lawrence Trilling (14 episodes), Harry Winer (10 episodes), **J. J. Abrams** (2 episodes), et al.

Series Writers: Jennifer Levin (20 episodes), Josh Reims (19 episodes), et al.

Series Cinematography: Michael Bonvillain (47 episodes), Marshall Adams (22 episodes), et al.

Series Production Design: Woody Crocker (36 episodes), Denny Dugally (22 episodes), et al.

Series Art Direction: Kenneth J. Creber (16 episodes), Dawn Swiderski (13 episodes), et al.

Series Costumes: Linda Serijan (61 episodes)

Series Editing: Stan Salfas (22 episodes), Mary Jo Markey (14 episodes), et al.

Series Music: W.G. Snuffy Walden (52 episodes), Joseph Williams (22 episodes), et al.

Series Casting: Janet Gilmore (40 episodes), Megan McConnell (40 episodes), et al.

Cast: Keri Russell (Felicity Porter), Scott Speedman (Ben Covington), Scott Foley (Noel Crane), Tangi Miller (Elena Tyler), Greg Grunberg (Sean Blumberg), Amanda Foreman (Meghan Rotundi), Amy Jo Johnson (Julie Emrick)

35mm, Widescreen (2.35:1), Color

60 minutes

2001–2006

ALIAS

Production Companies: Touchstone Television and Bad Robot

Creator: **J. J. Abrams**

Series Producers: Sarah Caplan (88 episodes), Lawrence Trilling (66 episodes), et al.

Series Executive Producers: **J. J. Abrams** (105 episodes), Ken Olin (105 episodes), Jesse Alexander (105 episodes), et al.

Series Associate Producers: Meighan Offield (61 episodes), Scott Collins (49 episodes), et al.

Series Co-Producers: Nicole Carrasco (63 episodes), Bryan Burk (61 episodes), et al.

Series Directors: Ken Olin (23 episodes), Lawrence Trilling (15 episodes), **J. J. Abrams** (5 episodes), et al.

Series Writers: Jeff Pinkner (12 episodes), Jesse Alexander (11 episodes), et al.

Series Cinematography: Donald E. Thorin Jr. (60 episodes), Michael Bonvillain (44 episodes), and Bing Sokolsky (1 episode)

Series Production Design: Scott Chambliss (42 episodes), et al.

Series Art Direction: Cece Destefano (43 episodes), Ray Yamagata (12 episodes), et al.
Series Costumes: Laura Goldsmith (85 episodes)
Series Editing: Maryann Brandon (27 episodes), et al.
Series Music: Michael Giacchino
Series Casting: Mandy Sherman (105 episodes), et al.
Cast: Jennifer Garner (Sydney Bristow), Ron Rifkin (Arvin Sloane), Carl Lumbly (Marcus Dixon), Kevin Weisman (Marshall Flinkman), Victor Garber (Jack Bristow), Michael Vartan (Michael Vaughn), Greg Grunberg (Eric Weiss), David Anders (Julian Sark), Merrin Dungey (Francie Calfo), Bradley Cooper (Will Tippin)
35mm, Widescreen (1.78:1), Color
42 minutes

2004–2010
LOST
Production Companies: Bad Robot, Touchstone Television, ABC Studios and Grass Skirt Productions (uncredited)
Creators: **J. J. Abrams**, Jeffrey Lieber, and Damon Lindelof
Series Producers: Ra'uf Glasgow (115 episodes), Patricia Churchill (51 episodes), et al.
Series Executive Producers: Bryan Burk (117 episodes), **J. J. Abrams** (116 episodes), Damon Lindelof (116 episodes), Carlton Cuse (108 episodes), et al.
Series Associate Producers: Noreen O'Toole (32 episodes), Jim Triplett (24 episodes), et al.
Series Co-Producers: Samantha Thomas (67 episodes), Melinda Hsu Taylor (32 episodes), et al.
Series Directors: Jack Bender (39 episodes), Stephen Williams (26 episodes), **J. J. Abrams** (2 episodes), et al.
Series Writers: Carlton Cuse (35 episodes), Adam Horowitz (21 episodes), Edward Kitsis (21 episodes), et al.
Series Cinematography: John S. Bartley (51 episodes), Michael Bonvillain (25 episodes), Cort Fey (18 episodes), et al.
Series Production Design: Zack Grobler (57 episodes), James H. Spencer (14 episodes), Jonathan A. Carlson (12 episodes), et al.
Series Art Direction: Tim Beach (39 episodes), et al.
Series Costumes: Roland Sanchez (90 episodes), Billy Ray McKenna (13 episodes), and Kathryn Morris (11 episodes)
Series Editing: Stephen Semel (41 episodes), et al.

Series Music: Michael Giacchino (117 episodes)
Series Casting: April Webster (104 episodes), Veronica Collins Rooney (60 episodes), Mandy Sherman (46 episodes), et al.
Cast: Jorge Garcia (Hugo "Hurley" Reyes), Josh Holloway (James "Sawyer" Ford), Yunjin Kim (Sun-Hwa Kwon), Evangeline Lilly (Katherine "Kate" Austen), Terry O'Quinn (John Locke), Naveen Andrews (Sayid Jarrah), Matthew Fox (Dr. Jack Shepard), Daniel Dae Kim (Jin-Soo Kwon), Emilie de Ravin (Claire Littleton), Michael Emerson (Benjamin "Ben" Linus), Henry Ian Cusick (Desmond Hume), Dominic Monaghan (Charlie Pace), Harold Perrineau (Michael Dawson)
35mm, Widescreen (1.78:1), Color
44 minutes

2006–2007
WHAT ABOUT BRIAN
Production Companies: Bad Robot and Touchstone Television
Creator: Dana Stevens
Series Producers: Liz Tigelaar, Robert M. Williams Jr., David Graziano, Carol Dunn Trussell, and Robert Duncan McNeill
Series Executive Producers: **J. J. Abrams**, Bryan Burk, Jonathan Pontell, Dana Stevens, Josh Reims, Jeff Judah, Gabe Sachs, Thom Sherman, et al.
Series Associate Producers: Jason Harkins and Jake Aust
Series Co-Producers: Michael Foley, Stan Salfas, Stephen Hootstein, Debra Lovatelli, Cathy Mickel Gibson, and David Schulner
Series Directors: Dan Lerner (4 episodes), Bethany Rooney (2 episodes), Allison Anders (2 episodes), Jonathan Pontell (2 episodes), et al.
Series Writers: Kate Angelo (4 episodes), Ross Canter (2 episodes), Micheal Foley (2 episodes), Stephen Hootstein (2 episodes), et al.
Series Cinematography: Joe Pennella (19 episodes), Russ T. Alsobrook (4 episodes), and Uta Briesewitz (1 episode)
Series Production Design: Jeremy Cassells (25 episodes), Derek R. Hill (1 episode), and Jonathan A. Carlson (1 episode)
Series Art Direction: Brian Jewell (14 episodes), Jonathan A. Carlson (4 episodes), and Karen Steward (1 episode, uncredited)
Series Costumes: Kathryn Morrison (19 episodes), Debra McGuire (4 episodes), and Ana Crabtree (1 episode)
Series Editing: Paul Dixon (5 episodes), Jon Dudkowski (4 episodes), Barbara Gerard (3 episodes), Tanya M. Swerling (2 episodes), et al.
Series Music: Bennett Salvay (13 episodes), Blake Neely (8 episodes), Michael

Giacchino (4 episodes), Grant Lee Phillips (4 episodes), and Jim Dooley (2 episodes)

Series Casting: Mandy Sherman (19 episodes), John Brace (5 episodes), Linda Lowy (5 episodes), Natalie Hart (4 episodes), et al.

Cast: Barry Watson (Brian Davis), Matthew Davis (Adam Hillman), Rick Gomez (Dave Greco), Rosanna Arquette (Nicole Varzi/Nicole O'Hara), Amanda Detmer (Deena Greco), Payton Spencer (Geneva), Mikaila Baumel (Larissa), Jason George (Jimmy), Sarah Lancaster (Marjorie Seaver), et al.

Widescreen (1.78:1), Color

60 minutes

2006–2007

SIX DEGREES

Production Companies: Bad Robot and Touchstone Television

Creators: M. Raven Metzner and Stuart Zicherman

Series Producers: Peter Elkoff and Jane Raab

Series Executive Producers: **J. J. Abrams**, Bryan Burk, M. Raven Metzner, Stuart Zicherman, Kenneth Biller, Carol Flint, and Thom Sherman

Series Associate Producers: Tamara Isaac and Julia Rask

Series Co-Producers: David Dworetzky and Kathy Ciric

Series Directors: Eric Laneuville (2 episodes), Jace Alexander (1 episode), Juan José Campanella (1 episode), Rodrigo García (1 episode), et al.

Series Writers: Peter Elkoff (4 episodes), Peter Parnell (2 episodes), Julie Rottenberg (2 episodes), Elisa Zuritsky (2 episodes), et al.

Series Cinematography: John Thomas (11 episodes) and Phil Abraham (1 episode)

Series Production Design: Dan Davis (12 episodes)

Series Art Direction: Adam Scher (10 Episodes) and Michael Auszura (1 episode)

Series Costumes: Patricia Field (12 episodes)

Series Editing: Tanya M. Swerling (3 episodes), Lisa Willinger (3 episodes), Stan Salfas (2 episodes), and Sue Blainey (2 episodes)

Series Music: Michael Giacchino (13 episodes), Atli Örvarsson (6 episodes), and Adam Cohen (5 episodes)

Series Casting: Beth Blanks (8 episodes), Mary Jo Slater (8 episodes), Steve Brooksbank (7 episodes), Gayle Keller (4 episodes), et al.

Cast: Jay Hernandez (Carlos Green), Bridget Moynahan (Whitney Crane), Erika Christensen (Mae Anderson), Dorian Missick (Damian Henry), Campbell Scott (Steven Caseman), Hope Davis (Laura Morgan), M. Xavier O'Connor (Ralston Employee 2006), Ruby Jerins (Eliza Morgan), Deborah S. Craig (Melanie), et al.

Color

43 minutes

2008–2013
FRINGE
Production Companies: Bad Robot, Warner Bros. Television, FB2 Films and Fringe Element Films
Creators: **J. J. Abrams**, Alex Kurtzman, and Roberto Orci
Series Producers: Tamara Isaac (96 episodes), Tanya M. Swerling (86 episodes), Kathy Lingg (78 episodes), Athena Wickham (56 episodes), et al.
Series Executive Producers: **J. J. Abrams** (100 episodes), Bryan Burk (98 episodes), Jeff Pinkner (86 episodes), J.H. Wyman (85 episodes), et al.
Series Associate Producers: Noreen O'Toole (33 episodes), Jay Worth (33 episodes), et al.
Series Co-Producers: Vladimir Stefoff (56 episodes), Graham Roland (35 episodes)
Series Directors: Joe Chappelle (16 episodes), Brad Anderson (12 episodes), Fred Toye (8 episodes), Jeannot Szwarc (7 episodes), et al.
Series Writers: J. H. Wyman (28 episodes), Jeff Pinkner (26 episodes), Akiva Goldsman (19 episodes), Graham Roland (13 episodes), et al.
Series Cinematography: David Moxness (29 episodes), Thomas Yatsko (25 episodes), David Geddes (13 episodes), Michael Wale (8 episodes), et al.
Series Production Design: Ian D. Thomas (67 episodes), Steven J. Jordan (14 episodes), Anne Stuhler (6 episodes), and Carol Spier (2 episodes)
Series Art Direction: Peter Andringa (50 episodes), et al.
Series Costumes: Jenni Gullett (52 episodes), Marie Abma (20 episodes), et al.
Series Editing: Jon Dudkowski (30 episodes), Luyen Vu (23 episodes), Timothy A. Good (20 episodes), Scott Vickrey (7 episodes), et al.
Series Music: Michael Giacchino (74 episodes), Chris Tilton (54 episodes), and Mike McCready (1 episode)
Series Casting: April Webster (53 episodes), Sara Isaacson (36 episodes), Ross Meyerson (14 episodes), Julie Tucker (14 episodes), and Cindy Tolan (7 episodes)
Cast: Anna Torv (Olivia Dunham), Joshua Jackson (Peter Bishop), Jasika Nicole (Astrid Farnsworth), John Noble (Dr. Walter Bishop), Lance Reddick (Phillip Broyles), Blair Brown (Nina Sharp), Michael Cerveris (The Observer), et al.
35mm, Widescreen (16:9), Color
46 minutes

2010
UNDERCOVERS
Production Companies: Bad Robot, Good Butter, and Warner Bros. Television
Creators: **J. J. Abrams** and Josh Reims
Series Producers: Kathy Lingg (13 episodes) and Robert M. Williams Jr. (13 episodes)

Series Executive Producers: **J. J. Abrams** (13 episodes), Bryan Burk (13 episodes), and Josh Reims (13 episodes)
Series Associate Producers: Stephen Semel (11 episodes) and Geoff Garrett (2 episodes)
Series Co-Producers: Anthony Sparks (12 episodes)
Series Directors: Stephen Williams (3 episodes), Tucker Gates (2 episodes), **J. J. Abrams** (1 episode), et al.
Series Writers: Michael Foley (2 episodes), Elwood Reid (2 episodes), Phil Klemmer (2 episodes), Tracy Bellomo (1 episode), et al.
Series Cinematography: John B. Aronson (12 episodes), John S. Bartley (6 episodes), and Michael Bonvillain (1 episode)
Series Production Design: Doug J. Meerdink (12 episodes) and Martin Whist (1 episode)
Series Art Direction: Ray Yamagata (11 episodes)
Series Costumes: Laura Goldsmith (13 episodes)
Series Editing: Jill D'Agnecia (6 episodes), Mark Conte (4 episodes), Mark Goldman (4 episodes), et al.
Series Music: Andrea Datzman (12 episodes), Michael Giacchino (1 episode), and Chris Tilton (1 episode)
Series Casting: Veronica Collins Rooney (13 episodes) and April Webster (1 episode)
Cast: Gugu Mbatha-Raw (Samantha Bloom), Boris Kodjoe (Steven Bloom), Ben Schwartz (Bill Hoyt), Gerald McRaney (Carlton Shaw), Mekia Cox (Lizzy Gilliam), Carter MacIntyre (Leo Nash), Brad Grunberg (Charlie), et al.
Redcode RAW, Widescreen (1.78:1), Color
60 minutes

2011–2016
PERSON OF INTEREST
Production Companies: Kilter Films, Bad Robot and Warner Bros. Television
Creator: Jonathan Nolan
Series Producers: Athena Wickham, Melissa Scrivner-Love, Margot Lulick, et al.
Series Executive Producers: **J. J. Abrams**, Bryan Burk, Jonathan Nolan, and Greg Plageman
Series Associate Producers: Chris Risner, Amanda Lencioni Barnett, and Ben Brafman
Series Co-Producers: Joshua Levey, Noreen O'Toole, Stephen Semel, and Erik Mountain
Series Directors: Chris Fisher (17 episodes), Richard J. Lewis (12 episodes), Frederick E. O. Toye (11 episodes), Jeffrey G. Hunt (7 episodes), et al.

Series Writers: Sean Hennen (47 episodes), Lucas O'Connor (38 episodes), Erik Mountain (32 episodes), Michael Sopczynski (27 episodes), Nic Van Zeebroeck (27 episodes), Dan Dietz (27 episodes), Tony Camerino (16 episodes) et al.
Series Cinematography: David Insley (37 episodes), Teodoro Maniaci (22 episodes), Manuel Billeter (20 episodes), Stephen McNutt (11 episodes), et al.
Series Production Design: Rick Butler (74 episodes), Dan Leigh (28 episodes), Kalina Ivanov (1 episode)
Series Art Direction: C. J. Simpson (37 episodes), Sarah Frank (30 episodes), Neil Prince (28 episodes), Ola Maslik (1 episode), et al.
Series Costumes: Gary Jones (49 episodes), Frank L. Fleming (31 episodes), John Glaser (21 episodes), et al.
Series Editing: Mark Conte (35 episodes), Ray Daniels III (18 episodes), Ryan Malanaphy (17 episodes), Scott Powell (11 episodes), et al.
Series Music: Ramin Djawadi
Series Casting: Mark Saks (67 episodes), Jessica Kelly (35 episodes), Suzanne Smith (35 episodes), and April Webster (1 episode)
Cast: Jim Caviezel (John Reese), Kevin Chapman (Lionel Fusco), Michael Emerson (Harold Finch), Amy Acker (Root/The Machine/Caroline Turing/Samantha Groves), Taraji P. Henson (Joss Carter), Sarah Shahi (Sameen Shaw), John Nolan (John Greer), Enrico Colantoni (Carl Elias/Charlie Burton), Robert John Burke (Officer Patrick Simmons), Al Sapienza (Detective Raymond Terney), Boris McGiver (Hersh/George Hersh), et al.
SxS Pro, Widescreen (1.78:1), Color
43 minutes

2012
ALCATRAZ
Production Companies: Bonanza Productions, Bad Robot (in association with), Warner Bros. Television (in association with), and Alcatraz Films (uncredited)
Creators: Steven Lilien, Elizabeth Sarnoff, and Bryan Wynbrandt
Series Producers: Athena Wickham (13 episodes), Robert M. Williams Jr. (13 episodes), Robert Hull (12 episodes), and Alison Balian (6 episodes)
Series Executive Producers: **J. J. Abrams** (13 episodes), Jack Bender (13 episodes), Bryan Burk (13 episodes), et al.
Series Associate Producers: Geoff Garrett (13 episodes) and Noreen O'Toole (13 episodes)
Series Co-Producer: Stephen Semel (13 episodes)
Series Directors: Jack Bender (5 episodes), Paul A. Edwards (2 episodes), Brad Anderson (1 episode), et al.

Series Writers: Robert Hull (4 episodes), Jennifer Johnson (3 episodes), Toni Graphia (2 episodes), et al.

Series Cinematography: David Stockton (7 episodes) and Stephen McNutt (6 episodes)

Series Production Design: Mark S. Freeborn (9 episodes), Tony Wohlgemuth (3 episodes), and Zack Grobler (1 episode)

Series Art Direction: Tony Wohlgemuth (10 episodes), Peter Ochotta (3 episodes), Rodrigo Segovia (3 episodes), et al.

Series Costumes: Roland Sanchez (8 episodes), Susan De Laval (5 episodes), and Maya Mani (2 episodes)

Series Editing: Hibah Schweitzer (4 episodes), David Eisenberg (3 episodes), Andrew Seklir (3 episodes), et al.

Series Music: Michael Giacchino (11 episodes), Andrea Datzman (10 episodes), and Chris Tilton (10 episodes)

Series Casting: Sara Isaacson (12 episodes) and April Webster (9 episodes)

Cast: Sarah Jones (Det. Rebecca Madsen), Jorge Garcia (Dr. Diego Soto), Jonny Coyne (Warden Edwin James), Parminder Nagra (Dr. Lucy Banerjee), Sam Neill (Emerson Hauser), Leon Rippy (Dr. Milton Beauregard), et al.

ProRes 4:4:4, Widescreen (16:9), Color

60 minutes

2012–2014

REVOLUTION

Production Companies: Kripke Enterprises, Bad Robot, and Warner Bros. Television

Creator: Eric Kripke

Series Producers: Athena Wickham (37 episodes) and Robert M. Williams Jr. (37 episodes)

Series Executive Producers: **J. J. Abrams** (37 episodes), Bryan Burk (37 episodes), Jon Favreau (37 episodes), Eric Kripke (37 episodes), et al.

Series Associate Producers: Geoff Garrett (37 episodes) and Noreen O'Toole (37 episodes)

Series Co-Producers: Matt Pitts (22 episodes) and Oanh Ly (7 episodes)

Series Directors: Charles Beeson (9 episodes), Steve Boyum (7 episodes), Fred Toye (4 episodes), Helen Shaver (3 episodes), et al.

Series Writers: Paul Grellong (13 episodes), Matt Pitts (11 episodes), David Rambo (11 episodes), Anne Cofell Saunders (8 episodes), et al.

Series Cinematography: Jimmy Lindsey (11 episodes), William Wages (11 episodes), David Moxness (10 episodes), et al.

Series Production Design: Cary White (22 episodes), Doug J. Meerdink (19 episodes), and Zack Grobler (1 episode)
Series Art Direction: Yvonne Boudreaux (22 episodes), William G. Davis (13 episodes), Matthew C. Jacobs (1 episode), et al.
Series Costumes: Roland Sanchez (21 episodes), Mari-An Ceo (20 episodes), and Ha Nguyen (1 episode)
Series Editing: Anthony Pinker (14 episodes), Harry Jierjian (7 episodes), Nona Khodai (7 episodes), David Eisenberg (6 episodes), et al.
Series Music: Christopher Lennertz (37 episodes)
Series Casting: Erica S. Bream (42 episodes) and April Webster (37 episodes)
Cast: Billy Burke (Miles Matheson), Tracy Spiridakos (Charlie Matheson), Giancarlo Esposito (Tom Neville), Zak Orth (Aaron Pittman), David Lyons (Sebastian "Bass" Monroe), Elizabeth Mitchell (Rachel Matheson), JD Pardo (Jason Neville), Stephen Collins (Dr. Gene Porter), Daniella Alonso (Nora Clayton), Maureen Sebastian (Priscilla Pittman), et al.
Widescreen (16:9), Color
43 minutes

2013–2014
ALMOST HUMAN
Production Companies: Frequency Films, Bad Robot, and Warner Bros. Television
Creator: J. H. Wyman
Series Producers: Athena Wickham (13 episodes) and Tanya M. Swerling (12 episodes)
Series Executive Producers: **J. J. Abrams** (13 episodes), Bryan Burk (13 episodes), J.H. Wyman (13 episodes), and Naren Shankar (8 episodes)
Series Associate Producers: Dieter Ismagil (13 episodes), Noreen O'Toole (13 episodes), and Amanda Lencioni (4 episodes)
Series Co-Producers: Vladimir Stefoff (13 episodes)
Series Directors: Sam Hill (2 episodes), Brad Anderson (1 episode), Kenneth Fink (1 episode), Omar Madha (1 episode), et al.
Series Writers: Princeton Kennedy (5 episodes), Alison Schapker (3 episodes), Ingrid Kenning (2 episodes), Sarah Goldfinger (2 episodes), et al.
Series Cinematography: David Geddes (7 episodes), Michael Wale (6 episodes), and Thomas Yatsko (3 episodes)
Series Production Design: Ian D. Thomas (13 episodes)
Series Art Direction: Peter Andringa (13 episodes)
Series Costumes: Jenni Gullett (13 episodes)

Series Editing: Nicholas Erasmus (6 episodes), Michael R. Fox (6 episodes), Lola Popovac (6 episodes), Gregg Featherman (5 episodes), et al.
Series Music: The Crystal Method (13 episodes)
Series Casting: Sara Isaacson (13 episodes) and April Webster (13 episodes)
Cast: Karl Urban (Det. John Kennex), Michael Ealy (Dorian), Minka Kelly (Det. Valerie Stahl), Mackenzie Crook (Rudy Lom), Micharl Irby (Det. Richard Paul), Lili Taylor (Capt. Sandra Maldonado), Darren E. Scott (MX-43 '2'), Anthony Konechny (MX-43 '1'), Garfield Wilson (MX-43 '3'), et al.
Widescreen (16:9), Color
60 minutes

2014
BELIEVE
Production Companies: Bad Robot, Bonanza Productions, Esperanto Filmoj, and Warner Bros. Television
Creators: Alfonso Cuarón and Mark Friedman
Series Producers: David DeClerque (13 episodes), Tamara Isaac (13 episodes), Athena Wickham (6 episodes), Seamus Kevin Fahey (5 episodes), et al.
Series Executive Producers: Hans Tobeason (12 episodes), **J. J. Abrams** (6 episodes), Bryan Burk (6 episodes), Alfonso Cuarón (6 episodes), et al.
Series Associate Producers: Jill Risk (11 episodes), Noreen O'Toole (9 episodes), and Jay Worth (1 episode)
Series Co-Producers: Timothy A. Good (12 episodes) and Cecilia Kate Roque (1 episode)
Series Directors: Sam Hill (2 episodes), David Boyd (1 episode), Alfonso Cuarón (1 episode), Roxann Dawson (1 episode), et al.
Series Writers: Nick Antosca (11 episodes), Sneha Koorse (11 episodes), Ned Vizzini (5 episodes), Jonas Pate (4 episodes), et al.
Series Cinematography: Gonzalo Amat (8 episodes), Chris Norr (4 episodes), and Eric Gautier (1 episode)
Series Production Design: Roshelle Berliner (7 episodes) and Lester Cohen (1 episode)
Series Art Direction: Matteo De Cosmo (12 episodes) and Sarah Frank (1 episode)
Series Costumes: Stephani Lewis (11 episodes) and Stacey Battat (1 episode)
Series Editing: Rich Fox (5 episodes), Jennifer Van Goethem (4 episodes), Annette Davey (3 episodes), Michael R. Fox (1 episode), et al.
Series Music: Steven Price
Series Casting: Jessica Kelly (8 episodes), Suzanne Smith (5 episodes), April Webster (1 episode), and Hunter Lydon (1 episode, uncredited)

Cast: Jake McLaughlin (William Tate), Johnny Sequoyah (Bo Adams), Jamie Chung (Janice Channing), Kyle MacLachlan (Dr. Roman Skouras), Delroy Lindo (Dr. Milton Winter), Kerry Condon (Dr. Zoe Boyle), Katie McClellan (Lila Leeds), Arian Moayed (Corey), Trieste Kelly Dunn (FBI Special Agent Elizabeth Ferrel), et al.
Widescreen (16:9), Color
43 minutes

2016–
WESTWORLD
Production Companies: Bad Robot, Jerry Weintraub Productions, and Kilter Films
Series Producer: Cherylanne Martin
Series Executive Producers: **J. J. Abrams**, Bryan Burk, Lisa Joy, Jonathan Nolan, and Jerry Weintraub
Series Co-Executive Producers: Athena Wickham, Richard J. Lewis, Kathy Lingg, and Roberto Patino
Series Directors: Jonathan Nolan (2 episodes), Fred Toye (2 episodes), et al.
Series Writers: Jonathan Nolan (10 episodes), Lisa Joy (10 episodes), et al.
Series Cinematography: Brendan Galvin (4 episodes), Robert McLachlan (4 episodes), et al.
Series Production Design: Zack Grobler (9 episodes) and Nathan Crowley (1 episode)
Series Art Direction: James Bolenbaugh (10 episodes), Jonathan Carlos (7 episodes), et al.
Series Costumes: Ane Crabtree (9 episodes) and Trish Summerville (1 episode)
Series Editing: Andrew Seklir (3 episodes), Tanya M. Swerling (3 episodes), et al.
Series Music: Ramin Djawadi
Series Casting: John Papsidera
Series Cast: Evan Rachel Wood (Dolores Abernathy), Thandie Newton (Maeve Millay), James Marsden (Teddy Flood), Jeffrey Wright (Bernard Lowe), Ed Harris (Man in Black), Louis Herthum (Peter Abernathy), Anthony Hopkins (Dr. Robert Ford)
35mm, Widescreen (16:9), Color
60 minutes

2016
11.22.63
Production Companies: Carpenter B, Bad Robot, and Warner Bros. Television
Creator: Bridget Carpenter (developed for television by)

Series Producers: Joseph Boccia, James Franco, and Athena Wickham
Series Executive Producers: Bryan Burk, Bridget Carpenter, **J. J. Abrams**,
Stephen King, and Kevin Mcdonald
Series Associate Producer: Noreen O'Toole
Series Directors: James Strong (2 episodes), Frederick E.O. Toye (2 episodes),
John David Coles (1 episode), James Franco (1 episode), James Kent (1 episode),
and Kevin Mcdonald (1 episode)
Series Writers: Quinton Peeples (3 episodes), Brigitte Hales (1 episode), Joe
Henderson (1 episode), and Brian Nelson (1 episode)
Series Cinematography: Adam Suschitzky (7 episodes), David Katznelson (2
episodes)
Series Production Design: Carol Spier
Series Art Direction: Kimberley Zaharko (7 episodes), Elinor Rose Galbraith (3
episodes), and Elizabeth Beck (2 episodes)
Series Costumes: Roland Sanchez
Series Editing: Sue Blainey (3 episodes), Michael R. Fox (3 episodes), Plummy
Tucker (3 episodes), and Dorian Harris (2 episodes)
Series Music: Alex Heffes
Series Casting: Erica S. Bream (8 episodes) and April Webster (3 episodes)
Cast: James Franco (Jake Epping), Sarah Gadon (Sadie Dunhill), George MacKay
(Bill Turcotte), Chris Cooper (Al Templeton), Cherry Jones (Marguerite Oswald),
Daniel Webber (Lee Harvey Oswald), Kevin J. O'Connor (Yellow Card Man),
Lucy Fry (Marina Oswald), Jonny Coyne (George de Mohrenschildt), et al.
35mm, Widescreen (2.35:1), Color
60 minutes

2016
ROADIES
Production Companies: Bad Robot, Dooley & Company Productions, Vinyl
Films, and Warner Bros. Television
Creator: Cameron Crowe
Series Producers: Kelly Curtis, Peter Schindler, and Iain Paterson
Series Executive Producers: **J. J. Abrams**, Bryan Burk, Cameron Crowe, Winnie
Holzman, and Len Goldstein
Series Associate Producer: Noreen O'Toole
Series Co-Producers: Andy Fischer, Tamara Isaac, Greg Mariotti, and Vladimir
Stefoff
Series Directors: Cameron Crowe (4 episodes), Jon Kasdan (2 episodes), Sam
Jones (1 episode), Allison Liddi-Brown (1 episode), Jeffrey Reiner (1 episode),
and Julie Anne Robinson (1 episode)

Series Writers: Winnie Holzman (3 episodes), David Rosen (2 episodes), Hannah Friedman (1 episode), and Tom Kapinos (1 episode)

Series Cinematography: Thomas Yatsko (9 episodes) and Nicola Marsh (1 episode)

Series Production Design: Clay A. Griffith

Series Art Direction: Kiel Gookin (9 episodes), Roger Fires (1 episode), and Jeremy Stanbridge (1 episode)

Series Costumes: Christine Wada (7 episodes) and Deborah Lynn Scott (3 episodes)

Series Editing: David Bilow (3 episodes), Jon Dudkowski (3 episodes), Shannon Mitchell (3 episodes), and Joe Hutshing (1 episode)

Series Music: Jordan Cook (1 episode), Jim James (1 episode), and Lucius (1 episode)

Series Casting: Gail Levin (10 episodes) and Candice Elzinga (1 episode)

Cast: Luke Wilson (Bill Hanson), Carla Gugino (Shelli Anderson), Imogen Poots (Kelly Ann), Rafe Spall (Reg Whitehead), Keisha Castle-Hughes (Donna Mancini), Peter Cambor (Milo), Machine Gun Kelly (Wesley), Ron White (Phil Valentine), Christopher Backus (Rick Bayless), et al.

Digital, Widescreen (16:9), Color

60 minutes

J. J. Abrams: Interviews

Beardless Wonders of Film Making

Robert Young / 1982

"I got a call from a fifteen-year-old filmmaker who said he had seven years' experience with feature films," says Cable TV show host Gerard Ravel, president of Word of Mouth Productions. "I just couldn't believe it! I couldn't stop laughing."

Ravel laughs no longer. That filmmaker, Jeffrey Abrams, persuaded Ravel to take a look at his work. "I was amazed at how professional it was," Ravel says.

"We aired about an hour of Jeffrey's stuff and got a lot of response from other teen filmmakers, some of them very good. So I put together a showcase of their best work to see how it would do in the theaters."

Abrams's latest film, *High Voltage*, screened at the Best Teen Super 8mm Films of '81 recently at the Nuart Theater.

Created by Ravel a year and a half ago as a vehicle to encourage young filmmakers, the festival has recently evolved into an end in itself—a career steppingstone that Ravel plans to release nationwide on 35mm film.

"We have received many offers from studios and talent agencies," Ravel says. "Disney Studios, which collaborated with us on the soundtrack to (thirteen-year-old) Mussa Mustafson's *Casagrain*, has expressed interest in helping us promote the next festival. Also, Creative Artist Agency, a top Hollywood talent agency, scouted the show."

Ravel, self-described mother hen and not-so-gentle prodder, has assumed a militaristic control over the situation in order to protect his young protégés. "I got them to sign exclusive contracts placing them under the management of Word of Mouth," he says. "I want to mold these filmmakers like a military organization because I'm a perfectionist. What I'm putting them through right now is basic training."

Abrams is one of the centerpieces of Ravel's army. His drive in life is to emulate his idol, John Carpenter. "I see stuff by Steven Spielberg and John Carpenter, and

I want to do it too," Abrams says. "I've always wanted to be a director. I did a clay animation thing on my parents' home movie camera when I was seven, and I've been making films ever since. This experience with Gerard is a big step for me."

High Voltage, a forty-five-minute horror/comedy, was, by popular ballot, the audience favorite at the Nuart screenings. The audience approved its tongue-in-cheek look at high school stereotypes.

Abrams's current project is *Little Nothings*, a collection of shorts he has created since he was twelve. "Before I was twelve, I used to do everything myself: write, direct, produce, everything. But I've broken down lately and let my friend, Jonathan, help."

"It's hard to believe," Ravel says. "I can't figure out where these kids find the time."

Matt Reeves, whose murder mystery, *Stiletto*" is rated second among teenage films in the nation by the Photographic Society of America, keeps a grueling weekend schedule.

"My mind moves very quickly. I'm tired of *Stiletto* already. It bores me. I don't want to see it again. I just wish my new film, *The Loser*, could have been finished in time for the festival," says the fifteen-year-old. "It's ten times better than *Stiletto*. I'm never going to do another horror film again." Gore, implied or explicit, makes him uncomfortable.

The contradiction of teens playing detectives and police sergeants in *Stiletto* bothers Reeves. His next film, he promises, will feature "kids playing kids."

"I eventually want to get into stories with a purpose, with a message like *Ordinary People*," he says.

For *The Loser*, which is set in the 1950s, Reeves has obtained the services of ex–Mandrell Sisters' choreographer Ken Grant.

"I'd have to say that Matt is the most professional of the kids," says Ravel. His casting sessions and rehearsals are videotaped; several copies are made of the script; and the makeup, lighting, and directing are carefully supervised.

"I want to be a director just like Martin Scorsese," Reeves says. "And this exposure can't hurt."

Larry Fong, who made *Toast Encounters of the Burnt Kind* when he was seventeen, feels the exposure may help his career ambition which he feels is slightly off-beat.

"Don't laugh, but my goal is to someday go to China and teach filmmaking," the twenty-one-year-old movie buff says. "I really don't know why, but it's appealing for some reason. The people over there would probably think I was a jerk though. I'm just too Southern Californian. Heck, I don't even know their language."

Toast Encounters is Fong's only completed work to date. The special effects, including an intergalactic toaster and a miniature neighborhood replica, required three months of work and a budget of $20.

His current interest is the study of screenplay formats and makeup technique. "Right now, I just want to go back to UCLA and get my degree in film studies. Somehow, I don't think *Toast Encounters* will make me rich," Fong says.

Although most of the young filmmakers' work is shot with cameras in the $1,000 range equipped with fade-out and stop-action capabilities, poor picture quality is a major detriment to Super 8mm film, according to Fong.

Special Xenon projectors, designed to project 20' x 20' Super 8mm images, minimize this problem. "A lot of people are surprised by the quality," Ravel says. "We're not dealing with the standard 8mm home-movie technology."

"Transferring the films to 35mm will upgrade the clarity to professional standards," says Ravel. "It's a world of difference."

The entire Best Teen Films program will be available shortly on half-inch videocassette.

Presently, Word of Mouth has a feature-length suspense thriller, five karate films, and a comedy feature in preproduction. The students will handle the various duties on a rotating basis with Ravel as technical assistant and, of course, iron-fisted general.

The Best Teen Super 8mm Films of '81 will become a monthly event at local revival theaters beginning in April.

From the Archives: J. J. Abrams Interview Regarding *Superman*

Ed Gross / 2002

Interview conducted by and copyright Ed Gross. Published October 27, 2009.
Reprinted by permission.

With MTV's new interview with J. J. Abrams about how he would potentially be interested in revisiting the Superman movie script he had written at the beginning of the decade, VFK decided to dip into the archives to resurrect this 2002 interview with Abrams in which he talked a (tiny) bit about the project.

As fans may recall, a review of his script was posted on Ain't It Cool News, and it was truly shredded. Shortly thereafter, Warner Bros., based on fan outcry based on the review, shelved the script. Of course, given Abrams's current status in Hollywood, WB could very seriously reconsider that screenplay.

Back in 2002, while Abrams was in the midst of production on the second season of *Alias*, he spoke to VFK Editor Edward Gross about the project. He doesn't reveal much in the way of details but certainly expresses his enthusiasm over the project.

This was the version that was supposed to be directed by McG and potentially starring Brendan Fraser as Superman.

VOICES FROM KRYPTON: The real question, of course, is how you came to be signed on as the writer of the new Superman film.
J. J. ABRAMS: Pretty simple, really. They approached me about doing the movie. I took a meeting. For me, I miss doing movies. I love doing TV, but I wanted to do another film. What's been nice is working with producers with incredible records, like Jerry Bruckheimer and my idols. What's wonderful about working on *Superman* is that as a kid I was the biggest fan. My three-and-a-half-year-old son goes to bed almost every night wearing a Superman shirt. I couldn't pass it up.

VOICES FROM KRYPTON: What's the approach to the material?

J. J. ABRAMS: What's nice is that after a lot of years of trying to get this going and not succeeding, everyone's coming at it with a very fresh, open mind. What's exciting for me is that we've got some incredible, really big ideas that go beyond just the one story we're telling. *Alias* has actually been an amazing training ground for me. In this *Superman* we're talking a lot about where he's come from and where he's going. I can't talk about specifics, but I can tell you that there are a lot of exciting, big ideas. I think it's Superman for everyone and not just for people who already know the character. It's for the uninitiated.

VOICES FROM KRYPTON: Do you feel the first two Christopher Reeve films are a tremendous shadow to overcome, or do you basically just ignore them?

J. J. ABRAMS: I think it's really a question of embracing what has come before it. This, in many ways, is a retelling of *Superman*. They did four of those movies, then they did *Supergirl*—you have to start fresh. I don't think this should be looked at as the fifth sequel.

VOICES FROM KRYPTON: From what I've gathered from people I've spoken to in the past, producer Jon Peters isn't much of a fan of the Superman costume or the image of Superman flying. This, of course, begs the question: why bother making a Superman movie?

J. J. ABRAMS: It's safe to say that if Superman doesn't fly, it would be a disappointment. I do think that we're approaching this in a very fresh way, but there are certain things that people have come to realize are important. You have to have the costume and you want to do a Superman movie that will be so satisfying. I'm so sick of going to big blockbuster movies and leaving feeling like I died a little bit, like, "Oh, my God, how disappointing was that?" What's so exciting for us is that we're approaching this thing knowing and feeling the kind of movie that as kids we used to see. I feel that we're going to try as hard as we can to make this a satisfying experience.

TV Producer J. J. Abrams on Creating *Lost*

David Bianculli / 2004

Transcript of *Fresh Air* radio show, October 14, 2004. Published by permission of WHYY, Inc. *Fresh Air* with Terry Gross is produced at WHYY in Philadelphia and distributed by NPR. Podcasts are available at www.npr.org/podcasts and at iTunes.

One of the most critically acclaimed shows of the new TV season is *Lost*. It's about what happens after a commercial airline crashes, leaving the survivors stranded on a mysterious island where they face dangers, some of them supernatural, lurking in the jungle. We learn about the characters gradually through flashbacks. *Lost* was created by J. J. Abrams, who also created the series *Alias*, about a CIA agent leading a double life. Another Abrams creation is *Felicity*, a TV series following a college student in New York. Abrams wrote the screenplays for the films *Armageddon* and *Forever Young*. Our TV critic, David Bianculli is enthusiastic about Abrams's new series *Lost* and spoke with him about it. Here's a clip from the pilot: Matthew Fox, from *Party of Five*, plays a doctor who takes care of others before taking time to tend to himself and a nasty gash in his side. He takes a travel sewing kit and asks a dazed survivor walking by, played by Evangeline Lilly, to stitch him up and close the wound.

NPR: David Bianculli asked J. J. Abrams to describe the filming of *Lost*.

J. J. Abrams: We went to Hawaii, where we shot for forty days, which sounds great but it is sort of tough when there are no interiors and you're out there. It was a pretty grueling but incredibly challenging and fun shoot.

David Bianculli: What are some of the things about location filming that are so difficult?
Abrams: Well, there's a sequence that's in the first hour of the show where, as an example, they are in the rain in the jungle, and they go to find the cockpit of the

plane which has fallen into the jungle. They go to retrieve a transponder that they hope to be able to send a signal. They get to the cockpit, and it's leaning against this enormous tree. They climb up the cockpit, and inside there's a pilot that's actually still alive. But the entire scene—the whole sequence was shot—if it had been a film, they would have built a set; they would have the interior of the cockpit. It would have been somewhat feasible and comfortable. We had a cockpit of a plane in the jungle placed against this tree, and it was, essentially, "Good luck." So, we literally shot the sequence in this enormous cockpit at a sixty-degree angle, and we had all the rain—a lot of it was real rain. It was muddy and smelled horrendous, and we were in this can. It was one of those things where the fun level was so high that it didn't matter that it was just, you know, sort of hard to do. We had all the crew in there, all the lighting. It was hot, but it was just one of those things. I'm not complaining. It was a great time, but at the end of the day, it was doing that for four or five days shooting. It was a real jumbo jet that was laying there, dressed remarkably realistically so it looked as if this thing had just crashed. The fact is, it's a horrifying sight, and with all the smoke and rubber burning, it just wears on you. After two, three, four, five, six, seven weeks, you're out there, and you're shooting this stuff. It was just exhausting. So, we did the shoot there, and, when you don't have any interiors and you're shooting outside for that length of time, it can be one of those things where it's like, "God, I miss *Felicity*." Those kids in that dorm room? You can't believe how easy it was to do those scenes.

Bianculli: How prominent are the *Twilight Zone* elements of *Lost* going to get as we get further into the season?

Abrams: There are a lot of elements to the show that excited me, and the primary one, really, is the cast of characters. The people who are on the island, to me, are kind of the only reason to tell the story. They've all got a history, and we're using flashbacks in order to see who these people were just prior to and long before this flight, in every episode. So, you're going to get a chance to see who these people were and who they are now, which is for me part of the pleasure of getting to work on this show. Simply speaking, visually, just spending one hour in the jungle or just on the beach, it is gorgeous, but you've got to modulate it a little bit. So, the flashbacks help in terms of getting us off the island. The *Twilight Zone* aspects, to me, are going to always be present, but the show is no way a straight forward, sci-fi show. I've had a lot of discussions about this. What is straight sci-fi? What does that mean exactly? Is it something that is more obviously science fiction like *Alien* or comedically science fiction like *Back to the Future* or more subtly science fiction like the stuff David Cronenberg might do. To me, the use of extraordinary circumstance colliding with ordinary people is the most interesting storytelling.

Bianculli: Let me ask you some questions about *Alias* now. You pulled off a very strange plot twist a couple of seasons in by adding two years in-between seasons, changing things, and then going back from there. How was that received by most fans? What are you doing to start this season?

Abrams: We've always done weird things on the show. I mean, *Alias* is such a specific—it's like having a kid that's really quirky, and people kind of look at the kid and go, "That's interesting." I think the thing about *Alias* is that given the kinds of twists and turns you do, you've got to be careful what you do. Because saying that someone is dead and then learning that they're not or saying that a character who has a roommate that then gets killed and is replaced by an evil double—these are the most embarrassing things to say. You say them, and you feel like an idiot. I mean, literally, just now, I'm sweating, so we trade in a very strange place on that show. The key to that show is it's done well when we commit to the "A" version of what is ultimately a "B" premise. When you say, "spy show," when you say, "college girl by day, spy by night," you're creating a world that clearly cannot exist in real life without having an attitude. The thing about the twist we did, that two-year jump, to me was one of the twists that I feel wasn't quite thought out as well as I wish I had thought it out. The two-jump, to me, was an amazing reversal at the end of an episode. She literally wakes up, and you don't know where you are. I think the character was lost and scared, and she ends up finding out that the man who she loved three scenes earlier had this great weekend planned and everything was rosy. She discovers that two years have passed, and this guy is married. It was sort of a great way to end the year because now we're like, "Oh, God, now what?" For me, the "now what" didn't live up to the response to the question. The show, to me, in that last season got away from the thing that I loved about the show, which is that the characters relate to each other in a specific way. I felt that we were misusing almost every key relationship on the show. We had eliminated two relationships that I really did love, with her friends. She and her father didn't really have much of a story, which is a mistake, and despite all that, we did some entertaining episodes and some stuff that people [liked]. It's some people's favorite season, so I have no idea what the hell people want. But this season begins in January, of *Alias*, and we did a lot of cool stuff to kind of click back into place where it was in the beginning.

Bianculli: How do you do that? How do you course-correct?

Abrams: Well, we looked at what we had, and we said, "What's the best version of this show? How can we get back to everything we love about this show?" We realized that there were some fundamental choices that we could make that would almost make the paradigm of the show that of the first two seasons. It was really a question of saying—look, someone like David Kelly, who is one of the masters of

TV writing, this guy, he'll do anything he wants, and you'll believe it because he did it. For example, he'll have a character who was always the secretary in the law firm show up in an episode and say, "I've been going to law school for the last couple years, and now I'm a lawyer." What the hell? You know? In the next episode, she is a lawyer, and you're not sitting there wondering—I've only done these couple shows. I have so much to learn, and I'm still watching what other people do. What you realize is you can debate forever over how you do something. If you know it's the right thing to do, you've got to figure out how to do it, and [you] just need to do it and commit to it. The key is you can't make it so far-fetched that the audience, whether new or a loyal viewer, feels like it's something that's too preposterous. Given that sort of hyperreality of *Alias*, these adjustments that we've made are some of the least egregious things we've done and immediately the show reaps the benefits of those choices.

Bianculli: Another *Alias* thing that I'm sort of fascinated by is sometimes you introduce the theme song and the title credits ten, twelve, fifteen minutes into the show where they shock me because I've forgotten that they haven't been here yet. I've never seen this before. Why do you do this?

Abrams: It's one of my favorite things to do: is to have the show play and have a long first act. We've had first acts that have gone twenty-one minutes long, and we'll do the opening credits—it's this bizarre thing that—I can't really explain it. At first, I thought, "Oh, we're going to be really clever when we do this. People will get sucked in; the ratings will be higher." It never helps our ratings. There's never been a benefit to it other than I think it's just funny to me. There's no real reason other than if an act is working, let's not cut away. Remember *The Fugitive*, the Harrison Ford movie?

Bianculli: Sure.

Abrams: I remember seeing that movie and having the same reaction when the credits came up fairly late into the film. I had that same reaction, "Oh, my God, this is so cool. This is all preamble? Oh, my God!" There's a very interesting psychological interaction, for the audience, where they're watching something and there are credits on. For some people, it's irrelevant to even look at them or recognize them. For me, at least, when I'm watching a scene and there are credits underneath it, it oddly takes the onus off that scene, having to be an excellent scene. So, a lot of times, we'll have a scene, and it's a little clunky; it's not quite the greatest scene. Well, if we make that scene the opening of the second act and we put credits over it, it kind of takes the edge off that scene having to be just the greatest thing you've ever seen. Credits can be a shellac or something to make it look a little shinier than it is.

Bianculli: You got interested in writing, specifically writing for film, very early, and you got exposed to more television than most young people do. How did that happen?

Abrams: My father is a TV movie producer, Gerald Abrams, and as a kid, he had an office at the Paramount lot. I would go with him to work on occasion and just wander around the lot. It was a fantasy, the greatest thing. My favorite thing was walking into the facades of buildings, looking around the back side, and seeing they were nothing—actually, storage rooms, usually. But it was that weird, desolate thing, sort of *Twilight Zone* feeling. In fact, the first episode of *The Twilight Zone*, which is my favorite show of all time, is called, "Where Has Everybody Gone?" or something like that, with Earl Holliman. It was essentially inspired, I learned later, by when Rod Serling was walking around a backlot, much like I did when I was a kid, and he, of course, came up with a genius idea. For me, it felt cool to walk around a place where movies had been shot.

Bianculli: How old were you, and what years were these?

Abrams: I was born in '66. I can tell what happened, which is I'd go into *Happy Days*, *Laverne and Shirley*, and *Mork and Mindy* would be rehearsing these shows, and no one would be in the bleachers. I would get to know the guards a little bit. They'd let me in, I'd sit in the bleachers, and I'd watch them rehearse these series. It's very odd because you're watching a show at home as a kid. You're watching *Happy Days*, and there's the Fonze and there's Richie, and you go there. You're sitting in the bleachers, and they're wearing their civvies, the clothes they'd wear any day of the week. It was this odd, play rehearsal, like watching Robin Williams rehearsing for *Mork and Mindy*, seeing him just go off, and it was just so crazy. It was just such an insight into the process, so I always loved watching the half-hour show being put together. And, later, my father actually told me we were watching *Mary Tyler Moore* one night, and there was this laugh, this classic, distinct laugh that you heard. It was like "Ha, Ha, Ha"—

Bianculli: James L. Brooks?

Abrams: James L. Brooks! That's James L. Brooks; he's the creator of the show. Being aware of that and listening to that laugh over the years on *Mary Tyler Moore*, on *Rhoda*, and on *Taxi* and hearing, not just the laugh, but the timing of the laugh. He would laugh in places that no one else was laughing. It was a laugh about the process, putting it together. I was acutely aware—"Why would he be laughing there?" I realized that when they were rehearsing, the actors must have been working on some piece and it was the build-up to what the audience laughed at the joke, but he would laugh. He was very unselfconscious about his laugh; it would kind of come loudly in some places. Growing up, I always felt like whenever I heard his laugh, I was in on how he was putting together, even though I might have been wrong. Years later, I got to know Jim Brooks, I talked to him about this, and he just smiled. He understood what I meant.

J. J. Abrams—*Mission: Impossible III*

Peter Canavese / 2006

From GrouchoReviews.com, February 11, 2006. Reprinted by permission of Peter Canavase.

After developing the story of *Taking Care of Business*, writing the screenplays for *Regarding Henry*, *Forever Young*, *Gone Fishin'* (with Jill Mazursky), and *Joy Ride* (with Clay Tarver), and contributing to the screenplay for *Armageddon*, J. J. Abrams found unexpected success on television. Abrams co-created the WB college soap *Felicity* (with Keri Russell) and created the ABC spy thriller *Alias* (with Jennifer Garner). Most recently, Abrams co-created *Lost*—and won an Emmy for directing the show's pilot—before landing the plum job of directing and cowriting *Mission: Impossible III* (a mission that thwarted directors David Fincher and Joe Carnahan). Abrams spoke to me on the occasion of the 2006 WonderCon, at San Francisco's Moscone Convention Center.

Groucho: Can you talk about your experience with the original TV series, and were there storytelling elements that you felt like you really wanted to bring back from that show? Also, was there anything you cherry-picked from the previous films that you thought, "That's cool. I want to keep that element"?

J. J. Abrams: There's no question for me that one of the most fun aspects of the TV show, as a kid always loving it, was this team. Even though in many ways that show was sort of the *CSI* of its time in that it was a very emotion-free, incredibly story-heavy show that wasn't about the inner lives of these people. What I loved about the show is that it was this group, and it was how their relationships—even though the relationships were things that you can kind of—you had to sort of intuit or extrapolate based on incredibly, you know, subtle human behavior. "Oh look, they have a relation—oh, he likes her. Oh, he's mad at—" You have to figure this shit out—it's never text. But that kind of stuff to me was always like—I love the dynamic of these people who happen to be—and seeing the roles they would play and often the roles they would play with each other in front of other people. So you were in on the whole play of it. There were episodes where, like, there would be one or two people in a room who wouldn't know that those two or three people were all working together to convince them of some—and I love that kind of stuff! And, look, there were moments of it in—like in the first movie, you had moments like that. In the very, very opening or in the embassy scene, there were moments where you kind of had it. But it never to me—I love when you go, "Okay wait a minute. I know what they have to do. I don't know how they're going to do it, but I know that—" And then, "Let's see. Oh, my God, the thing they never anticipated goes wrong." Or they didn't—I just loved that feeling of this group working together for a very specific goal. So there was that. And I think that we brought that back passionately because that was a really fun thing. The other thing is I loved elements of the first two films. I certainly am in no way knocking them. In fact we embrace them and make reference to a couple things in this movie. One is an homage to the going down just 'cause I thought, "You've got to do it almost as a joke." But it's such a throwaway moment in the movie with everything else—but I wanted to do it just because it was there. Then the other thing is we make a couple references to some story stuff, but it's very oblique and truly only we will appreciate it. You know what I'm saying? Like, seriously—

G: Is it true [Tom Cruise] made a mock trailer of the stunts—did you ever see that?—a video, kind of pre-vis of his own for—?
JJA: He made a trailer very early on when they were going to do the Joe Carnahan incarnation, and it was—there weren't stunts in it, but it was sort of images and stuff, just to express the feeling for what he felt the trailer should be like. It was a different story, a different movie—

G: What is Ethan Hunt's home life really like?
JJA: Well, here's the thing. You know, the first two movies I thought were a lot of fun, but the thing for me . . . when Tom asked if I wanted to do this, beyond saying, "Yes," before he finished asking me, you know, "Do you want to dir—?" "Yes."—I thought the opportunity to do a version of *Mission: Impossible* was actually . . . it would actually realize the promise that I think the TV series delivered upon. Not to say the first two weren't great, but they were different. The show is so great because it was about this team. The first movie and, certainly, the second movie—it was basically just about Ethan Hunt. So to me, the way in was, "How do you actually exist as a human being and do the stuff that this guy supposedly does? How are you a man and a spy?" because all we know from the first two movies is his mom and dad are dead and he likes to rock-climb. You don't know anything else. So I thought, "Oh, my God, I get to do the third in the series where you don't know dick about this guy. You could make up anything you want—you could just say, "He has nutty hobbies." You could say anything. So, in asking, "At forty years

old, who is this man?" he's going to be a different guy than he was in the first film. And there have been amazing spy movies and shows made since then. The *Bourne* films, *24*, you look at the James Bond films that have been made since then: it's a different arena. So when you say *Mission: Impossible III*, yes, you've got the huge star, you've got the franchise, but that's obviously not a reason to make a movie. So the question is "How do you make a movie that's good regardless of those things?" Our ambition—and it's up to you to decide if we succeeded—was: tell a compelling story, and that to me was about "Who is he as a man? What is his home-life like?" So, the endless answer to your question is: it's very familiar, and it's very relatable. He happens to—when he goes to work—go to that bridge. This is what makes the story interesting to me.

Interview: J.J Abrams and Michelle Monaghan

Clint Morris / 2006

From *MovieHole*, May 2006. Reprinted by permission of Clint Morris.

He might be the force behind two of the biggest TV shows on television, *Alias* and *Lost*, but creator/writer J. J. Abrams is clearly a fan before he's a filmmaker. In Australia to promote his feature directorial debut *Mission: Impossible III*, the good-natured Abrams explains that he's still a garrulous manic fan when it comes to crossing paths with celebrities.

Clearly even a bit of a geek at heart (though he jokes that the glasses he wears don't actually have glass in them—they're mainly to help him "look smart" in photographs), the bespectacled wonder kid—now one of the most in-demand writers in Hollywood—says the highlight of any day for him is getting an email from British comics Simon Pegg or Ricky Gervais.

"If I don't get an email from Simon (who has a small role in *M:i:III*) or Ricky Gervais—who I met through *Alias*—I get so bummed. It's like 'Ohhh.' It's like my favorite thing," gushes Abrams, smiling like someone whose just been notified of a raffle win. "Simon is maybe the happiest biproduct of doing this movie for me. He and I email each other all the time now."

An email or phone call from Tom Cruise, on the other hand, didn't just excite him—it almost put a swift impede to his heart.

When he was informed that the A-list superstar wanted him to direct the third instalment of the *Mission: Impossible* franchise—the first was helmed by Brian De Palma, the second by John Woo—he was convinced it was a prank. After all, who would want a self-confessed "TV boy" handling one of the biggest movie franchises in the world?

"When Tom offered me the movie, it was the most unexpected thing—on every level," explains Abrams, who wrote the films *Regarding Henry* and *Roadkill*, among others, earlier in his career. "The weirdest thing was I had gotten to know Tom, we had become friends, and he had never bought it up. I knew he was getting ready to do *Mission: Impossible*. I thought maybe he might ask me to help with the script, or something, if they had problems with it, but he gave me the impression there were no issues at all. He seemed quite happy with what was happening with it."

A short time later, Abrams was out for a dinner with a friend when a call came through from his agent. "[He] asked me, 'Are you aware that Tom wants you to direct this movie?.' I thought it was a misunderstanding or a prank. I had just talked to Tom, like, a week earlier or something, and he didn't say anything about it."

Abrams went directly to the source to find out what was going on. "I walk in [to Cruise's house], and he just gives me that Tom Cruise smile and says, 'So, you wanna do it?' I was like 'Are you kidding me? This is insane. What happened to the guy that was supposed to direct the movie?'"

It was a fair question to ask. *Mission: Impossible III* had been in the works, at the point, for a couple of years. A number of different writers and directors, including David Fincher, Frank Darabont, and Joe Carnahan, had been attached at some time or another in the project's development phase.

When Abrams was asked to come onboard, it was assumed he would direct from one of the existing scripts.

"When I read the script that they had written, I really liked it; it was really cool. I just wasn't the right person to direct it. It wasn't the version that I'd be the best director of. So I said, 'Yeah, I'd like to do *Mission III*, but this isn't the version that I think I'm suited for.' I thought Tom would say, 'Oh, well, we'll find someone else.' But, he said, 'Well, what do you want to do?' I said, 'My version would be a more personal version, a more intimate movie, funnier, and it would be more heartbreaking.' He said, 'Well, that's the version I've wanted to do from the beginning.'"

Because of his TV commitments—*Lost* had just started, and he didn't want to take leave from that so early on in its infancy—Abrams said it would take him a year to put something together. Cruise was prepared to wait.

"It was like every day . . . it got weirder," smiles Abrams, so obviously in awe of Cruise's kindness. Cruise didn't stop at merely giving Abrams an elongated deadline—he also told him he had free reign to do whatever he wanted with the movie.

"Tom said from the beginning that he wanted it to be 'J. J. Abrams's *Mission: Impossible*.' I was skeptical, it just didn't seem right for an actor or producer of his stature to let me do what I want, but he really did. . . . He let me just go for it. He even let me cast the movie. For instance, I brought in Keri Russell, whom I've wanted to work with again since we did *Felicity*, and I also bought my regular crew over—my editors, my production designers, my composer. He let me make the movie I wanted to make. All Tom had to do was to be a little bit of a jerk, a little less kind or even collaborative, and it could've derailed the whole thing."

Abrams never approached the film any differently to [what] he did working on one of his TV shows because he always shot *Alias* and *Lost* like a film—even if the network didn't show them in the wide screen format that they were shot in.

"I directed in wide screen, as if it were a movie, knowing it would be on DVD and live on forever. So, I never thought of it as TV stuff compared to film stuff."

In the same sense, he also didn't feel pressured to bring in huge stars to costar opposite Cruise in *Mission: Impossible III*. He cast the film as he did any of his TV shows—simply signing those who were right for the part and, for the most part, all fresh faces.

"Michelle Monaghan's character [Cruise's on-screen love interest] is a good example. I didn't want people to necessarily know the actress and go, 'Oh, that's so and so from so and so,'" says Abrams, who's responsible for giving both Jennifer Garner and Keri Russell their big breaks on his TV shows, *Alias* and *Felicity*, respectively. "I remember when I saw *Jerry Maguire* with my wife—then girlfriend—and I believed the relationship between Tom and Renee Zellweger. It was because we didn't know Renee Zellweger at the time. I believed that she really was this woman somehow. It wasn't like 'Oh, look, its Demi Moore in that part,' you know?"

Monaghan was just as shocked as her director was when she was asked if she'd like to be involved in the movie. She had good reason, though—the only thing Abrams had seen her in was her audition tape for the film *Constantine*—a film she was ultimately cut out of.

"He saw my audition tape and called up out of the blue and asked to have a meeting. He wanted me to audition with Tom!" says the animated young actress who first gained attention in last year's action-comedy *Kiss, Kiss, Bang, Bang*.

"I met Tom on the set of *War of the Worlds*, so not only was I meeting Tom, I was meeting Steven Spielberg! I just thought 'What am I doing here?' A year ago, this Easter Sunday, I was told I got the job. I started crying. J. J. was like 'What? Is there a scheduling conflict?' I was like 'No, I just got the job.' He was like 'Don't cry about it, my God!'"

And was Tom Cruise exactly how she'd imagined he'd be?

"I already had my own perception of what Tom was going to be like. I thought, "He probably won't talk to me that much, and he'll probably spend all his time in his trailer." I couldn't have been more wrong. I almost wanted to call him another name—like Harry, for instance—because it's as if there's Tom Cruise the entity, and then this other guy. 'But you're not Tom Cruise, Tom Cruise is this,' I'd tell him."

What Abrams wanted to do with this sequel was to make it a little more human, and not necessarily a straight-up action film.

"The first movie was so much about plot and suspense; the second movie is so much about action; and this movie, I think, takes a more realistic approach than a stylistic approach," says the director.

"Whilst this is a movie that's full of action—more than the first two combined, when you count the sequences—it's not an action movie. It's a love story, and there's a lot of comedy and heartfelt stuff in it too. *Die Hard* is a good example of a movie that was a great movie that just happened to have action in it, but I don't think of it is an action movie. The reason that film was so effective, and the reason you tune into it whenever it's on, is because of the characters."

"I don't think you knew anything about Ethan Hunt other than his parents were killed," adds Michelle Monaghan. "What's appealing about this film . . . is that you do care about him. It really sets the scenes for the super spy's private life—what does he tell his family?—it really explores interpersonal relationships.

"Everything is really character-driven, and you're so invested in these characters. Unless you care about them, you don't really care about all the blowing up and all those special effects," she says. On a personal level, the actress was also relieved to discover that her character, Hunt's fiancée Julia, wouldn't be your typical clichéd damsel in distress.

"Yeah, I don't like to be that girl!" laughs the actress who claims she had to play one such character in the film *North Country*. "As a woman in Hollywood, you don't always want to be that damsel in distress or that victim. There is a point in which she is threatened, but this is the thing—J. J. really likes strong female characters."

While Abrams eagerly awaits the world's response to his first film as director ("It's like I've got this secret, and I just want to share it with all of you."), he returns to the world of TV. The first thing he's doing there is saying goodbye to *Alias*, which comes to a close shortly.

"It was the right time, but it was also bittersweet. It's so much better to be here than for the network to get to the end of the season and say, 'OK, that's it.' We wanted to end it right," he says, adding, "The ending is fantastic . . . it's really, really good."

Monaghan, on the other hand, is going straight into another project. She'll play a lead role in Ben Affleck's directorial debut *Gone, Baby, Gone*, based on the book by Dennis Lehane.

"It's going to be set in Boston, and it'll star Casey Affleck and Ed Harris. I play a private investigator . . . kind of like a low-rate private investigator and something really serious happens in South Boston."

Until rehearsals for that start, though, she'll spend some time in Australia with her Melbourne-born husband. "We're going to football on the weekend. I've really wanted to go to a game for a very long time. He's not a big footy fan, but I said, 'Someone better join me, or it'll be just me and the VB.'"

J. J. Abrams

George Stephanopoulas / 2006

Transcript from *Charlie Rose*, May 2, 2006. Published by permission of Rosemary Guerin, coordinating producer, *Charlie Rose*.

GEORGE STEPHANOPOULAS: I am now joined by J. J. Abrams. You probably know him as the creator and executive producer of two big hits on television, *Alias* and *Lost*, and now he's about to make his director's film debut with *Mission: Impossible III*. It comes out this Friday, and of course it stars Tom Cruise as IMF agent Ethan Hunt. J. J. Abrams is here in the studio and so what is it, is it Hilary or Giuliani? I saw you listening to that political panel, and you wanted to jump in on that.

J. J. ABRAMS: I think I'm the perfect next guest. I'll explain why. When you look at Iran's nuclear program—What am I doing here?

STEPHANOPOULAS: You don't want to weigh in?

ABRAMS: No. Listen. It was a fascinating discussion. I was about to just run away and not be there in the room.

STEPHANOPOULAS: Well, I was about to run away. You talk about Iran's nuclear program, the big weapon in *Mission: Impossible III* is something called the Rabbit's Foot?

ABRAMS: It stands for anything that scares us. You know what I mean? It's the classic McGuffin. The thing that the characters are going after.

STEPHANOPOULAS: We never find out how it's going to destroy us all?

ABRAMS: There's speculation in the movie. For me, when I see movies like that, every time they get too expositional and you hear the characters explaining in great detail what some of the technical stuff is, I always zone out.

STEPHANOPOULAS: Either technical or politics. We were just joking about the politics.

ABRAMS: That's true.

STEPHANOPOULAS: If you bring too much politics into movies, that's something that you think hurts it, or it's just not what you do?

ABRAMS: It was important that—it's *Mission: Impossible III*. There's a three in the title, so we have to address that. You don't go to see that movie to see a manifesto. It's not going to be, but I think that this movie was made in a different time than the first two movies. I didn't want it to be vapid either. I didn't want to—

STEPHANOPOULAS: The last one was pre-9/11?

ABRAMS: Oh, yeah. Exactly. I wanted to make sure that at least the movie, without hitting it over the head, acknowledged the context in which it was released.

STEPHANOPOULAS: It is still a *Mission: Impossible* movie. Let me just show a little clip from last night, and I'm just going to get you to comment on it. . . .

Now, my wife and I are watching that last night. It's unbelievable. You've got a mile-long bridge, a convoy of cars, a helicopter, and heat-seeking missiles. I have a how question! Where does it first come from?

ABRAMS: In this movie—

STEPHANOPOULAS: Are you actually sitting looking at a pad of paper and marking this out?

ABRAMS: The thing that was fun for us in this movie is that we knew that the playground in *Mission: Impossible* is pretty limitless in terms of what you could do, but the reason I was excited about doing this, not just because it was an opportunity to make a movie which in and of itself is enough for me to jump at it, but the truth is when Tom asked me if I was interested in directing this movie I immediately said, "Yes," and the reason why is I felt, as much as I enjoyed the first two *Mission: Impossible* movies—and I did—they didn't really concern themselves with who his character was, like, who he was as a person. I just felt that was really exciting to me. I wanted to just play with that idea, which we touched upon in *Alias*. How do these two worlds coexist? The sort of hyperreal, larger than life, super-spy, and just the mundane—

STEPHANOPOULAS: Real life.

ABRAMS:—Yes, the mundane every day, the stuff that you and I have in our lives. That was critical to me, so with these kinds of action sequences, we knew we would have these kinds of moments. My one mandate with the other two writers was I didn't want to start with those. I didn't want to begin with "Okay. We have a bridge sequence, and let's figure out a story around a bridge." I said, "What's a story about this man? A man who is a spy, who is in love, who is lying to the woman he loves. How does he live with himself? What is it like when those two worlds collide?"

STEPHANOPOULAS: That's why Tom Cruise wanted you; in fact he wrote—
ABRAMS: Oh, no.

STEPHANOPOULAS: —in this week's *Time* magazine, you're named one of the most influential people in the United States. Big, big honor. Tom Cruise writes about it, he says he wanted you right away, but there were a lot of sundry movie executives who were worried about it.
ABRAMS: Look, I worked in television, but this is, like, a huge franchise movie, so what Tom did and what I am so grateful to him for, is he gave me an opportunity that no one would have given me. I've been very lucky in the past six or seven years to give opportunities to different writers or editors, actors, composers—and they've been very grateful—but I always feel like I'm lucky because I got these people-

STEPHANOPOULAS: Educate me here a little bit. You've created television shows; you've directed television shows. Why is it such a big leap to direct a film?
ABRAMS: When Damon Lindelof and I created *Lost*, we knew this was a two-hour pilot. We knew it was like making a little movie. We were very excited about that. Like, I directed it. It felt, like, a little bit bigger—

STEPHANOPOULAS: That is a movie.
ABRAMS: It was like a movie. When you do a movie of this scale, there's a different thing going on because it's a lot more expensive. The stakes are much higher. There's an unwritten rule that TV is over here and film's over here and the bridges are hard to find. I feel like what Tom did for me was give me that opportunity that I just feel beholden to him for letting me—and not just the opportunity—but we got to make the movie the right way. He was supportive the entire time. It was a big shoot. He never demanded anything. He was never micromanaging. It was an incredibly happy and creative environment to go to work in.

STEPHANOPOULAS: For you personally then, was it that big a leap, or did you feel like you were doing the same work you do every day?
ABRAMS: To be totally honest, I felt incredibly comfortable, and I think part of it was that support, part of it was the crew was so good. I worked with a lot of people I'd worked with before since *Felicity*, *Alias*, *Lost*. I'm sure you've been in situations

where, when you're trying to do your job and there's someone looking over your shoulder saying, "No," you kind of shut down a little bit. This was the opposite. This was, like, people were free, not just me, but the entire crew was free to do their job and do it well. And they did.

STEPHANOPOULAS: When you're working with someone of the scale of Tom Cruise, he's working for you because you're the director, yet you're working for him because he's the producer. How does that work?

ABRAMS: A lot of people said, "Careful. Star-producer. This is going to be a disaster." I got to tell you, he was—like I said, every day, and it's a long shoot, you see the best and the worst of people over that many months and that kind of pressure, and he said from the very beginning, "I want this to be your movie. I'm your actor. You're the director. Let's make the movie." I thought, you know, "Let's see—"

STEPHANOPOULAS: You didn't believe it?

ABRAMS: I thought, "How could that really be possible?" But every step of the way—I knew Tom—I didn't think he was going to suddenly turn and become that controlling, and he was true to his word. It was amazing.

STEPHANOPOULAS: You joked in the *New York Times* a couple of weeks ago, the question you get most now is "What's Tom Cruise really like?" I'm not going to ask you that question, but what I want to get at is where does the creativity—where is the line between creativity and commerce because obviously Tom Cruise is a huge star, obviously his personal life over the last year has been reported on, talked about probably more than his work in the last year, and does that effect either the work you're doing in the movie or change the shape of the movie in any way?

ABRAMS: It didn't at all, and the thing is, a lot of the stuff you're referring to happened. We were just about to start shooting; this was into preproduction, so we had written the movie, prepped the movie, cast the film. It wasn't like we were suddenly responding to stuff. We did very few adjustments along the way to be honest with you. A lot of movies of this scale start shooting prematurely, and, suddenly, a script is being written a month into shooting. We were very lucky to have a solid script and a schedule. We finished ahead of schedule and under budget, and it was, relatively speaking, very responsible. I was aware of the Tom Cruise baggage before he went on *Oprah* and before all the stuff you're referring to. The baggage for me is he's such a megastar that any movie he does, it's like you have to figure out a way to deal with what people know about him going in. I wanted to start the movie in a way that was just so unexpected and so shocking. Not a James Bond, huge action sequence, with the skiing and the Union Jack parachute. I wanted to do something that was—which would have been odd since it's American, but—

STEPHANOPOULAS: It was a real *Alias*-type start.

ABRAMS: I wanted to do something that thrust you into the story so quickly you were like, "Wait a minute. I don't, you know. What's going on here?" He's such a good actor. I wanted him to be so vulnerable that it kind of broke through all the preconceived notions that you might have of him, and it starts the movie. You're like, "Wait a minute. He's really scared, and I've never seen him so scared. And what's . . . ?"—just unnerve you a little bit and that was really about Tom Cruise the icon, not Tom Cruise the headline maker.

STEPHANOPOULAS: We're not going to show the opener. We're not going to give the opening away, but we do have another clip that shows part of what you were talking about before, making his character, Ethan Hunt, a real person. . . .

You know I promised I wasn't going to do something before we went on the air and now I'm going to do it—

ABRAMS: You're going to cry, aren't you?

STEPHANOPOULAS: I'm going to cry. I was going to say *Mission: Impossible* the love story, but the truth is—and my wife and I both know both you and your wife Katie McGrath—Michelle Monaghan looks an awful lot like your wife.

ABRAMS: You know, I—

STEPHANOPOULAS: Don't blush.

ABRAMS: No. No. No. Look, I admit that, and it's people who know us have said whether it's Jen Garner in *Alias*, Evangeline Lilly, or Michelle Monaghan, that there's a sort of a certain type that I tend to cast in situations. What I've been getting a lot lately is "She looks like Katie Holmes."

STEPHANOPOULAS: In that angle she did a little bit, yeah.

ABRAMS: I have to say we cast her in the movie two months before Tom met Katie. It's not like we were looking for a Katie Holmes look-a-like.

STEPHANOPOULAS: But it was important to make this a love story in addition to making it an action film?

ABRAMS: My favorite movies when you look at the big action films, like *Die Hard* or *Aliens*, or even something like *Jaws*. These are characters; they're people before whatever their job is. For example, in *Die Hard* he's a cop but in that first movie they spent a good half hour investing in who he was as a man on the verge of divorce, and you really cared about that couple. It was touching; it was funny, so all the stuff that happened you went with it because you actually cared about the characters. I just think action's irrelevant now. Given what computer graphics can do, I think we're just desensitized to spectacle and to action, so for me unless you care about a character and someone that makes you laugh or makes you feel something, none of that action means anything. All that stuff on the bridge is cool, but it's only fun and emotional if that character means something to you and you feel like you are that guy.

STEPHANOPOULAS: Exactly, right. The thing though that I was wondering about, you say this was all done a while ago, what happens when it's turned over to Paramount, because in the last couple of days I've read a couple of stories in the paper about how Paramount's really concerned. Tom Cruise is doing as well as ever with men, but they're worried that women aren't going to come. You're saying that didn't shape the script at all but it might shape how they're going to market it?

ABRAMS: From the beginning, they had a strategy that was—this is months ago—which was make sure that the people who knew this is an action movie know it's an action movie, because I guess that's a base, but that there are all sorts of other—I don't know, the different demographics that they go after. It's a very technical thing. To be honest with you, my approach was Tom had a lot of strong points of view about what and how this was going to happen. Paramount did as well. I just said, "Look, I'm making the movie. I'm finishing the movie. Sell the movie."

STEPHANOPOULAS: Did you ever think about doing anything else, or was this it?

ABRAMS: This is what I always wanted to do, but I felt, when I was a senior at college, I realized, "How the hell am I going to do this?" I know what I want to do, and what was lucky is I was in LA over my Christmas break my senior year of college. I ran into a friend of mine, Jill Mazurky, who was a writer. She had sold some scripts, and her father's Paul Mazurky and he was at—

STEPHANOPOULAS: *An Unmarried Woman*, right?

ABRAMS: That's right. He was at Disney at the time. Jill and I came up with a story, and we wrote an outline. Her father showed it to Jeffrey Katzenberg, who at the time was the head of Disney, and he bought it. It was the luckiest thing in the world. Thank God for Jill because I got an agent through her, and I just feel so lucky to have worked with her.

STEPHANOPOULAS: So, from college on you were doing this for a living?
ABRAMS: Yeah.

STEPHANOPOULAS: That is pretty lucky.

ABRAMS: It's insanely lucky. The thing I said to the first big production meeting on *Mission: Impossible*, and it was a huge group of people. I mean, more people in that room, I couldn't believe. It was the first time I realized how big this production was. It was more people than had ever seen *Felicity* were in that room. It was a huge group of people, and I was looking out at this group. I just said, "Look. I want us to all acknowledge, especially me, how lucky we are to be here and to be doing this," and that I wanted the set to be a respectful place. I wanted people to acknowledge that we were all just doing the best we could. I just hate the idea of going to work and having it be an abusive, angry place. I knew that all I needed was for Tom to be a little bit less kind, or a little bit less collaborative, and everything would just fall apart.

STEPHANOPOULAS: Fall apart.

ABRAMS: He was literally, not just to me but to everyone on the crew, so kind and so appreciative of what they were doing as we all were of what he was doing, because no one works harder than that guy; it's unbelievable.

STEPHANOPOULAS: Sounds like it.

ABRAMS: It ended up being a really—talk about lucky, amazing experience.

STEPHANOPOULAS: I was watching Ving Rhames yesterday, and he compared you to Quentin Tarantino.

ABRAMS: Look, it's incredibly flattering, and I've worked with Quentin. He was actually an actor in a couple of episodes of *Alias*, so obviously any comparison I'm flattered, but as fast as I talk he talks much faster than I do.

STEPHANOPOULAS: Who are your influences, though? Which directors do you think, "That's who I want to be like," or no one?

ABRAMS: It's sort of embarrassing to say it because it's the most obvious thing to say, but Steven Spielberg is the god for me. I mean the work that he has done is—

STEPHANOPOULAS: What is it about him?

ABRAMS: His visual storytelling—when you look and see what he does with a shot, how much information, purely informationally, if you look and see how much you're getting per shot that he does. It's a remarkable thing, and in *Munich*, which by the way I think was an extraordinary movie, what blew me away was, even Steven Spielberg, who you think, "How can he get better?"—you know what I mean? Look what he did. I thought that some of the stuff he did in that movie was just off the charts, even for him. I couldn't believe the amount of information and behavior—

STEPHANOPOULAS: When you say that as a director, what are you seeing in *Munich* that is a departure for you?
ABRAMS: Well, there is a certain—there was an approach that I thought felt rough, and there was a spontaneity to it. Not only that, there was an ability to, within one shot—and it wasn't show-offy; it wasn't like, "I'm going to do this one thing, and you're going to realize you're watching one shot over two," but you'd realize an entire story was being told between the characters with reflections in the cars. He was doing these incredible shots that I found myself absorbed by the film, but I found myself hungry to just dissect every choice he made. I was just inspired by that movie, but I've been inspired by almost every movie he's made. He's someone who, when I'm on the set working on something, I invariably try to figure out—

STEPHANOPOULAS: What would Steven want? What would Steven do?
ABRAMS: Kind of. I just feel like I want—it's a weird thing. You can't look at it from the outside-in like that. He's always in the back of my mind. The work that he's done, and I feel like it's such an obvious answer, and maybe because he's so crazy successful, it seems sort of—

STEPHANOPOULAS: For our generation, he looms over everything.
ABRAMS: That's right, but it might sound like an unartful answer because he's just so taken for granted. I think if any other filmmaker had made *Munich* it would have been heralded as just the greatest thing of all time, but it's a movie by Steven Spielberg. Suddenly, there's this expectation or something that I think is enormous. I just don't know how he does that.

STEPHANOPOULAS: What would you like to do different? You've now done the big action film; you've done a lot of television hits. Is there a challenge out there, a form that you haven't tried that you just want to try?
ABRAMS: The fun of doing this job, and as long as I'm able to do it I look forward to it, is that every time out it's a different experience. It's like you; every time you talk to someone else it's a totally different thing. For me it's not like, "Well, I've done TV, and I'm done with movies now." It's a thrill every day, and I feel so lucky to have this job at all.

STEPHANOPOULAS: You're not even forty yet. You turn forty in June right?
ABRAMS: Yep.

STEPHANOPOULAS: Pretty soon. Enormously successful in Hollywood. How do you keep—I was going to say "sane" but I think that's too strong a word. How do you keep perspective in a town where when you've got some success you're rewarded in unbelievably out-sized ways?

ABRAMS: I think that any kind of success, maybe especially in Hollywood, magnifies who you are by nature, and, clearly, the people who surround you say a lot, if not everything about you. Anything good in my life I attribute to my wife. She is someone—Katie is just a remarkable litmus test for everything that's true and right. She just has an incredible, immediate ability to just know the right thing to do and does it and reminds me every day how to be a better person. I know that as much as I love our children and as much as we are this incredibly tight family, the work is seductive—the amount of work, the energy. Not just the attention. It seems like, "Oh, it's the accolades, or it's money." The work itself is actually this drug, and it is critical that you not get seduced by that and get sucked into that vortex. It's an insidious thing, and Katie is—my friend, my best friend from kindergarten. Another friend, Matt Reeves, I've known since I was twelve. I'm someone who is a creature of habit, so all my friends and especially Katie and our kids are the most important things. And, so, as big as the work gets and as crazy as it is and as much as we're shooting this movie and it's Tom Cruise and it's all the noise of that and everything. At night, we're doing the dishes, and the kids are screaming; they're not brushing their teeth like they should be. It's all the madness that everyone has, and it's the best part of life.

STEPHANOPOULAS: Thanks very much.
ABRAMS: Thank you so much. Appreciate it.

The Mystery Box

J. J. Abrams / 2007

From TED2007, March 7–10, 2007. Reprinted by permission.

I want to start today—talk[ing] about the structure of a polypeptide.

I get a lot of people asking me, in terms of *Lost*, "What the hell's that island?" It's usually followed by, "No, seriously, what the hell is that island?"

Why so many mysteries? What is it about mystery that I seem to be drawn to? And I was thinking about this, what to talk about at TED. When I talked to the kind rep from TED, I said, "Listen, you know, what should I talk about?" He said, "Don't worry about it. Just be profound."

I took enormous comfort in that. So, thank you, if you're here.

I was trying to think, "What do I talk about? Good question. Why do I do so much stuff that involves mystery?" I started trying to figure it out. I started thinking about why do I do any of what I do, and I started thinking about my grandfather. I loved my grandfather. Harry Kelvin was his name, my mother's father. He died in 1986. He was an amazing guy. One of the reasons he was amazing: After World War II, he began an electronics company. He started selling surplus parts, kits, to schools and stuff. So, he had this incredible curiosity. As a kid, I saw him come over to me with radios and telephones and all sorts of things. He'd open them up; he'd unscrew them and reveal the inner workings—which many of us, I'm sure, take for granted. But it's an amazing gift to give a kid. To open up this thing and show how it works and why it works and what it is. He was the ultimate deconstructor, in many ways. My grandfather was a kind of guy who would not only take things apart, but he got me interested in all sorts of different odd crafts, like printing, like the letter press. I'm obsessed with printing. I'm obsessed with silk-screening and bookbinding and box making. When I was a kid, I was always taking apart boxes and stuff.

And last night in the hotel, I took apart the Kleenex box. I was just looking at it. And I'm telling you it's a beautiful thing, I swear to God, when you look at the box and you sort of see how it works. Rives is here, and I met him years ago at a book fair; he does pop-up books. I'm obsessed with engineering of paper—the scoring of it, the printing of it, where the thing gets glued, the registration marks for the ink. I just love boxes. My grandfather was the guy who kind of got me into all sorts of these things. He would also supply me with tools. He was this amazing encourager—this patron, sort of, to make stuff. He got me a Super 8 camera when I was ten years old. And in 1976, that was sort of an anomaly, to be a ten-year-old kid that had access to a camera. He was so generous; I couldn't believe it. He wasn't doing it entirely without some manipulation. I mean, I would call him, and I'd be like, "Listen, Grandpa, I really need this camera. You don't understand. This is, like, I want to make movies. I'll get invited to TED one day—"

And my grandmother was the greatest because she'd get on the phone. She'd be like, "Harry, it's better than the drugs." She was fantastic. So, I found myself getting this stuff, thanks to her assist, and suddenly I had a synthesizer when I was fourteen years old—this kind of stuff. It let me make things, which, to me, was sort of the dream. He sort of humored my obsession to other things too, like magic. The thing is, we'd go to this magic store in New York City called Lou Tannen's Magic. It was this great magic store. It was a crappy little building in Midtown, but you'd be in the elevator, the elevator would open—there'd be this little, small magic store. You'd be in the magic store. It was a magical place. So, I got all these magic tricks. Here. I'll show you. This is the kind of thing. So, it would be like, you know—which is good, but now I can't move. Now, I have to do the rest of the thing like this. I'm like, "Oh, wow. Look at my computer over there!"

So, one of the things that I bought at the magic store was this Tannen's Mystery Magic Box. The premise behind the Mystery Magic Box was the following: $15 buys you $50's worth of magic, which is a savings.

Now, I bought this decades ago, and I'm not kidding, if you look at this, you'll see it's never been opened. But I've had this forever. I was looking at this; it was in my office, as it always is, on the shelf, and I was thinking, "Why have I not opened this? Why have I kept it?" because I'm not a pack rat. I don't keep everything, but for some reason I haven't opened this box. I felt like there was a key to this, somehow, in talking about something at TED that I haven't discussed before, and bored people elsewhere. So, I thought, "Maybe there's something with this." There was this giant question mark. I love the design, for what it's worth, of this thing. And I started thinking, "Why haven't I opened it?"

And I realized that I haven't opened it because it represents something important—to me. It represents my grandfather. Am I allowed to cry at TED? Because—no, I'm not going to cry.

The thing is that it represents infinite possibility. It represents hope. It represents potential. What I love about this box, and what I realize I sort of do in whatever it is that I do, is I find myself drawn to infinite possibility, that sense of potential. I realize that mystery is the catalyst for imagination. Now, it's not the most ground-breaking idea, but when I started to think that maybe there are times when mystery is more important than knowledge, I started getting interested in this.

So, I started thinking about *Lost* and the stuff that we do, and I realized, "Oh, my God, mystery boxes are everywhere in what I do! In the creation of *Lost*, Damon Lindelof, who created the show with me, and I were basically tasked with creating this series that we had very little time to do. We had eleven-and-a-half weeks to write it, cast it, crew it, shoot it, cut it, post it, and turn in a two-hour pilot. So, it was not a lot of time. That sense of possibility—what could this thing be? There was no time to develop it. I'm sure you're all familiar with those people who tell you what you can't do and what you should change. There was no time for that, which is kind of amazing. So, we did this show, and for those of you who haven't seen it or don't know it, I can show you one little clip from the pilot, just to show you some stuff that we did.

Ten years ago, if we wanted to do that, we'd have to kill a stuntman. It would be harder. Take two would be a bitch. So, the amazing thing was, we were able to do this thing. Part of that was the amazing availability of technology, knowing we could do anything. We could never have done that. We might have been able to write it; we wouldn't have been able to depict it like we did. So, part of the amazing thing for me is in the creative process; technology is mind-blowingly inspiring to me. I realize that that blank page is a magic box. It needs to be filled with something fantastic.

I used to have the *Ordinary People* script that I'd flip through. The romance of the script was amazing to me; it would inspire me. I wanted to try and fill pages with the same kind of spirit and thought and emotion that that script did. I love Apple computers. I'm obsessed. So, the Apple computer—the PowerBook—this computer, it challenges me. It basically says, "What are you going to write worthy of me?" I feel this—I'm compelled. I often am like, "Dude, today I'm out. I got nothing." You know? So, there's that.

In terms of the content of it, you look at stories; you think, "What are stories but Mystery Boxes?" There's a fundamental question—in TV, the first act is called the teaser. It's literally the teaser. It's the big question. So, you're drawn into it. Then there's another question. It goes on. Look at *Star Wars*. The droids meet the mysterious woman. Who's that? We don't know. Mystery box! Then you meet Luke Skywalker. He gets the droid; you see the holographic image. You learn it's a message. She wants to find Obi Wan Kenobi. He's her only hope. But who the hell's Obi Wan Kenobi? Mystery box! So then he meets Ben Kenobi. Ben Kenobi is Obi Wan Kenobi. Holy shit! So, it keeps us—

Have you guys not seen that? It's huge! Anyway—so there's this thing with mystery boxes that I started feeling compelled. Then there's the thing of mystery in terms of imagination—the withholding of information. Doing that intentionally is much more engaging. Whether it's like the shark in *Jaws*—if Spielberg's mechanical shark, Bruce, had worked, it would not be remotely as scary; you would have seen it too much. In *Alien*, they never really showed the alien: terrifying! Even in a movie like a romantic comedy, *The Graduate*, they're having that date, and they're in the car. And it's loud, and so they put the top up. You don't hear anything they're saying! You can't hear a word! But it's the most romantic date ever. And you love it because you don't hear it.

So, to me, there's that. Then, finally, there's this idea—stretching the paradigm a little bit—but the idea of the mystery box, meaning, what you think you're getting, then what you're really getting. It's true in so many movies and stories. Look at *E.T.*, for example—*E.T.* is this unbelievable movie about what? It's about an alien who meets a kid, right? Well, it's not. *E.T.* is about divorce. *E.T.* is about a heartbroken, divorce-crippled family, and, ultimately, this kid who can't find his way. *Die Hard*, right? Crazy, great, fun, action-adventure movie in a building. It's about a guy who's on the verge of divorce. He's showing up to LA, tail between his legs. There are great scenes—maybe not the most amazing dramatic scenes in the history of time, but pretty great scenes. There's a half an hour of investment in character before you get to the stuff that you're expecting.

When you look at a movie like *Jaws*, the scene that you expect—we have the screen? These are the kind of scenes that you remember and expect from *Jaws*. And she's being eaten; there's a shark.

The thing about *Jaws* is, it's really about a guy who is sort of dealing with his place in the world—with his masculinity, with his family, how he's going to make it work in this new town. This is one of my favorite scenes ever, and this is a scene that you wouldn't necessarily think of when you think of *Jaws*. But it's an amazing scene.

Come on. "Why? 'Cause I need it"? Best scene ever, right?

Come on! So, you think of *Jaws*—that's the kind of stuff—the investment of character, which is the stuff that really is inside the box. It's why when people do sequels, or rip off movies, you know, of a genre, they're ripping off the wrong thing. You're not supposed to rip off the shark or the monster. If you rip something off—rip off the character. Rip off the stuff that matters. Look inside yourself and figure out what is inside you because, ultimately, the mystery box is all of us.

So, there's that. Then the distribution: what's a bigger mystery box than a movie theater? You go to the theater; you're just so excited to see anything. The moment the lights go down is often the best part. And you're full of that amazing—that feeling of excited anticipation. Often, the movie's there, and it's going. Then something happens, and you go, "Oh—," and then, "Mmm . . ." When it's a great movie, you're along for the ride because you're willing to give yourself to it.

So, to me, whether it's a TV, an iPod, computer, cell phone—It's funny, I'm an—as I said—Apple fanatic, and one day, about a year or so ago, I was signing on online in the morning to watch Steve Jobs's keynote because I always do. He came on; he was presenting the video iPod, and what was on the enormous iPod behind him? *Lost*! I had no idea! I realized, holy shit, it'd come full circle. The inspiration I get from the technology is now using the stuff that I do to sell technology. It's nuts!

I was going to show you a couple of other things I'm going to skip. I'll show you one other thing that has nothing to do with anything. This is something online; six years ago, they did this. This is an online thing done by guys who had some visual effects experience. The point was that they were doing things that were using these mystery boxes that they had—everyone has now. What I've realized is what my grandfather did for me when I was a kid, everyone has access to now. You don't need to have my grandfather, though you wish you had. But I have to tell you—this is a guy doing stuff on a Quadra 950 computer—the resolution's a little bit low—using Infinity software they stopped making fifteen years ago. He's doing stuff that looks as amazing as stuff I've seen released from Hollywood.

The most incredible sort of mystery, I think, is now the question of what comes next because it is now democratized. So now, the creation of media—it's everywhere. The stuff that I was lucky and begging for to get when I was a kid is now ubiquitous. So, there's an amazing sense of opportunity out there. When I think of the filmmakers who exist out there now who would have been silenced—who have been silenced in the past—it's a very exciting thing.

I used to say in classes and lectures and stuff to someone who wants to write, "Go! Write! Do your thing." It's free; you don't need permission. But now I can say, "Go make your movie!" There's nothing stopping you from going out there and getting the technology. You can lease, rent, buy stuff off the shelf that is either as good, or just as good, as the stuff that's being used by the, you know, "legit people." No community is best served when only the elite have control. I feel like this is an amazing opportunity to see what else is out there.

When I did *Mission: Impossible III*, we had amazing visual effects. ILM did the effects; it was incredible and sort of my dream to be involved. And there are a couple of sequences in the movie, like these couple of moments I'll show you. There's that.

Obviously, I have an obsession with big crazy explosions. So, my favorite visual effect in the movie is the one I'm about to show you. It's a scene in which Tom's character wakes up. He's drowsy. He's crazy. And the guy wakes up, and he shoves this gun in his nose and shoots this little capsule into his brain that he's going to use later to kill him, as bad guys do.

Okay, now, when we shot that scene, the actor who had the gun, an English actor, Eddie Marsan—sweetheart, great guy—he kept taking the gun and putting it into Tom's nose, and it was hurting Tom's nose. I learned this very early on in my career: Don't hurt Tom's nose.

There are three things you don't want to do. Number two is: Don't hurt Tom's nose. So, Eddie has this gun—and he's this sweet English guy. He's like, "Sorry, I don't want to hurt you." I'm like, "We have to make this look good." I realized that we had to do something because it wasn't working. I thought back to what I would have done using the Super 8 camera that my grandfather got me sitting in that room, and I realized that hand didn't have to be Eddie Marsan's. It could be Tom's. Tom would know just how hard to push the gun. He wouldn't hurt himself.

So, we took his hand and we painted it to look a little bit more like Eddie's. We put it in Eddie's sleeve, and so the hand that you see—that's not Eddie's hand, that's Tom's. Tom is playing two roles.

And he didn't ask for any more money. So here. Here. Watch it again. There he is. He's waking up. He's drowsy, been through a lot.

Tom's hand. Tom's hand. Tom's hand. Anyway. So . . .

Thanks.

You don't need the greatest technology to do things that can work in movies. And the mystery box, in honor of my grandfather, stays closed. Thank you.

J. J. Abrams

Noel Murray / 2008

Writer-director-producer J. J. Abrams was born into a show-business family as the son of a TV executive, and he started his own career immediately after college, selling screenplays for *Taking Care of Business*, *Regarding Henry*, and *Forever Young* while he was still in his twenties. He moved from feature films to television in 1998, first cocreating the collegiate drama *Felicity*, and then heading up the twisty twenty-first-century spy thriller *Alias*. In the 2000s, Abrams has divided his time between movies and TV—and between offbeat fantasy and straight drama—having a hand in such disparate projects as *Lost*, *What About Brian*, *Cloverfield*, *Six Degrees*, *Joy Ride*, and *Mission: Impossible III*. While putting the finishing touches on the new big-screen version of *Star Trek*—due in theaters next summer—Abrams is also working with Robert Orci and Alex Kurtzman on the new science-fiction mystery series *Fringe*, which debuts September 9 on Fox.

The A.V. Club: How do you generally feel when a new TV show of yours is about to premiere? Anxious? Confident?

J. J. Abrams: Well, it's a cocktail of excited for people to see it, terror that no one will watch it, and relief that something I've been working on for so long will finally be out there. Oh, and panic that I can't make more of the little changes we've been making all along. All the times I've been lucky enough to be a part of a show that's actually gotten on the air. It's always that same mixture of excitement and utter fear, which is kind of what I hope people will feel when they watch *Fringe*.

AVC: One thing about TV that's different than movies is that you can adjust as you go, and if you're on the air long enough, you can respond to the audience response. Do you pay a lot of attention to what critics and fans say when they write about your work?

JJA: Oh, sure. The noise you hear after people see something you do—whether it's a TV show or a movie—that always makes you see that thing slightly differently, without question. The ability of a television series to make adjustments is something you've got to take advantage of. Test-screening a movie can be helpful too. The part that can be dangerous is when you take those notes as gospel, instead of taking them with a grain of salt. The key is to use the response as one of the tools in your box, as opposed to using it to determine what you do.

AVC: You didn't direct the *Fringe* pilot.
JJA: No, I was directing *Star Trek*, and the studio didn't want me to put that on hold so I could go do my TV thing.

AVC: Do you want to direct an episode?
JJA: Well, I'm hoping, maybe a season finale or a season opener or something. I've been wanting to do it since the pilot. We have great directors working on *Fringe*, but when someone else directs something that you're involved with, it's always their vision. And the director in my head is definitely wanting to get involved.

AVC: Which hat do you like to wear the most: director, producer, or writer?
JJA: Directing's the best part. Whenever I've directed something, there's this feeling of demand and focus that I like. Secondly, it means that you've gotten through all the writing stuff, the producing stuff, casting, prep, and all those stages that are seemingly endless. So, directing is sort of the reward for all the work you put in before. Then there's the editing, which is another amazing stage of the process. It's incredible the moments you can create.

AVC: Where do you think your strengths lie?
JJA: I wish I had a clue. My guess is nowhere, but I do the best I can.

AVC: The pilot of *Fringe* opens up with an airplane in trouble, which is similar to the opening of *Lost*. Was that a conscious nod or just a coincidence?
JJA: We were discussing what the opening of the show should be. We talked about so many different things, so when the plane idea came up, the last thing on my mind was *Lost*. Later, we realized it sounded an awful lot like what we did on *Lost*, but by that point, honestly, I thought, "Who cares?" It's appropriately creepy and large enough in scale to fit the bill for an opener.

AVC: How much day-to-day input do you still have on *Lost*?
JJA: Almost none. Damon Lindelof's been running the show since the first season.

I went off to make a movie, and Damon's been running *Lost* brilliantly since then, so my day-to-day involvement is about as much as yours.

AVC: Do you watch the show as a fan? Are you surprised by what happens?
JJA: Oh, yeah, I watch episodes, and I get the scripts. What's cool is that I was there when it was created, and now I'm watching it grow into something else.

AVC: Back when you were doing *Felicity*, on the heels of writing movies like *Regarding Henry* and *Taking Care of Business*, not many people would've pegged you as an SF/fantasy guy, but that's become a big niche for you. Is that something you'd planned all along?
JJA: I could not have less of a plan. I've just been lucky to work on things that I felt would be cool to see. It's not that I had a strategy or anything. Growing up, I loved *The Twilight Zone* as much as I loved *The Mary Tyler Moore Show*. I loved the *Superman* TV show when I was a kid and *Batman* and *Speed Racer* and all the pop-culture icons that everyone in my generation lived on. But I also remember loving the version of *The Hunchback of Notre Dame* with Charles Laughton. I watched it when I was ten or eleven and was just sobbing over the story, while also being blown away by the makeup. My favorite things have nearly always been extreme and fantastical, involving some kind of visual effects, but also very emotionally driven. I loved *Ordinary People* and *The Philadelphia Story* and a lot of dramas and comedies based on plays that could not be farther from science fiction. At the same time, I was obsessed with the horror movies of the early '80s and late '70s. So, in the end, the things I've worked on professionally have really been whatever I've been lucky enough to get produced, not stuff that I planned out years in advance.

AVC: How do you put your varied interests to work in a franchise like *Star Trek*, which has fans deeply devoted to certain immutable core elements? How do you make it yours?
JJA: Well, I was never the type of *Star Trek* fan that had expectations or limits about what the "right" version of a *Star Trek* movie should be. At the same time, one of the reasons I got involved with *Star Trek* was because it has such devoted fans, so I felt it was critical to honor them and honor the series. I learned as much as I could about the show and looked for help from Bob Orci, one of the creators of *Fringe*, who was also one of the writers of *Trek* and an avowed Trekker. He knows all the arcane details, so he was the one kind of keeping me honest on the set.

Ultimately, though, I wasn't making this movie just for the dedicated fans. I was making the movie for fans of movies. The final product, I think, doesn't require any prior knowledge of the show *Star Trek*. Almost anyone, if you stopped them on the street and asked who Kirk and Spock are, they'd know. I think people will typically have some sense of those two guys. Then there are fans who know every episode and argue about what the *Star Trek* canon is. This movie does acknowledge a world that has preexisted off the screen for decades, but when you see it, it's not going to be quite what you'd expect and definitely not just a rehash of things you've seen before. It's a very new take on the thing that it's also beholden to. It's a very interesting balance.

AVC: You grew up in a TV family, correct?

JJA: My father was a retail commercial contractor who became a TV producer, and then my mother became one later, after I went to college. When I was growing up, she was a lawyer.

AVC: Did growing up in those surroundings demystify showbiz at all or make it seem more exciting?

JJA: It completely demystified it in a way that was sort of strange. My dad had an office at Paramount, and when I was eleven, twelve years old, I would go to the office with my father. I would wander around the lot. I got to know the guards who were there, so they'd let me in. I'd sit in the empty bleachers and watch *Happy Days* or *Laverne and Shirley* or *Mork and Mindy*. I vividly remember seeing Robin Williams in civilian clothes, rehearsing and doing a bunch of crazy accents. I remember watching Ron Howard and Henry Winkler and those guys, and it's a strange thing when you're a kid and there's The Fonz, such a hugely important part of your childhood. Yet, you go to the set and see Henry Winkler, and in real life, he's nothing like the Fonz. It was disconcerting and confusing, but at the same time demystifying and fun.

Really, it was great just watching my father, I would go to sets with my dad, and just watching what he did, seeing how production really works, asking adults questions . . . It's one of those things that's fueled me. I'd been making Super 8 films since I was eight years old and seeing how it was really done, even though I still didn't understand a lot of it, was something I could use.

AVC: Having met Henry Winkler, can you still watch *Happy Days* and see the Fonz, or do you just see Henry Winkler?

JJA: Well, I actually didn't meet him until a couple of years ago. I just watched him, but of course, once you know how it's done, once you know what it looks like when you're on a set, watching the finished product is no longer the same experience. It's like a magic trick. Once you know how that trick is done, it ruins the experience of watching it. On the other hand, there's a bigger thing that starts to happen, and you start to appreciate the presentation. Even though it's not the same anymore when you watch the show you were present for rehearsals for or watch a movie that you were on the set for, you start to see another thing. It doesn't negate being entertained.

AVC: If you look at a lot of the TV and movies you've been involved with, like *Cloverfield* or *Lost* or now *Fringe*, you seem to be trying as hard as you can for as long as you can not to reveal the trick.

JJA: I think that that's partially true. Like with *Cloverfield*, the whole idea with the marketing and the quick release was for people to have an experience as it happened, instead of pre-experiencing it by reading all about it. But I feel like with *Fringe*, the mandate is to try to do something week-to-week that's a procedural like *CSI*, but a skewed procedural, that's as creepy as humanly possible. While with *Lost*, on the one hand, it is a show that seems to duck answering questions. At the end of the pilot, you have Charlie asking, "Where are we?" and that's something the audience still wants to find out. Week-to-week, that show answers a lot of questions, just not always the ones people feel are the ones that matter.

I think that even if you're wondering if two characters are ever going to kiss, drawing out the inevitability is part of the fun, whatever the genre happens to be. Now, in a movie, you get all the answers by the end, except in *Pulp Fiction*, where you don't ever really get to know what's in that case. But even in movies—a great example is *North by Northwest*, where you don't really know what the microfilm is, but who cares? By the end of the movie, the answer that you get is not really the answer that you thought you wanted to know. The answer you get is: "Oh, they're in love, and now they're married. And these were the circumstances that led up to that. They almost died a number of times, but they survived. And they found each other," I feel like in telling stories, there are the things the audience thinks are important, and then there are the things that are actually important.

Star Trek: J. J. Abrams Interview

John Hiscock / 2009

From the *Telegraph*, April 30, 2009. © Telegraph Media Group Limited.
Reprinted by permission.

Director J. J. Abrams has been entrusted to breathe new life into the moribund *Star Trek* franchise. Here, he explains how he set about wooing the old stars of the original series—as well as Trekkies around the world.

It wasn't an easy job, but if anyone could do it, figured the executives at Paramount, it was the prolific film- and TV series–maker J. J. Abrams.

His mission was to breathe new life into the moribund *Star Trek* franchise and plant the seed for a whole new generation of Trekkies; and Abrams, who wrote and directed *Mission: Impossible III* and created the television series *Felicity*, *Alias*, *Lost*, and the new *Fringe*, is not one to turn down a challenge.

"I wanted to go back to the beginning and start afresh," he recalls, talking just before the Los Angeles premiere and soon after, rave reviews of the movie had appeared in the US. As producer and director, he knew he had to walk a fine line between creating a fresh *Star Trek* for the twenty-first century while avoiding alienating die-hard Trekkies, who still revere the old series as an icon of modern pop culture.

"I wanted to take the spirit of what was created forty-three years ago and use it to make it relevant for today, but the key was that we wanted to make it ours and not feel constrained by too many rules that were almost half a century old," he says. "The spirit of what came before had to fuel the movie, and yet the specifics of the film needed to be ours."

He enlisted his co-producers from *Lost* and writers Roberto Orci and Alex Kurtzman, who had written *Mission: Impossible III* and *Fringe* for him. "I wanted them to create a story about where the young James Kirk and Mr. Spock came from and what sparked their hopes and dreams," he says.

The writers came up with a story that follows the rebellious young Kirk, whose father sacrificed himself at the helm of a spaceship, and Spock, the troubled half-human, half-Vulcan, as they enlist in the Starfleet Academy, join the Starship *Enterprise* and become colleagues in combating the ferocious Nero (Eric Bana), who wants to annihilate the Federated planets, most notably Vulcan and Earth.

Then, armed with the screenplay and with much trepidation, Abrams approached two Star Trek veterans to seek their cooperation and, if possible, lure them aboard in cameo roles.

William Shatner, who played Captain Kirk in the original series and in seven of the subsequent movies, was not interested in taking a cameo role but wanted a larger part. "One of the problems was that Captain Kirk had been killed off in the seventh *Star Trek* movie, and we didn't know how to bring him back because we wanted to honor the canon of *Star Trek*." Shatner declined an offer to meet with his successor, twenty-eight-year-old Chris Pine, who plays the young Kirk, but wrote him a letter wishing him well.

Then, with fingers firmly crossed, Abrams went to Leonard Nimoy, whose emotionless Spock was one of the mainstays of the original series and six of the movies. He offered him a small but important role in the movie and showed him footage of thirty-one-year-old Zachary Quinto, one of the ensemble cast of the TV series *Heroes*, whom Abrams had chosen as the young Spock.

"We knew if he said, 'No,' we were screwed," Abrams says, "because the story is about Spock. We knew Leonard was going to be the key thing for this story to work because the fans of *Trek* are so passionate and so vocal that if we didn't get this movie blessed by someone from the original *Trek* they would probably reject it sight unseen. It must have been very emotional for him because here was this kid who looked crazily like him coming in assuming the role Leonard originated almost half a century ago."

Nimoy says that after reading the script and seeing footage of Quinto, he had no hesitation in giving his approval. "I think he's excellent," says Nimoy, seventy-eight. "Obviously, he looks enough like me to make it work and, more important, he has an intelligence and an inner life he projects as an actor. And I found that very appropriate for the character."

The excitable and garrulous J. J. Abrams vividly remembers Nimoy's first day on set. "He came out with the ears on, his hair had been done, he was wearing the outfit, and Spock was in the house. We shot the scene and he did his first reading and it was amazing, but I had some things to tell him. I'm walking up to him, and it hits me: 'What the hell am I doing trying to explain to Leonard Nimoy how Spock should say that line?' So I say, 'Mr. Nimoy, I have some ideas, but I'm not sure how to tell you.' He grabbed my shirt and said, 'Tell me; tell me; tell me.' He's a great actor and a fine gentleman, a wonderful collaborator."

Nimoy and Quinto have become firm friends, and Quinto, whose father died when he was seven, says he looks on the older actor as a surrogate father figure.

"His life is so rich and full, and he's been incredibly supportive. And it was a great opportunity for me to get to know the man as well as the character."

Like Nimoy, Quinto is eloquent and erudite and, also like Nimoy, has a background in theater. He is currently one of the ensemble cast of the television series *Heroes*, and he sees certain similarities in his portrayal of both Spock and the mysterious serial killer Sylar of *Heroes*. "Both characters are very contained and are striving for control over themselves and over a directly rooted emotional life that has a power of its own," he says.

Chris Pine, whose father was the actor Robert Pine, a regular in the seventies *CHiPs* TV series, walks with a swagger that suits the cocky young James Kirk. Pine, whose biggest claim to fame so far has been a role in *The Princess Diaries 2*, was offered the *Star Trek* role at the same time as he was offered a substantial part as a detective in a gritty crime drama starring George Clooney.

"I wasn't sure which one to take, and I thought about it long and hard," he recalls. "The one thing that really struck me was whether, in five years' time, I would be upset if I'd said, 'No,' to *Star Trek* and wished I'd said, 'Yes.' That's an awful thing to have hanging over your career—asking yourself why you said, 'No.'"

He has almost certainly made the right choice because, although no one is openly discussing the possibility of sequels yet, all the main actors have signed on for two more movies, and it is a good bet that the Starship *Enterprise* will be boldly going where no man has gone before for a good many years to come.

J. J. Takes on a Soaring Franchise

Paul Fischer / 2009

From Femail.com, May 2009. Reprinted by permission.

J. J. Abrams has created some of TV's most successful shows, from *Felicity* to the compelling *Alias*, *Lost*, and recently, *Fringe*. So it was inevitable that he would take the leap to the big screen, first with the last in the *Mission: Impossible* franchise and now helming the risky reboot of the iconic *Star Trek*. The gamble has paid off, with the film already receiving early buzz. The once non-Trek fan has clearly gone where no director has gone before. He spoke to Paul Fischer.

QUESTION: J. J., you really took it on yourself to take on one of the most beloved franchises, probably in the history of television, and I'm just wondering, first of all, why you felt so compelled to do this—and why now, in the year 2009, is it the right time to revisit this world?

J. J. ABRAMS: I think that the embarrassing truth is that because I was not a *Star Trek* fan, my initial reaction when they asked if I'd be interested in producing was, "Oh, that would be cool, to try and work on a version that did appeal to me." I immediately called Alex and Bob. They had already been talking to Paramount about *Star Trek*, and they were trying to figure out how to do it. Alex and Bob and Brian and Damon Lindelof, who couldn't be here today—he's doing a *Lost* thing in France—we all got together and started talking about what *Star Trek* could be, for now. Because I was not a huge fan, because Brian had never seen an episode, and because Bob and Alex were big fans, and Damon as well, we had a range of sort-of relationships with *Star Trek*. The key was to find a story that we all embraced. And again, you know, knowing that *Star Trek* inherently was an optimistic story—it told a future that was about collaboration, about survival, about working together across cultural and political and racial lines, and special lines—and the idea that we wanted to maintain that, spoke to the tone of the movie. And—which is to say that there have been many films in recent years, many of which we have all loved, that have depicted a very dark, dismal, cynical, grim future. That's not what Roddenberry created. That's not what we were interested in doing. The idea to go back to Kirk and Spock, tell their origin story, create an emotional way that would give people like myself a way to love these characters, was an exciting one. To tell a story that was ultimately optimistic, and—with a big heart, felt like the movies we loved as kids, that was one of the things that was the most exciting to work on.

QUESTION: Did you get Greg Grunberg into this movie?
J. J. ABRAMS: You know, when Young Kirk is driving, his stepdad calls him? Greg Grunberg.

QUESTION: Okay. What's up with the big red balls?
J. J. ABRAMS: Excuse me?

QUESTION: Everything you do has a big red ball in it.
J. J. ABRAMS: Not everything. There are a couple of shout outs to some of the stuff that we've worked on before, and one of them is the big sort of Rambaldi ball from *Alias*, which was also a cameo.

QUESTION: And now we know what the ball is.
J. J. ABRAMS: That's right. It was just a cameo.

QUESTION: I was really struck by how you incorporated a lot of iconic things about the characters and the show, like certain lines, and this and that. But you did it in a way that wasn't cheesy, or winking to the audience. How did you do that? Were you worried about putting in those lines and making them seem natural?
J. J. ABRAMS: Well, even as a nonfan, "I'm giving her all she's got." You know, "Beam me up." There are certain lines that if I were to see a *Star Trek* movie and didn't see those things, I would feel like I was cheated somehow. But the brilliance of Bob and Alex's script was that it didn't have those lines in scenes that would not have existed without those lines, meaning they were situations that were real and urgent and specific, and necessary. Those lines organically came out of those moments. You had those kinds of little peaks of recognition, but they were justified. They were intrinsically connected to the scene. So you didn't ever feel like "Oh, yeah, that line." They came out of the blue. They would surprise you. When I read the script, I thought, "This is genius." So, it's funny how—it was not—doing those lines was beside the point. Yet, we all knew, "Yeah, yeah, yeah." A by-product of including those lines will be sort of that appreciation and nod to what people have—fans of *Trek* have loved for years.

QUESTION: J. J., your movie really is a love letter to these characters, but you do make a pretty big change in the canon with the destruction of Vulcan. Do you think any of these characters are expendable? Also, if you were a kid in the backyard playing *Star Trek*, which one of these characters would you be?

J. J. ABRAMS: Well, I think you're right. The movie is all about the characters and is a love letter to the characters. That's why I wanted to direct the movie. When I read the script, I just fell in love with it. At the beginning of the process, if you'd said, "Who is your favorite? Which one would you play?" I would say, "Well, probably none of them. I don't really connect to any of them." Now, I'd say I couldn't choose one because I love them all. I never felt like I was Spock. I never felt like I was Kirk. I wasn't Bones, I wasn't Scottie. I wasn't Uhura. I wasn't Sulu. I wasn't any of them, really. Now, I sort of feel like I love all of them, and I know all of them. I don't think any of them are expendable. I think that the genius of what Roddenberry created is that paradigm of all of these characters. You've got the id, the ego, the superego. The group went obviously beyond just Kirk and Spock and Bones, with—this film especially, the end of the movie—you realize that they wouldn't be there if all of them hadn't done their job, meaning that each one of them contributed in a critical way. Each one of them has put their lives into the other's hands, not to say that if we were to do another film—who knows what the story would be. But I would say that in this one, I loved how each character was absolutely critical, and you got to know them in a way that, personally, I felt that I hadn't had a chance to do before.

QUESTION: How did you come to cast Tyler Perry in his role? That was interesting, to have him in this movie.

J. J. ABRAMS: Tyler's someone who I've admired for years, not just in his abilities as a writer, director, and actor, but as an industry. This guy is amazing. Quite frankly, I've been jealous of him for a long time because the work that he's done has been incredible. We have people in common, and I just used those connections to reach out to him and sent him an email just to say, "Hey, it's J. J. Abrams. Would you be interested in playing a role in this movie?" He was intrigued—never seen *Star Trek* before, so he didn't really know. I kind of pushed it a little bit, and I sent him the script. He said, "Yes," but he'd never seen *Star Trek*, still. He did this part, and he'd never been on anybody else's set before. He's never acted in anybody else's movie. The way that he's created his business, his industry, his studio, and done his work, TV and film, is unbelievable to me. And I just—again, I'm just a fan. So, working with him was an honor, as it was working with Leonard Nimoy and Eric Bana, both of whom I'd also wanted to work with. To be the first person that he collaborated with in this way was a thrill. And I was just telling—there was a—one day we were shooting one of his scenes, and he was doing his lines. In the middle of it, he didn't like it. He said, "Cut," and he said, "Oh, sorry! So sorry." He was just so used to doing his thing. I love Tyler. And what was nice— the last thing about it: What was nice about it is that—and this has happened a few times where there are actors or composers or writers or, you know, directors, whose work you appreciate. Musicians, too. There's a weird thing, where you go, "I don't know that person. It's presumptuous, but I bet I'd get along with them." You know? And literally, on the set with him, it was like he was a brother. We had the same kind of references. It was the weirdest thing. Working with him just felt like it was—bless you. Felt like it was just one of those—you know. It couldn't have gone better, and I had high hopes for it. So, you know, I'm just a fan.

QUESTION: All of the actors today have demonstrated an amazing camaraderie with each other. Obviously, it was apparent on set. It translated. There are a lot of funny moments on screen. Any funny moments on set that happened to kind of bond with the actors? Any practical jokes that went on, on the set?

J. J. ABRAMS: The thing about this cast is—and we all saw a ton of actors. The key was that they all needed to have a sense of humor. I knew that was going to be the most important thing because if they were too serious—*Star Trek* already exists in that place. It's been parodied so many times. If it was too self-serious—and the original show had great wit. The best things in some episodes of the original series was that amazing repartee between the characters. It was just too good. Every single actor, including Eric Bana, Bruce Greenwood, and Mr. Nimoy, are funny. So, that was awesome. It wasn't awesome on one particular day when we were shooting this one scene, and they were all together. It was one of those things where we just had no time. It was really late. We were way over schedule. We had all this work to do. The next day it was going to be a disaster. It was one of those few scenes on the bridge where they were all together because a lot of times it's like, two actors here, three actors here. But it was one of those scenes. They were just all in the mood to goof off. The first AD, whose job it is to make sure that we make our day and ride me so that we finish scenes, was looking at me like, "We're screwed." Like, "This is a disaster." The actors literally could not get through their lines without laughing. By the way, on any other day, I would have been like, "Hey, this is fun." No. They were all goofing off, and I was trying to—I have three kids. So, it's not a completely unusual situation, to try and wrangle. I was trying to wrangle, and they were doing their thing. Finally, I was like, "When you guys are ready, come get me." I just walked off. And I'm walking, and I'm thinking, "Wow, I just went and did it." I went back, and I got some water. Somebody was like, "Are you okay?" I'm like, "Yeah, I'm fine. We'll see what happens." Then they were all like, "Ooh, we've got to," and then they came back and said, "Okay, they're ready to go." I came back literally, like, three minutes later. They were totally serious, and they did their scene. It was the only time where their amazing sense of humor, camaraderie, and sort of natural personalities were actually a pain in the ass. Other than that, it was awesome.

QUESTION: J. J., you seem to have a certain kind of creative restlessness that you are always moving from one idea to the next or from one kind of storytelling to the next. Do you have a certain identified—either in retrospect or as you go forward—do you have an identifiable or, sort of, conscious idea or concept that you are trying to explore or something that you especially like to bring to each new thing? Or is the difference in each of them the thing that appeals to you?

J. J. ABRAMS: Personally and obviously, I never think about stuff from the outside in like that. So, I have no idea what the hell I do. I know that when there's something that interests me, it's undeniable. I guess if I deconstruct things, I can find connections. But then it feels too mannered, or sort of self-aware. I would hate to be logical about why I'm approaching a project or something. To me, if there's an idea—literally, the idea of doing *Star Trek*, which is another sequel to a series of films based on a television show that Leonard Nimoy starred in—I'd done that with *Mission: Impossible*. I didn't think, "Oh, I'm going to do another one of those." It just happened to be that when I read the script after we worked together for a while—and I just read it, I thought, "I will literally be so envious of whomever directs this movie." I just knew I'd go to the set, and it would kill me, not that they couldn't do it better but that I'd just be frustrated that I didn't say, "Yes," to an opportunity to do it. It wasn't an intellectual thing at all. It was actually counterintellectual. It was an emotional thing. So, the key for me—and I think the way that these guys work, too—is when you work on something that you truly love, that is undeniable—even if it ends up not being any good, at least the ambition was right. But if you ever work on something, you think, "Oh, they will like this," I think you're in such dangerous territory because you have no idea what—then it's false pretenses from the beginning.

QUESTION: I just want to ask you a little bit about the casting because you didn't necessarily go with actors that looked exactly like the original actors that portray those characters. What were you looking for—say, for Simon Pegg portraying his character, and also, of course, Chris, who doesn't look exactly like William Shatner, but he was able to kind of convey that swarthiness.

J. J. ABRAMS: Right, right. Well, the only one that we needed to cast that really had to resemble was Zachary because he was playing the same character, and we knew there was going to be a scene with the two of them. If they looked nothing alike, it would just be too distracting. The fact that Zachary is an eerie doppelganger didn't hurt. That was sort of the only literal—look. The fact is, at a certain point, it's a movie. It's called *Star Trek*. And we knew that the audience needed to accept certain artistic license. We had to be able to say to the audience, "Look, it's different actors playing these parts. It's not going to be . . ."—you have to just go with us. What we always knew—not looking at this as a series of films at all—but we just knew that this movie was a bridge between the *Trek* that people know and this new group that's starting this five-year mission so that, to me, was the critical thing. We needed to—as much as we could—assume the audience would go along with us on this ride. The actors who played the other characters needed to embody them. They needed to be inspired by what was created forty-three years ago, and, at the same time, own it. The only way it would work is if they really owned it, so although Zachary could walk on the set, he wouldn't need to talk. They'd be like, "That's Spock." It got to a place where I literally would forget what the original Spock looked like a little bit because that was—it was a weird thing. I was like, "Oh, that's Spock." Then I'd see a picture of Nimoy and go, "Oh, I see." It was very strange. With the other characters, it was really about just finding great actors who could give—make those roles come alive. So, finding John Cho—I was a little worried at first because—okay, he's not of Japanese descent. But I thought, "This is ridiculous." It's like he's right for the part. I knew that we inherited these characters, so they had to—I knew that Uhura needed to be of African descent. That didn't mean that she needed to be exactly like Nichelle Nichols. In fact, that issue of relevance, the master we needed to serve was—what makes it vital for now—and not try and do a skit. So, it was—on every level from the casting you're discussing to the props to the ship design to the production design—everything was a choice, filtering it through that. Like, "How do we make it work for now, even though it was inspired by a half-a-century-ago idea?"

QUESTION: You had Majel Barrett-Roddenberry working on set for the last little while, didn't you?
J. J. ABRAMS: Yes.

QUESTION: How was that? It was just before she died, wasn't it?
J. J. ABRAMS: Yes, it was. We were very lucky to have Majel come and do the voice for the Star Fleet computer, which she had done in the series and the films. She came to the set one day when we were shooting on the *Narada*, and she was just lovely. She was elegant and funny and supportive. It was—it's that crazy thing. We were working with Nimoy, so we knew we had someone who had been there and was part of it. Walter Konig visited the set, and that was great. Nichelle visited the set. We had had breakfast with George Takei. But to have Majel come, it was a different kind of thing because she was part of the behind-the-scenes of it, as well as being on camera. To have her say to us, "This is what . . ."—basically, she said

that Gene would have approved of what we were doing. That meant more than I can say. We always knew we were dedicating the movie to Gene Roddenberry because we never would have, obviously, been doing any of this if it weren't for him. Sadly, when Majel passed away, we added her name to the card at the end.

QUESTION: Was there any discussion at all about bringing Shatner into this? Was there an early draft of William Shatner?

J. J. ABRAMS: Sure. Oh, sure. We had a scene with him in it that they wrote. It was sort of a flashback-y thing. Bill made it clear he didn't want to just do a cameo. So we ended up realizing we'd have to change the whole story to bring him back to life—we just had to bite the bullet and say, "It's going to be Nimoy and not Shatner." We would have loved to work with him.

QUESTION: Would you like to direct the series finale of *Lost*?

J. J. ABRAMS: I would love to, but Jack Bender's been directing the whole series, the producing director. I wouldn't presume to take that away from him. He was the director. I would love to do it, selfishly.

QUESTION: What's next for you?

J. J. ABRAMS: We're producing a movie, and it starts shooting next month in New York. And I'm working on a script for something, so we'll see if it works out.

QUESTION: Karl Urban. How did you know if he would be able to do McCoy?

J. J. ABRAMS: I didn't. I actually thought he wouldn't. I thought, "This is a waste of everyone's time," because he's the stud from *The Lord of the Rings* and he's that bad guy from *Bourne*. It's like, "Come on." Could not be less Bones. He walked in and was Bones. It was insane.

QUESTION: Did he campaign for it, or was it just a casting director's idea?

J. J. ABRAMS: He walked in and just started being Bones. It was the last thing I ever thought was going to happen. He channeled the character in a way that—he left, and there was never anyone else to play that part.

Star Trek: J. J. Abrams Interview

Rob Carnevale / 2009

From IndieLondon.co.uk, May 2009. Reprinted by permission.

J. J. Abrams talks about some of the challenges of rebooting the *Star Trek* movie and working with Leonard Nimoy, who reprises his iconic role as Spock.

He also outlines some of the reasons why he chose to ignore *Star Wars* as a reference point when it came to reconstructing set pieces that may bear similarities and whether he'd be open to returning to the franchise for a sequel.

Q: What aspects of the original *Star Trek* TV series or subsequent incarnations seemed the most insurmountable at the outset of this project, and how did you approach dealing with that?

J. J. Abrams: I think that the world of *Star Trek* is so much bigger than anything I've worked on before and the scope is so crazy. Despite it being *Star Trek* and being a fantasy, our goal was really to make the film feel real and alive. It's a strange one because you're dealing with a lot of obviously over-the-top science fiction fantasy, but I really want you to believe in it. And the only way you can do that is with the characters. So, the biggest challenge was to take something that has preexisted us for decades and make it feel legitimate and vital and relevant for today. The only way to do that was through the characters that these actors brilliantly portrayed. None of the visual effects and spectacles would matter if you didn't care about and believe those characters, and that was the goal we had.

Q: To what extent did you feel that you had to be a historian of *Star Trek* to dot the *i*'s and cross the *t*'s? To what extent did you take poetic license and redraw it the way you wanted to?

J. J. Abrams: I was never a huge *Star Trek* fan when I started working on this, so I didn't have that feeling of it being a sacred text that I couldn't make creative decisions that would make for a better movie. The risk there, obviously, was alienating fans of the original *Star Trek*. I didn't want to do that, but I also felt that if we did our job and we made a movie that was entertaining it would include *Star Trek* fans. Things like the exact look of a certain species—that's changed in the history of *Star Trek* anyway. You can even look at the original series and find inconsistencies that they had, but it's part of the charm and the reality of an ongoing series—it's fiction. At a certain point, you have to make the right choice for the right movie, and if we had only gone after pleasing the original *Trek* fans I think our movie would have been a very different film. So, things like that were really a question of: "What feels right for now? What feels interesting?" We knew that we would always upset someone.

There's always someone that will say it's sacrilege that we changed this or that, or with this adjustment or that adjustment, but I couldn't approach this film— none of us could—from the point of what one particular fan wants. We had to look at the film and try and put blinders on and not listen to the noise of that kind of nitpicking stuff. The overall concern we had—I think we were protected by Roberto Orci, one of the writers, who is a huge *Trek* fan, and he made sure that we weren't slapping the face of the die-hard fan. We're beholden to that person. We wouldn't be making a *Star Trek* movie if those people hadn't kept it alive for so many years. So, it was a tightrope to walk.

Q: I think the film is extraordinarily topical in terms of modern politics and the way that we've got two guys really developing their characters in the heat of battle. If either of them were to run for president—Spock or Kirk—which one would you vote for, bearing in mind the qualities you've discovered in them while making this film?

J. J. Abrams: Well, I would say Kirk but only because Chris [Pine] is sitting right next to me. If Chris weren't here, I'd say Spock. I think the thing about Kirk and Spock is that they're both separately full of great potential, but it's not until they come together as a team that they can accomplish almost anything. To me, the key to the movie is that friendship. In fact, my approach to the movie was almost like a story of two brothers. I felt it was their relationship that was the spine of the film.

Q: I noted a couple of big similarities between this and *Star Wars*. Were they deliberate?

J. J. Abrams: The thing about *Star Wars* is that across those six films they've done everything. They've done every weather system, every character, every weapon, every ship—the shadow looms so large that for us—my guess is that everything in any space movie will feel somewhat derivative of it. That was almost more of a threat to this movie—the fear of ripping off *Star Wars*. It was more of a concern I had than any sort of *Trek* fan concern I had. The only way to deal with that was to not worry about things like, "Oh, they've done snow; we can't do snow." If we did that, we wouldn't do anything. So, it was really about focusing on the characters and knowing that if you have a character that might be small . . . I can name a number of characters from *Star Wars* that might be small, but that wasn't an inspiration on any of the things we were trying to do. We were just trying to keep our focus on our people and our objectives and just accept the fact that they've made these amazing *Star Wars* movies that we have to live after. Although *Star Trek* did come first, I'll point out.

Q: You're obviously a competitive person, so there must be a bit in you that thinks in reinventing this *Star Trek* tale you're going to make it the best in the genre?
J. J. Abrams: Again, my own point of view, and this was something that because I wasn't a fan going into it I felt like there had not been a version of *Star Trek* that was as appealing to me as I would have liked to have seen. For example, *The Twilight Zone* was my favorite show growing up, and I would never want to even try to do a *Twilight Zone* show or movie because I feel like it had been done in a way that I could never outdo them. What's come before in *Star Trek* is forty-three years, tons of hours, amazing stuff, and huge fans . . . just because it didn't work for me as it did for many other people doesn't mean that it's not far better than what I could do. This is my own point of view and working with this cast and this amazing crew, our goal was to make the best possible version ever. The key to that was just the emotional way in. I've become a lover of *Star Trek*, which I can't even believe, but it's out of examining these characters and getting under the skin of these characters. I never knew why I should care about Kirk. Now I do, and it's not because I directed it; it's because I appreciate now what Gene Roddenberry created. He was amazing, and the dynamic of the characters, we didn't change that. We just brought them back to life by casting amazing actors and luckily had a script that they were able to turn to.

Q: How did you tackle the issue of whether or not to bring back any original cast members? And why Leonard Nimoy?
J. J. Abrams: Did Bill [Shatner] ask you to ask this question? My first reaction when they asked me to be a producer was to do the Kirk and Spock story because there had been so many versions and iterations of *Star Trek*. It felt like doing another ship, a whole new group of characters wasn't the way to go. I thought starting on the ground floor, where I never felt like there was an emotional way in, was what interested me. I called the writers, with whom I'd worked before—Roberto Orci and Alex Kurtzman and the producers, Bryan Burk and Damon Lindelof, and the five of us got together—one of whom was, Orci, a huge fan; one of whom, Bryan Burk, had never seen the show before. We had this range of experiences on *Star Trek* and by talking about story and finding a story that worked for all of us

that was sort of the way in. We knew that we needed to embrace what had come before, and we knew we needed to tell a story that involved Spock, who would be a catalyst in the story. That required Leonard to be in the movie, so we met with Leonard and pitched him a story—we sat with William Shatner and did the same—and Leonard was interested but didn't commit. So, we thought, "Okay," and wrote the script. We gave him the script and crossed our fingers. Amazingly, he did. He'd said, "No," so many times in the last couple of decades that we were thrilled. So, that was the way in.

Q: What was it like actually working with Leonard and directing him?

J. J. Abrams: Even as a nonfan going in, the first day of shooting with Leonard—he had the ears on, the hair; he was in wardrobe. You just felt this legend on set. Here was this guy who's been playing this for forty-two years. I remember he did his first line-reading. I was backstage behind the camera watching him, and I had some notes. I started walking towards him, and as I'm doing so, I started to ask myself, "What the hell am I doing? How the hell do I tell Leonard Nimoy how Spock should talk? This is the dumbest thing." So, I slowed down and realized I was sweating. I get there. He's got the ears on, and he's like, "Yes?" And I said to him, "Mr. Nimoy, I want to give you a note. I just don't know how to do it . . ." He grabbed my shirt and said, "Tell me. Tell me. Tell me." I just saw in his eyes that he's an actor, he's an artist, and he's a collaborator. I cannot tell you how wonderful it was to work with him. He was just a gentleman; he's incredibly cooperative, and the most amazing thing is that he was so supportive—not just of what we were all doing, but specifically of Zachary. Here's a guy, if you can imagine, who has played this role for almost half a century and here's this young, handsome actor who is just starting in his career coming in and taking over that character. I just think it could have been a lot of things, but what it was was the definition of grace. He was so wonderful and so supportive to the whole crew and especially in a wonderful way to Zachary.

Q: Did you ever give in to the temptation to seek tips from him about how you were doing?

J. J. Abrams: I remember when we were doing the scene with the two Spocks together I pulled Leonard aside and said, "I have to ask you this because you were in the scene and you were watching him [Zachary] play Spock, so what do you think? Is there anything I should be telling him? Is there something you're not seeing because no one knows this character better than you?" And he just said, "He's pretty good."

Q: Will you be back for a sequel?

J. J. Abrams: Nothing would be more fun than to work with them again, but I think what Chris Pine has said is right. It is insanely presumptuous to be talking about it. The good news is that if people like it and there's demand for another one, the actors and the writers and I will be back. But we don't have a story. We don't have a script; we don't have an outline or a thought. We just have this movie.

J. J. Abrams

Charlie Rose / 2009

Transcript from *Charlie Rose*, May 4, 2009. Published by permission of Rosemary Guerin, coordinating producer, *Charlie Rose*.

Charlie Rose: His work as writer, director, and producer has made him Hollywood's master of mystery. His creations include the television shows *Alias*, *Fringe*, and *Lost*, which won the Emmy award for Outstanding Drama Series in 2005. He moved to films in 2006, directing Tom Cruise in *Mission: Impossible III*. Here is a look at some of his work.

His latest movie is *Star Trek*. *Variety* calls it a smart and breathless space adventure. Here's a look at the trailer.

I'm pleased to have J. J. Abrams at this table. Welcome.

J. J. Abrams: It's an honor to be here.

Charlie Rose: Thank you so much. Look at this, *Newsweek*.

J. J. Abrams: I couldn't believe that. I'm not kidding.

Charlie Rose: You don't want them to pull it back, do you?

J. J. Abrams: No.

Charlie Rose: "To Boldly Go, How *Star Trek* Taught Us to Dream Big." How does *Star Trek* teach us to dream big? I realize you didn't write the article, but—

J. J. Abrams: I didn't. I didn't. Actually, I should read it, and then, maybe, I can answer that question. I'm not sure—

Charlie Rose: Well, just talk about dreams and fantasy and genre and—

J. J. Abrams: The thing about *Star Trek* is, as someone who was never necessarily a fan of *Star Trek*, I've come to appreciate it, working on the movie in a way that friends of mine did, often smart friends. They loved the show. I always felt a little behind them. I didn't quite find a way in. What I realized is that one of the things that Gene Roddenberry did when he created the show forty-three years ago is he was showing us a version of our future that was optimistic. It wasn't a dark, cynical—it showed us—

Charlie Rose: Prophet of doom.

J. J. Abrams: Yes, and by the way, there have been in recent years many films, which I've loved but have been postapocalyptic or preapocalyptic and, ultimately, very cynical. I think that one of the things that *Star Trek* has intrinsically that allows us to dream is a hopeful future. That optimism was one of the things that actually got me excited about doing the movie.

Charlie Rose: How did you get to do it, even though you weren't a fan?

J. J. Abrams: Well, I just finished the *Mission: Impossible* film, and Paramount asked if I would be interested in producing a *Star Trek* film.

Charlie Rose: Producing?

J. J. Abrams: Producing. I thought, "You know what? Being involved as a producer, to kind of help shepherd a vision of *Star Trek* . . ." that was something that I could get into. It was interesting and a cool challenge. As I started working with the writers, Roberto Orci, Alex Kurtzman, the producers Damon Lindelof and Bryan Burk—the five of us, Bob Orci, one of the writers is a huge *Star Trek* fan, just loves it. One of the produces, Bryan Burk, had never seen an episode. So, we had this sort of range of experiences with *Star Trek*. I was sort of someone who knew of it but didn't really love it. I just fell in love with the script. When I finally read it, I thought, "This is nuts. I will be jealous of anyone who directs this movie. So, if I can do it, I should."

Charlie Rose: The producer's prerogative in this case.

J. J. Abrams: Exactly. I know who we should hire.

Charlie Rose: So, you set out to make it. What was the challenge? This was a television series, and you didn't want it to be just television series installments we haven't seen.

J. J. Abrams: Right. Do you remember when the *Superman* movie came out that Richard Donner directed?

Charlie Rose: Right.

J. J. Abrams: Up to that point, *Superman* had been this sort of cartoon. It had been a comic book; it had been a kind of campy show. But, the poster—I remember this when I was a kid—it came out, the poster for *Superman* was "You'll believe a man can fly." There was a kind of legitimacy with which he treated the subject. I just thought that would be a real cool thing to try and do with *Star Trek*. Not to say that they didn't try to do it before or do it, but the resources they had on the show were slim. The films didn't have much more, quite frankly. For the first time, we were actually given a really sizeable budget, plus the technology that exists now for visual effects is light years beyond what they ever had before. So, we were actually in a situation where we could realize *Star Trek* in a way where you would believe this ship could fly—

Charlie Rose: What's the equivalent of "You will believe a man can fly"?
J. J. Abrams: You will believe the ship can fly. The key for me was—

Charlie Rose: That there's a world beyond.
J. J. Abrams: Yes, but the genius about what Dick Donner did when he did *Superman* was the characters were—he respected the characters as much as the audience. They were funny, and they were real. They were mostly unknowns. You had this sort of sense of watching these characters. Clark Kent was no longer a comic book. He was—you believed this guy was real. I just loved that treatment. So, we were trying to tell a sort of epic tale—the birth of the character, the becoming of the captain, all that kind of stuff. That was a model.

Charlie Rose: My impression about you is that you want your audiences, whether it's *Lost* or wherever it might be, to understand where the character came from.
J. J. Abrams: Well—

Charlie Rose: And then use all the technology in the world to tell your story.
J. J. Abrams: That's right. What you just said is the key, and whether there's any technology or not—it's what *The Twilight Zone* did so well. That was my favorite show. I adored that show. One of the reasons it was so brilliant is, literally, you'd have Rod Sterling say "meet so-and-so"—you know how the character was—and then you actually get to meet the character.

Charlie Rose: Oh, I love that, yes.
J. J. Abrams: But it was such a wonderful narrative style, and it was a way to connect with the character who was broken in some way, who was, like, under it in some way. Then something extraordinary would typically happen. Usually, they would have no resources either, but it would just be an extraordinary story or a turn. Anyway, that was to me like the most exciting as a kid, the most exciting sort of inspiration.

Charlie Rose: First, you have got to cast this movie.

J. J. Abrams: *Star Trek.* Yes, I'd never had to do that before, cast characters that had been cast.

Charlie Rose: Right.

J. J. Abrams: And that was a weird thing, because I knew I didn't want this to be *Star Trek 11.* Although technically, it's *Star Trek 11.* But I wanted—

Charlie Rose: You didn't want this to be the characters—it couldn't be the characters that the audience at home who loved *Star Trek* had identified with.

J. J. Abrams: Well, it's a tricky thing because our story was in a continuum and, yet, was very much its own thing. As someone who was not a fan to begin with, I needed to make the movie for people like myself who would go to the film without any information. I didn't want to make a movie for *Star Trek* fans.

Charlie Rose: Right. Because they'll come anyway.

J. J. Abrams: Well, that—if we made a movie that was hopefully a good movie, that was exciting and fun, and we'd get them anyway. That's right. But, so, yes. I should just shut up. But I think that the key with casting this movie was finding people who could take the spirit of what was in the original characters, but not do impersonations, because *Star Trek* has been mocked so many times. We didn't want to do a skit.

Charlie Rose: Is that why you said at one point that people who make sequels rip off the wrong thing.

J. J. Abrams: Well, what I was referring to was that a lot of times, there will be a movie that will be scary—or a comedy or whatever it is, any genre—and you will always inevitably find the next year, two or three movies that feel somewhat like a Xerox of what you had seen in that successful film, and usually they fail because the thing that they're ripping off is the thing that they sold, meaning it's the gimmick of the plot. It's the pyrotechnics of it, for example. Inevitably, the movie was successful despite those things. My favorite movies are sort of B-genre films treated A. You can look at things like *Jaws*; you can look at things like *Tootsie.* And you can say, "Well, when you describe the plot, it's a little, 'Come on.'" Then you see how genius it was done. It was like you can't deny it. So, for me, that's the goal, to take the things, the characters, the inner life of the characters. That's the thing that you want to be mining and discovering and figuring out, all the kind of alien—

Charlie Rose: And how did you do this here?

J. J. Abrams: Well, the key for this, and the writers, obviously, I think, wrote a wonderful script. The key was to get inside, get under the skin of these characters. So, for example, with Kirk, I knew he was Captain Kirk, but I never knew why I should care about Captain Kirk. What we did is come up with a story where we see this is a broken guy. This is a guy who is—he's lost. He's aimless. He's sort of a punk when you meet him. He's in a bar; he's picking up some girl; he's getting into a fight, has nothing to lose. You kind of think, "Well, I know he's Kirk, so that's Captain Kirk, but he's hardly a captain." The journey of the story for his character is how he goes from a guy who's full of potential, but unrealized completely, and how does he become that character? So that was one way in. I felt that's a cool story anywhere. It doesn't have to be in space. That's an interesting story. How does a guy go from being this sort of bum to becoming someone who's proud, who's earned that captain's chair? That was an interesting way in.

Charlie Rose: Tell me this. Okay, so you were more of a *Star Wars* fan than a *Star Trek* fan because . . . ?

J. J. Abrams: Yes. Well, because *Star Wars* gave you a way in. *Star Wars* introduced this farm boy who's just in the middle of nowhere, and, suddenly, he's called to adventure. How can this kid—you got to know someone in a relatable way who is then taken on an extraordinary adventure. *Star Trek* always had characters in extraordinary-adventure mode.

Charlie Rose: Right. So *Star Wars* created a notion that you can imagine how this could happen because the beginning is average, normal.

J. J. Abrams: That's right. Right. It's funny. Even something like I was talking about, like movies that I liked when I was a kid, like *Die Hard* I remember seeing, and that's a story about this cop who, when you first meet him, he's got his tail between his legs. He's coming back to his wife because he's trying to keep their marriage alive, and it's a guy who's—he's never become the kind of hero he becomes in the movie. It's not like you have to start out a complete innocent, but you have to start out someone who is not—who hasn't gotten to the end yet. By the end of the movie, you think, "Wow, that's a whole experience, a whole journey that character's been on." I often think of movies as the dream the main character has that changes him or her, meaning if that main character at the beginning of the story were to fall asleep that night and have a dream and then wake up a better and changed person, what's that dream? And that's the film.

Charlie Rose: What was your dream?

J. J. Abrams: Just to be on *Charlie Rose*. All I—my goal—

Charlie Rose: Every night you went to bed, and you fell asleep—
J. J. Abrams: No, no, my—

Charlie Rose:—and you looked at this table and you said, "Someday." Do you know how many people come up to me on the street and say, "Someday I'm going to sit at your table"?
J. J. Abrams: When I said it's an honor to be here, I'm not kidding around. It's not a joke, I'm telling you. No, I think the ultimate dream really was to—and I'm not kidding—was to be here, meaning to get to make a movie, to get to do something that when I was an eight-year-old kid, I was making Super 8 films with my parents' camera. This is what I've always wanted to do—to be lucky enough to get a shot and get to do it, and literally be sitting here talking to you about a movie that I've got coming out is as surreal as it gets. Really.

Charlie Rose: I'll take your word for it. Tell me, what do you think was the spark between a camera, putting it on film, and you?
J. J. Abrams: I think part of it was when you're a kid, you do what kids do. So, kids are out playing, in the field playing ball or whatever. I was never an athlete, so I was never chosen first. When you're chosen near the end, you play less, and when you play less, you get worse. When you get worse, you get picked less. When you don't get picked . . . I mean, literally, it's a cycle.

Charlie Rose: Pretty soon you're looking for a Super 8 camera—
J. J. Abrams: That's right—it takes three days to—does somebody have a camera?

Charlie Rose: If I can't be it, I'll photograph it.
J. J. Abrams: That's right. You're not—even when I was in kindergarten, I re-member, I would watch kids through the jungle gym. I would do this all the time, and I had watched, to see what it would look like through a camera. My teachers would call my parents, very concerned, "I don't know what the hell Jamie is doing near the jungle gym—"

Charlie Rose: I wonder what they say now.
J. J. Abrams: Well, but that was—that was really my thing. I think that I remember going to Universal Studios' tour back when it was a real tour—not like an amuse-ment park kind of thing. It was just a simple—like Lucille Ball's dressing room was huge. They advertised that.

Charlie Rose: No rides, nothing?
J. J. Abrams: Nothing. It was incredibly bare bones—

Charlie Rose: Yes.

J. J. Abrams: But it was inspiring. I remember going home and starting to make movies that night.

Charlie Rose: In your mind or with your Super 8?

J. J. Abrams: I knew that my dad had a little JF boxed Super 8 camera and it, just a little thing. So, I went home, and I started making movies. I would just do all sorts of—build models and blow them up and film them.

Charlie Rose: Spielberg was the first hero. No?

J. J. Abrams: Spielberg is—

Charlie Rose: Steven Spielberg is, was, will always be—

J. J. Abrams: Spielberg is, yes, present tense to me. He's my idol. He's just the guy who—I watch what he does, and I just—any of his movies, every time I watch it, I discover. I learn something else.

Charlie Rose: What is it you learn? Because it's interesting to me, about him, that you're not the only person that says that—

J. J. Abrams: Sure.

Charlie Rose: Actors will say, "Marlon Brando," and you go down the line—

J. J. Abrams: Yes. I think that part of it is his unbelievable sense of the visual storytelling that he has, which he will do in one shot what directors need six, seven shots to do. He will tell stories; if you watch, he will tell stories without editing. There's a fluidity to what he does. In some of his films, there's a level of unbelievable, kind of, heartbreaking realism, and then in the same reel, there will be something that is just extraordinary and mind-blowing. That to me is like the nexus of where the mundane and the amazing connect. That to me is what he does with this facility that's truly just mind-blowing to me.

Charlie Rose: Was there a moment in which you met Spielberg and Tom Cruise because they wanted you to make *Mission: Impossible III*?

J. J. Abrams: I actually met Spielberg years earlier, but every time I would see him, it would just be—it was terrifying. I was always just—I was horrified because I just thought, "What if—? Am I going to say the wrong thing or—?" It's a weird thing to meet the person that you admire so much, most in anything. Anyway, so one day Tom Cruise, whom I had not met, and Mr. Spielberg and Paula Wagner, who is Tom's partner—

Charlie Rose: Tom and Mr. Spielberg.

J. J. Abrams:—show up to my office, and they're sitting on my sofa. They're asking if I would write a movie that they were going to do, which was *War of the Worlds*. Now, I was not available because I was going to do the *Lost* pilot. But I was sitting there with these people for an hour or whatever; we were talking, and it was that thing of looking—I was looking at Steven, and I'm like, "I can't look at him any-more because I'm too nervous. I'm going to—" I would look over at Tom, and I'm like, "Oh, dear God, it's Tom Cruise." I couldn't look anywhere. At a certain point, literally in the meeting—I swear this is true—I literally—I stopped it and said, "This is too weird for me." I was like, "This is—" I had to just take a second. "Okay, let's continue the meeting." I was overwhelmed with this ridiculous energy. Then, of course, I had to say I couldn't do it because I was doing *Lost*, which to say, "No," to either of these men is not the ideal scenario. But they were incredibly sweet and gracious about it. Then Tom ended up calling and asking if I would direct the *Mission: Impossible* film.

Charlie Rose: But didn't he ask to come on the set or something? What was—?

J. J. Abrams: Well, he called me when I was shooting the *Lost* pilot. He called me because he watched the first two seasons of *Alias*, and he was so—he loved it, and he was so sweet about it. He said, "Let's hang out when you get back." I was like, "Okay, Tom Cruise."

Charlie Rose: "We can do that."

J. J. Abrams: Yes. "Let's hang out." I thought, "Come on," as if we're going to hang out. I got back to LA. He called. He's like, "Let's hang out." We did. We became friends. He is the greatest. He gave me this shot to direct the film that no one else would give me. It was—

Charlie Rose: *Mission: Impossible III.*

J. J. Abrams: Yes, I can't believe—I still cannot believe it.

Charlie Rose: What was the budget? Like, $150 million or—

J. J. Abrams: Around that. A little bit more.

Charlie Rose: How different are movies today, 2009, because of technology? What can you do in *Star Trek* you couldn't have done in the year 2000?

J. J. Abrams: I often wonder, looking back on what we're doing now, if it won't feel as real as we think it is because when they started doing—when they did films in the sixties and they did visual effects, they must have looked pretty real. Now, we look at these films and think— But I have to say, I think we've gotten to a place where photoreal is photoreal, where it truly does look real. I think we can do now, even in the last ten years, things that would have been either unheard of or just prohibitive to do. You can do things now on television that would have been impossible to do in films nine, ten years ago. What you can do with computer graphics, it's gotten exponentially more possible. The question becomes just fascinating to me: You can do anything now, so what are you going to do?

Charlie Rose: The question also for me is: Does that feed your imagination or simply give you the tools to make your imagination real?
J. J. Abrams: Well, I think we have become sort of immune to spectacle. I think that the visual possibility has now become so open-ended that there is no shock value anymore in what you can see. It only matters if you have a human connection to it. So, a spaceship flying by, we've seen that hundreds of times. It doesn't matter. Nobody is going to go, "Ooohhh, a spaceship flying." If you don't love the people on the spaceship, the spaceship means nothing. So, the visual effects are huge and important and really fun, but they're only there to serve the humanity of the story.

Charlie Rose: There is scene two, Kirk and Sulu parachute onto planet Vulcan. Anything you couldn't do with this that you wanted to do?
J. J. Abrams: We actually got to make this movie. I have to say—

Charlie Rose: This is the movie you wanted to make.
J. J. Abrams: It is. I mean, it's a weird situation, especially with the sound. That was so important. We finished the movie and delayed the release of the film while we were shooting. They told me they were going to release it six months later. We finished the film on time for a December release, and we were done. It's kind of closet space; you use as much as you've got, so all of a sudden we had six more months. I was watching it, and the mix isn't good enough yet. We actually went back and mixed it for a couple more months, and I'm telling you, it made a huge difference. Anyway, so this is the movie.

Charlie Rose: Does it lead you to think about a certain kind of movie you want to make now?
J. J. Abrams: Well, having been lucky enough to make this movie and *Mission: Impossible*, both of which obviously were based on TV shows, and they were sequels—

Charlie Rose: That you would write.
J. J. Abrams: Yes, that would be good, yes. I would love to.

Charlie Rose: No, but it's more likely you'd want to write it, isn't it?

J. J. Abrams: Probably. Although I'm not precious about who writes it or where the thing comes from. If the thing is compelling, that's all that really matters.

Charlie Rose: What about television and other media?

J. J. Abrams: You mean the TED speech?

Charlie Rose: Yes.

J. J. Abrams: Yeah, that was really fun, actually—

Charlie Rose: The reason I'm bringing it up, there's a box. Did you bring a box on stage when you made that speech?

J. J. Abrams: Yes, that was sort of a—that was sort of a—

Charlie Rose: Which is mystery and secrets and everything.

J. J. Abrams: There's a box that my grandfather—I used to go to this magic store in New York City called Lou Tannen's Magic. We'd go there all the time. I bought, when I was a kid, this magic box that was $15. What they say is, there's like $50 worth of magic inside, but you can't know what you're getting. So you get this box, and I just never opened it. I didn't open it because I felt that keeping it closed made the box truly magical. There was something inside, I don't know what it is, and what's inside—to me—is my imagination right now, which is infinitely more powerful than whatever's in there, you know what I mean? I remember I actually got the boxes for my kids as well. I gave one to my daughter when she was three and one to my son when he was four. My son is ten now, and he still hasn't opened his. Our daughter opened hers the week I gave it to her. She—and I knew she would, too.

Charlie Rose: How do you explain the difference? Their personality?

J. J. Abrams: Well, you know, at three years old—

Charlie Rose: Or gender?

J. J. Abrams: My—you said that. My guess is that at three years old she couldn't—you get a box; you open the box. This is human nature. At four years old—I also I remember saying to my son, "You can open the box, but there's no more mystery."

Charlie Rose: What is it you want to say about mystery, other than it's magical?

J. J. Abrams: I guess the point is that—you know, I make this point in the magazine—that we sort of live in this age of immediacy, where if you have a question about something or you're curious about something, you can instantly—

Charlie Rose: Google it.

J. J. Abrams: Yes. You instantaneously can have a sense of knowledge and understanding about it. I think there's a certain point where people become entitled; they begin to feel entitled to get information immediately. The thing about mystery or a puzzle or even a magic trick that's being performed is that you have to surrender to it. It becomes—you have to solve this thing; you have to get it on its terms. It can't be just your desire to know the answer right now. So, when people say to me, "How does *Lost* end? Tell me," I always feel like they're missing the point of what the show is because, yeah, I can tell you the ending. I can tell you what's in the mystery box, but isn't the idea of it, isn't the experience of it more important than the answer?

Charlie Rose: So, what did you think of the ending of *The Sopranos*?

J. J. Abrams: It's funny; my wife and I have had a big debate about this. She—

Charlie Rose: You're not the only one.

J. J. Abrams: And, of course, I thought it was actually very interesting, and I loved the ambiguity of it. My wife will—in the middle of doing anything, she'll say, "God, that was genius," just out of the blue. She'll go on about—and I think she's right because it's incredibly provocative. It was one of those things where part of me feels like I kind of wish I knew more, and, yet, I so love that feeling. That's kind of what I'm talking about, that idea of engaging the audience. For example, like in *The Graduate*, when Ben and Elaine go on that date and they put the top up in the car, and they're in the car. You can't hear a word they're saying, but they're having this talk. What I love about it is you give that scene, you imbue that scene with the best version of a romantic date. To me, you could say it's a cheat; you could say, "Oh, but to me it's like that's what makes it so brilliant . . ."—is the audience filling the blanks, filling in the blanks between what you're seeing and what you're not seeing.

Charlie Rose: All right. *Lost*. People that I know just love it. Love it. Love it. They all come at me, saying, "Do you watch *Lost*? If you didn't like season one, here it is. If you didn't like season two, here it is."

J. J. Abrams: Oh, I'm sorry.

Charlie Rose: No, no, don't be sorry. But tell me what that is about.

J. J. Abrams: Well, first of all, it's about—

Charlie Rose: Mystery?

J. J. Abrams: First of all, it's about Damon Lindelof and Carlton Cuse. Those are the guys who run the show. When I went to do *Mission: Impossible*, I left working on that show day-to-day. So, they are brilliant. I think what it is, is that the show is weird. The show is an unusual show that doesn't give you all the answers. It's one of the few truly serialized shows on television. My guess is we're never going to get a new viewer from this point on. It's like we stopped trying to get new viewers because the show is very much a serialized show. I think that the characters are amazing. The actors are incredible. I think that it's a show that has at its core a mystery that people, on the one hand, want the answer to, and, on the other hand, it's a catalyst to learn about the characters and to have situations that make you—give you the feeling that I used to get when I was a kid and watched *The Twilight Zone*, which is, "Oh, my God, could that happen? What does that mean?" It's really—I think it's an interesting gray area.

Charlie Rose: Do you know what your next project is?
J. J. Abrams: I'm working on a script that hopefully will come together, but it's one of those things where—

Charlie Rose: How do you write? You go up in the room and shut the door. Don't let me out until I give ten pages.
J. J. Abrams: Usually, what I do is I just outline—write a million notes, and then try and find time. But we've got three kids, and there's a lot going on. So, it's sort of finding time is half the battle.

Charlie Rose: *Newsweek*, cover story, "To Boldly Go, How *Star Trek* Taught Us to Dream Big." J. J. Abrams's film opens this Friday, May 8.

J. J. Abrams—Director of *Star Trek: Into Darkness*, *Star Wars*, and the *Lost* Finale

Paul Byrne / 2009

Transcript from Movies.ie, May 4, 2009. Published by permission.

Paul Byrne: I know back in 1966, James T. Kirk said it was a five-year mission, but it turned out to be a little bit longer than that. I don't know whether you felt the need to go to every single adventure and misadventure over the last forty-two years to put yourself in this place where you could write this or whether you thought, "I know enough to a point to just be able to make this a fresh story for me"?

J. J. Abrams: *Star Trek* [was] met with a mixed reaction in many ways. In fact, their original five-year mission was cut short by a couple years in the original run of the series, but then it went on in syndication to become more popular. There have been so many iterations of *Star Trek* over time that when they first asked if I wanted to be involved, I thought, "It's a tough one to nail down because there have been so many versions and series." And I just thought, "Let's just go back to Kirk and Spock and tell their story," because I was never really a fan, and one of the reasons why is because I never felt there was a way in for me, emotionally. That was really the important thing for me that I really wanted to do.

PB: That great thing that you've been open from the start that you were never really a fan, that you're more of a *Star Wars* guy. Obviously, for you, it wasn't the case of pleasing "comic book guy," it was pleasing all those people who aren't yet *Star Trek* fans.

JJA: That was the priority for me in doing the movie, was to try and make a film that was a standalone movie that would work for people who want to go see a movie where there's action and adventure and romance and emotion. All the things that I love about movies in a movie. It happens to be a *Star Trek* film. The goal was to do a movie that would also appeal to that core fan base, but if we only focused on them and didn't try to expand what it is to be a fan of *Star Trek*, we would've been limiting ourselves, I think.

PB: Well, that notion, too, that you've got to boldly go into new areas for this franchise, and at the same time you have to embrace a certain amount of the familiar because there's such an iconic status to the characters and some of the hardware and so forth. That balance, I don't know whether that was something that was just a joy or was it kind of difficult to always know, "Well, this is the right level of . . ."
JJA: It was fun to try and balance what would work for a new audience and what would work for the established audience, but because I was coming at it more from the broader, mainstream audience point of view, I knew that it just had to work on its own. I couldn't rely on, and didn't want to rely on, any preexisting knowledge of *Star Trek*. It was never going to be about it being a continuum; it was all about, "What is this movie from the beginning?" Start at ground zero, begin with the birth of these characters. When you meet Kirk as a young man, he's hardly a captain; he's this aimless punk. When you meet Spock in the beginning, he's unreconciled with his half-Vulcan, half-human conflict. Who is he going to be? What is he going to be? How do those coexist? These two characters, the journey, the adventure, the movie is how these two characters, by finding each other, almost like two brothers, they end up basically being a team that could accomplish almost anything.

PB: That idea that you start ten years, pretty much, before the original series's "stardate" on the Captain's Log—you go back at least ten years—
JJA: It's a little bit less than that.

PB: A little bit less, but that kind of thing where you're in the Academy and you meet these people as teenagers, really, I don't know whether there was a danger that you were going to get "Fast Times at Starfleet High," that it wasn't just going to be crazy times with these young kids that you . . .
JJA: The truth is they're not much younger than the actors were when they started the series. It's around five years younger, in their twenties, thirties. There's one teenager in the bunch, which is Chekov played by Anton Yelchin. It's funny because the movies—obviously they went on for years, and we sort of remember them as older. But when you see the show, they were actually fairly young when they began. So, they're much closer in age to the original series actors than you think.

PB: The original movies—of course there were ten of them before, and they kind of went down a very dark hole with *Nemesis* [which] didn't do any kind of business. For you, that wasn't going to be any sort of inspiration; you went for something more like *Galaxy Quest* as kind of a reference point to say, "This is what can happen if you get too cheesy." Were there certain reference points for you, I don't know if there were, maybe just the original Gene Roddenberry series that you felt, "That's the key to my identity"?

JJA: *Star Trek* has been parodied so many times and been mocked enough that we knew if the movie didn't have a sense of humor built in, that people would have something to laugh at, that we couldn't be so self-serious and self-important that the film would lose oxygen and not have that levity that I think is critical to a story like this working and being believable. So, we made sure—one of the lucky things is the cast, all of them, have a great sense of humor. Working with them, working with everyone, it made it much easier to do that. The script had a lot of comedy in it, which is nice. But it was important, again, whether you're a fan of *Star Trek* or not, this movie was not just made for those fans. I think having the humanity of these characters is the key to everything. You're never going to care about this movie if you don't love these characters.

PB: You've built up quite a canon of work now with your Bad Robot company, and people know you a lot from the television. You've done *Alias*, *Felicity*, also *Lost*, this show which you cocreated with David Lindelof, is that how you pronounce it?

JJA: Damon Lindelof, yeah.

PB: There you go. It's a show that even David Lynch is confused about at this point, where he's not quite sure what's going on. For you, it's quite a definite line between you can dazzle people with brilliance and you can baffle them with bullshit. There's definitely a plan here, or is there a little bit free form? "I know the ending, but let's have a little fun before we get there"?

JJA: I left in the first season to go do *Mission: Impossible III*, *Cloverfield*, *Fringe*, and now *Star Trek*. Damon Lindelof, who I created *Lost* with, has stayed on the show the entire time. He produced *Star Trek*, as well, with me. He's been running the show with Carlton Cuse since I left, and I think the work they've done has been unbelievable. One of the smartest things that Damon did was convince the network to end the series after six years so that he would know how to pace himself. There wouldn't be that confusion: "Is it ten years? Is it five years?" When you don't know and you're doing a storyline that is linear, or serialized, you start spinning your wheels and doing things that are just BS, and you don't know what the point is. Because he knows where it's going to end, everything over the last two years has been paced to that end. There is an amazing ending that they're going to do. Like any series, you're flexible, and, as you go, you make adjustments. So, I'm not saying that they've written the last episode, but I can tell you it's going to be amazing. I think it will be very satisfying.

PB: The idea, too, that you're such a busy man, you've got so many different things going on. What I've been reading is you've got *The Dark Tower*, possibly; you've got *Mystery on 5th Avenue*; you've got an untitled Hunter Scott project; you've got *Anatomy of Hope* on TV, *Fringe*, and *Lost* and *Morning Glory*. I don't know whether this is twenty-four hours a day for you, or I don't know whether you can allow yourself time away from this because it does seem you've just got something going all the time.

JJA: There's a lot going on, but I also work with incredibly talented people who are doing, in some cases, most of the work, in other cases, all of the work. So, for example, with some of the projects you're mentioning, some aren't happening, but then there are others that are happening that you didn't mention. Our little company is trying to pick and choose specific things that we think, "Oh, we'd kill ourselves if we didn't have something to do with that. That sounds too cool, too much fun!" The good news is we're working with really talented people who are doing their job, and I try to help out as much as I can. But my wife and I have three kids; that's the most important thing. I take them to school every day. I put them to bed every night. I don't work on weekends. With the exception of a thing like this, a tour where I'm going around for a few weeks, or when we're shooting, which is not very often, it's a lot more like a job that I happen to love than it is anything else.

PB: I'm guessing—I think I've got to just wrap up now but, very quickly, you've always struck me, too, that you're much more kind of Spielberg than some European, Hans-Jürgen Syberberg or more *Star Wars* than *La Strada*. The idea that you just get an audience and hold them captive, and they're entertained completely, rather than [have] the festival circuit love you. Is that something early on that you decided? I just love the idea that you reach a lot of people, and you just knock them out.

JJA: I never made a decision to be one thing or another. The movies I've always loved have typically been more of those amusement park rides, whether it's a comedy or an action film or a drama. The [movies] that I remember as a kid going to see were those that would happen to have this huge audience, and we're all kind of roaring together. That was always the thrill ride; that was always the most fun. That has appealed to me. That's not to say when I wrote *Felicity* it was a very small, romantic, sweet little show or when I wrote *Regarding Henry*, that was much more of a straight drama. I love all sorts of movies, but the ones that have been those great impactful experiences seem to be the ones that are that huge audience thing, where you feel like you're on a rollercoaster. Those are always the most fun. That's not to say that they're better, or that's all I would want to do, but, it's certainly the stuff, as a kid, I remember as being the most fun I had at the movies.

J. J. Abrams Not Worried about Writer's Block on *Fringe*

Tyrone Warner / 2010

From CTV.ca, May 11, 2010. Reprinted by permission.

It's no mystery where some of the strange ideas on this sci-fi series come from. The series creator talks about his inspiration and how he juggles his mind-boggling list of projects.

J. J. Abrams founded Bad Robot Productions with Bryan Burk in 2001, and has produced films and series including *Cloverfield*, *Star Trek*, *Alias*, *Lost*, and *Fringe*. He directed his first feature film, *Mission: Impossible III* in 2006, and his second was *Star Trek* in 2009. Abrams created his first series, *Felicity*, in 1998.

In 2005, Abrams received Emmy Awards for Outstanding Directing in a Drama for the *Lost* pilot, as well as Outstanding Drama Series for *Lost*.

With so many irons in the fire, Abrams admits he's been fortunate to not have a serious bout of creative stoppage.

"I've been very lucky to not hit serious writer's block, but every day there is some version of writer's block that is horrible," Abrams tells CTV.ca.

"You just walk away from it for a little bit; then something usually comes up. Or usually someone in the room has the better idea than you do anyway. So I'm very lucky to work with great people."

Fringe stars Anna Torv as FBI agent Olivia Dunham, who investigates cases of "Fringe science" gone awry, with the help of Peter Bishop (Joshua Jackson) and his mad scientist father Walter (John Noble).

When asked about where his ideas come from, Abrams says inspiration can come from anywhere.

"Sometimes there are ideas that are about characters or situations that have no story at all, and you think, 'That's intriguing, but I have no idea what I would do when I got there.' And usually it's the combination of the two that make the idea something that works," says Abrams.

"The lucky thing is that I think a lot of people have these ideas and these thoughts, but when you do what we do, whether it's journalism or TV or film writing, you can take those ideas and actually turn them into something. Because if it's interesting to you, chances are it will be interesting to someone else."

Balancing his TV and film projects is no easy task for Abrams either.

"It's a little bit tricky. Sometimes it's reactive, which is never good when you're sort of like, 'What fire is bigger?' and running to put that out. The best version is when you realize, 'Well, here's where we are,' and it's kind of like plate spinning. You just sort of know that these are all—these four or five plates—I love all these plates, and they have to all kind of keep spinning. As soon as one feels like it's starting to wobble, you have to hit it to keep it going," says Abrams.

"But I think that part of it is working with people who are often better than I am at their job. It's a lot about if I have an idea for something, I want to try to execute it the best I can. But usually it's a question of finding the people who I think could help realize it in the best possible way. Other times it's not my idea at all, and it's someone else's idea. It's a question of helping that happen the best we can, so prioritizing is really about looking at trying to have a big-picture view simultaneously with the singular view and sort of the binary thing of 'What does that project need, or where is it?' Sometimes it could be literally figuring out what the story is. Other times it's editorial and final. You know what music should be in it. It's a fun thing. Usually there are a lot of different stages of projects.

"On *Fringe*—it's funny because I feel like *Fringe* is a show that it almost feels like, for me that it's just beginning. I feel like, in a weird way, getting the rhythm of the show and getting the story at the end of the second season is very much unlike a lot of series finales that are all about cliffhangers and asking questions. Although there's a little bit of that in this, this one provides answers but also is a real platform for where it's going. I feel like the first couple seasons have been slightly a kind of buildup and kind of backstory to where it's about to go. So we've got that plate that's spinning well for us. We have a new show that we're doing called *Undercovers* that we're just editing now. So I'm at that stage where I'm in the editing room."

Ultimately, Abrams credits his collaborators in making all of his projects become a success.

"I work with incredibly talented people. For example, on *Fringe* Alex Kurtzman and Roberto Orci and I wrote this pilot, and we produced that first show. I was doing *Star Trek* when we shot the pilot, so I couldn't direct the pilot of that series. But I thought the director did an amazing job. The point is we got that show sort of up and going in a certain trajectory and then worked very closely with Jeff Pinkner and Joel Wyman. They and also Akiva Goldsman have been amazing and wonderful on this. They're incredibly talented writers, so it's not like they need me to come in and help fix their problems," says Abrams.

"Sometimes we'll talk every day. Then there will be a period of a couple weeks where we don't speak, but we're emailing a lot. There's a lot of stuff that happens that way. Even like visual effects, I'm sent all the effects that we do for the show, and I give notes and tweak them and get it—it's a constant stream of sort of people reaching out and my reaching out to them. It's just—it's kind of this web. It helps a lot with people like Jeff Pinkner, with whom I worked on *Alias* for years. He was the first writer I think we hired on *Alias*. Jeff and I have a shorthand that makes it very easy, so he can call me and say, 'We're doing this kind of thing. What do you think about that?' And it's like in a very sort of short period of time, we get what we're talking about because we have many references. Josh Reims, with whom I wrote this show *Undercovers*, I worked with him on *Felicity* for years. Once again, there's a—almost like he's a brother. I know these people. There are some things we're doing with some other writers coming up that, again, we worked with before. So that, to me, is the key, like developing a family of people that you just know well. And you think those are people who—they don't need me to do what they're doing, you know. I need them more than they need me. Then we work together, and I can hopefully help them when they need help."

Abrams says he has been a lifelong fan of science fiction, starting with an early love of *The Twilight Zone*, which he says influenced his approaches to his other TV projects.

"It was very much a drama and a thriller that had, sometimes elements of horror, sometimes elements of science fiction. My relationship with science fiction, having been involved now with things like *Star Trek* and, obviously, with *Fringe* and *Lost*, I love it when it serves the purpose of the story. I think science fiction also has a wide net in terms of what really defines science fiction. I think that our lives increasingly are as much what science fiction has typically been when you look at the sort of technological advances, what science is capable of or at least promising. It's amazing how, working on *Fringe*, every week you'll look in the news, and you'll see stories that are maybe weirder than the story you're working on for the show, and you think, 'What?'

"And I can't tell you how often that's happened. I feel like in a way, where science fiction used to be wholly imaginative and kind of predictive, it is now much more our almost-mundane reality. So I feel like, though certain things like putting people on a star ship and sending them off where no one's gone before, that may not be quite where we are, but I feel like it's the thing that makes me the most interested, which is that place—whether it's David Cronenberg or Michael Crichton or even Mary Shelley, when you think of what writers have done, where they've taken the sort of possible. They've sort of said, 'Well, what if we just went a little teeny bit farther than actually what's happening?' That, to me, is the most exciting place where it feels like, 'Oh, that actually might be just around the corner.' And that is what *Fringe* does. It's crazy. The show is insane, but it deals with things that I think are often sort of oddly possible as opposed to completely fantastic," says Abrams.

"On *Fringe* I feel like there are so many stories there you think, 'Oh, my God, this is so much fun. What other show could do this specific story?' And I think, of course, there are other things that are out there. There's a lot of science fiction out there, a ton of other shows. But there's something about the show now that it's gotten to the core of the Peter/Walter thing, how Olivia—what she's come to realize about this and her role in this. It feels like what's moving forward that—I think the reason that it feels like the rest was sort of backstory is I feel like now these characters are no longer strangers. These characters are no longer—even the father and son, they've come through what they've come through. Now a certain understanding exists between them. And, like I was saying before, like with Jeff Pinkner, when I work with him, our history allows us to have a kind of forward momentum with our work. I feel like now after these stories are told at the end of the second season, there's a baseline, you know, familiarity with these characters that will allow the stories to have more meaning because they have a history."

An Interview with *Super 8* Director J. J. Abrams

Matthew Pejkovic / 2011

From *Matt's Movie Reviews*, June 2011. Reprinted by permission.

J. J. Abrams is no stranger to hero worship. As the creator of acclaimed TV series *Alias* and *Lost*, and the man responsible for successfully relaunching the *Star Trek* franchise (no mere feat considering its lengthy history and devoted fan base), Abrams has become a credible and lauded entertainer, garnering a legion of fans in the process.

Yet, with his latest film *Super 8*, the Los Angeles–raised producer/screenwriter/director has himself become a gushing fanboy, tipping his hat to the classic films of legendary filmmaker Steven Spielberg while also paying tribute to the adventure of youth and his love of creating movies.

Set in the late 1970s, *Super 8* tells the story of young Joe (Joel Courtney) and his group of misfit friends, who, while filming their own sci-fi movie, discover a vast conspiracy involving a covert military operation and an unknown entity terrorizing his small town.

For Abrams, the story evolved from a more autobiographical angle. "I was very much like these kids. The first impulse for me in doing the movie, was to revisit a time in my life when I was about that age, at that time, making films," said Abrams. "It was the first thought that I had, and I called Steven (Spielberg), who I knew and asked if he was interested in producing it with me."

Working with Spielberg proved at first to be an intimidating process for Abrams, who freely admits to idolizing the *Jaws* and *E.T.* filmmaker since he was a child. "At the very beginning it was surreal and intimidating and, probably, more about getting my sea legs a little bit and realizing that I had known him enough to know that it was going to be okay to have actual conversations," said Abrams. "But very early on it struck me that no one is going to benefit if this isn't a collaboration. I can't go into this, writing and directing a movie, doggedly following around a master. Once I got over the idea of working with someone who is a hero of mine since I was a kid, I just started focusing on the work and not the person with whom I was working."

Another new experience for Abrams was working with a cast mostly made up of children, many of whom had never worked on a film set before. "The kids were great! Joe Courtney, Riley Griffiths . . . they've never been on a set or done anything before, and they were just terrific. Riley was amazing! He was one of the first kids to come in, and it was like 'How do you not cast that kid?' They were all spectacular."

An actor who has worked on set before is Elle Fanning, the younger sister of Dakota and burgeoning child actress in her own right, who won rave reviews in Sofia Coppola's *Somewhere* and has again wowed critics with her turn as wild child Alice in *Super 8*.

"Elle is incredible!" enthused Abrams. "One of the things that struck me was how sophisticated she was in terms of understanding the emotional motivation of characters. But then she will also understand how to modulate her own performance. For example, there is a scene where she has to be sort of rehearsing for a scene which is emotional, but then there is a scene later in the film where she is genuinely emotional. We talked about how they need to be very different scenes because if she was using the same tricks in the scene where she is rehearsing and the scene where she is actually emotional, people will point and go, 'Oh, that's a trick! That's acting. I've seen her do that before.' We talked about ways to go deeper into the scene, where she is genuinely emotional, and she is twelve at the time. I'm having this conversation with this actress when she is twelve! It was insane."

Mere days from release, and *Super 8* is still shrouded in a veil of mystery, with Abrams conscious not to go overboard with promotional materials and plot leaks, a risky maneuver with "more" the motto for many blockbuster movies of late.

"I was in a situation where a script that I wrote for a movie was reviewed online before it was produced, which ultimately it wasn't, and it was an unfortunate situation and I became paranoid because of it," said Abrams.

"So there was a loose end in the way things were handled in that situation, and I thought 'We can actually prevent that.' It doesn't mean anything other than the movie won't be ruined for people before they see it. Actually, the audience benefits. It's not just about me being paranoid for paranoid's sake. . . . I actually don't like seeing trailers where after the trailer is over I feel like, 'Well! I don't want to watch the movie anymore. I just saw everything.' I would rather be interested and compelled. Go and see the movie and actually have the experience that I knew I had when I was a kid and saw movies, where not every single clip was available at every given moment, where information about the fights in the set, who was in the movie and who got injured, who's making the cameo you are not supposed to know about . . . all of this stuff. By the time movies are coming out I know far more than I want to."

What is known far and wide is the influence of classic Steven Spielberg movies in the creation and look of *Super 8*, with *Close Encounters of the Third Kind* and especially *E.T.* felt in every preview and poster. Yet, for Abrams, *Super 8* is more than just some retread of classic American cinema. This is his ode to a time when cinema was full of spirit, adventure, and classy novelty that was only worth seeing in the cinema, with family and friends for company.

"*Super 8* was about the experience of being one of those kids and making those movies in the late seventies, which was profoundly affected by the cinema of the time," said Abrams. "Going back to this time and writing the script and making the movie, it was never about looking at *Close Encounters of the Third Kind* or *E.T.* or *Poltergeist* or *Goonies* or *Stand by Me* or any of these movies that I loved. It was really about looking at that period of time and knowing especially with Steven's involvement as producer that I was completely free to embrace the Amblin-ness of the movie. I didn't feel self-conscious. It was like, 'It's an Amblin movie! I've got to make an Amblin movie.'

"That means if the kids have got bicycles, I shouldn't feel guilty. I should celebrate it. If this spectacular thing happens on Main Street, then that's cool. That's the genre of the movie. The great thing about Amblin is that it embraces heart; it embraces humanity; it embraces parent/child relationships; it embraces first love; it embraces best friendship. It embraces confronting the thing that scares you most and finding your own voice, becoming a leader and not a follower, and learning that you can deal with tragedy and survive it."

"It was all these things that I loved in the potential about the movie that Amblin gave me license, and Steven gave me license, to truly embrace and dive into, as opposed to treading lightly. I think that was really the thing that was the biggest impact. Clearly, you can site dozens of influences, like you can in anyone's movie. But the Amblin umbrella allowed every genre I love to coexist. Whether it is successful is someone else's place to determine."

An Interview with J. J. Abrams, Director of *Super 8*

Matthew Toomey / 2011

From the *Film Pie*, June 4, 2011. Reprinted by permission of Matthew Toomey.

Gifted filmmaker J. J. Abrams was recently in Australia for the premiere of *Super 8*, one of my favorite films so far this year. I was lucky enough to have a chat over the phone with him, and here's what he had to say . . .

Matthew Toomey: This morning I'm speaking with a writer-producer-director whose career keeps on climbing. He created television shows such as *Felicity, Alias,* and *Lost.* On the bigger screen, he's directed *Mission: Impossible III* and the latest *Star Trek* reboot. I'm excited because this is the first film that I've given an A-grading to in the last four months . . . so let me say good morning to J. J. Abrams.
J. J. Abrams: You've made my day. Thanks very much. It's great to be here.

Toomey: So many of the projects you're associated with take this approach, but it's great to see a film withhold so much from the audience prior to seeing it. The posters give away nothing, and the trailers are very cryptic. As the director, can you command that kind of control over the marketing and the promotion of the film?
Abrams: Thanks for all that. The idea for *Super 8* was to try and preserve the experience for the audience. I don't know if you've ever had this. But you see a trailer or watch a commercial, and you literally feel like you've seen the whole movie. And you don't have a burning need to go see it.

Toomey: I feel that all the time.
Abrams: I just think it is a little overbearing, and it speaks to an entitlement to information that people seem to have now with the computer age. For me, it's not a question of being coy and trying to play it overly clever. It's about saying, "Look, here are the characters, and here is the situation." Clearly, we're telling more as we

get closer to the release, but we don't want people to feel the experience is spoiled before they've even been there.

Toomey: I wish more filmmakers took that approach. I should ask, though, because I want to be careful not to give too much away about this film. What do we tell people that it's about?

Abrams: The story, which I'm happy to talk about, focuses on this kid in the late seventies in an American small town. He's got a ridiculous group of friends that all make these movies on Super 8 film. This particular boy, before the movie even begins, has recently lost his mother in an accident at the local steel mill. He's been left with his father with whom he doesn't have a very strong relationship. He's getting on with his life as best he can, but he's still devastated by the loss of his mum.

He's with his friends making movies, and while filming at a train station one night, they witness this crazy train crash. They don't see what it is, but something escapes from the train that will change everything in their town.

The story about this boy and the creature is really just a catalyst to tell the story of first love, the story of family, the story of going from a follower to a leader, and, ultimately, realizing that you can go through a horrible tragedy and be stronger afterwards.

Toomey: About halfway through the film I was thinking that it reminded me of one of my favorite movies growing up, *The Goonies*. Please tell me you're a fan . . .

Abrams: I am a fan of *The Goonies*, but it's funny, I wasn't a huge fan when I first saw it as a kid. I became a fan when I watched it with my kids. They just loved it, and I had this newfound respect for it.

The thing that I loved about it was how wonderfully messy the dialogue was with the kids and how it constantly overlaps. It made that movie feel like it was real—the kids were acting like kids. If you've ever watched a bunch of kids hang out that age, they're not polite, and they don't wait for the other one to finish before they talk. That was a great lesson from that film.

Toomey: I want to give you as much credit as possible, but I can't help but mention these kids. They're so relaxed and are having so much fun on the screen. How did you get them to do that and look so natural?

Abrams: First of all, they're just an incredible group. Part of it was casting kids that didn't feel like professionals acting as children. We were lucky to find among the group Joel Courtney and Riley Griffiths, both of whom had never been in anything or even on the set of anything before this film. It was wonderful to work with them and allow them to bring a natural dynamic and personality to the movie.

It was just a blast to work with them, and Elle Fanning is just off-the-charts brilliant. The whole experience was really wonderful with these actors.

Toomey: Is there one of these kids that you molded on yourself growing up and I can watch the film thinking that's the young J. J. Abrams?

Abrams: The truth is that I'm like the kid who makes the movies, but I was never as confident as he is. I was also, like, the main character but probably not quite as shell-shocked. I loved blowing things up too and filming them, but I wasn't as obsessed about it as Cary. I guess I'm somewhere in the middle.

Toomey: I mentioned the posters before, and one thing they do say in big blaring letters is Steven Spielberg's name as he is a producer on the film. I know a producer can have varying roles on a project, but I'm curious to know how involved Spielberg was with this particular project.

Abrams: You know, I still haven't met him . . . just kidding. This movie would never have happened without him for many reasons, and most are probably obvious. When I was a kid in that time making Super 8 movies, the work of Steven Spielberg was a profound influence. The films he made, the films George Lucas made, the films John Carpenter made were huge for me and my friends.

As soon as I had this idea to do the film, I called Steven and asked if he'd be interested. He immediately said, "Yes," as he remembered what it was like to make the movies he did when he was a kid. Over the course of development of the script, casting, production, editorial, scoring, mixing . . . he was part of every process and was incredibly helpful.

It is an Amblin film as was *The Goonies* and a number of other movies. It really allowed me to feel free to embrace the qualities of Amblin films—often involving children and stories of spectacle and other worldly events. They were stories about family and friendships that weren't afraid to get emotional and pull at the heart strings.

Toomey: Well, you've done a fantastic job, but I want to ask you one more question about what cool projects you're working on that we're going to see in the near future?

Abrams: We've got *Mission: Impossible—Ghost Protocol*, which comes out in December that Brad Bird is directing. We've got a couple of new TV shows—one called *Alcatraz* and the other called *Person of Interest*. We've got a number of other things we're playing with in various stages of development that hopefully we can talk about soon. One of those is another *Star Trek* movie that we'd love to get up and running sooner rather than later.

Toomey: When do you sleep? It sounds like you have so much going on?
Abrams: The hardest thing about sleeping is not my professional life, but it's having three kids—that's what makes sleep so precious.

Toomey: Well, I'm sure they're going to love this movie. J. J. Abrams, thank you for speaking with us this morning.
Abrams: Thank you so much for your kind words.

Interview: *Super 8* Director J. J. Abrams!

Chris Eggertsen / 2011

From *Bloody Disgusting*, June 8, 2011. Reprinted by permission of Bloody Disgusting, LLC.

One of the most anticipated films of the summer is writer-director J. J. Abrams's *Super 8*, about a small Ohio town in 1979 that suffers a rash of bizarre occurrences following an explosive train crash nearby.

In anticipation of the release of the movie—which was produced by Steven Spielberg's Amblin Entertainment and in many ways harkens back to the likes of early Amblin-backed films like *E.T.* and *The Goonies*—BD's Chris Eggertsen recently had the opportunity to attend a press roundtable with Abrams to get his take on the film, which comes out in theaters everywhere this Friday.

Many in my age range and older look back with fondness on the Amblin films of yore—a collection of eighties classics that are touchstones of the collective Gen X memory bank. Classic titles like *E.T.*, *Gremlins*, *The Goonies*, and *Back to the Future* were released by the company within only a few short years of each other, leading the production shingle that was founded in 1981 by Steven Spielberg, Kathleen Kennedy, and Frank Marshall to become known as *the* premiere purveyor of quality family entertainment during the first decade of its existence.

Though there hasn't been a classic, old school–style Amblin film released in many a moon now, the upcoming *Super 8*, written and directed by Spielberg friend and powerhouse-in-his-own-right J. J. Abrams, is a film that in some ways attempts to recapture some of that bygone Amblin magic, right down to a classic formula that sees a ragtag group of kids in late-seventies suburbia experiencing an otherworldly series of events while they're in the midst of shooting their very own Super 8 movie.

I and a few other eager journalists sat down with Abrams in a small room at the Four Seasons Hotel on Sunday afternoon to chat about the soon-to-be-released film, which surprisingly—at least given the ubiquity of the Abrams brand (mostly due to his role as creator of smash hit television series like *Alias* and *Lost*)—is only his third feature film as director, his two previous efforts being 2005's *Mission: Impossible III* and 2009's critically-acclaimed *Star Trek* reboot.

Wearing his trademark horn-rimmed glasses and sporting a full head of wavy dark brown hair, Abrams was an immediately warm presence as he entered the hotel suite and shook each of our hands in turn (a rare move for industry vets at his level of influence) before seating himself in front of a row of red-and-blue microphones at the head of the table.

Born in 1966, which would have made him a teenager during Amblin's early-mid-eighties heyday, Abrams—an engaging, lightning-fast speaker whose words often run into each other in his eagerness to get them out—admitted that the idea of Amblin homage didn't occur to him until later in the development process when he came to the realization that the brass tacks of his story shared quite a bit in common with the company's earliest cinematic efforts.

"The thing about *Super 8* is it was inspired initially by just the desire to go back in time and tell a story about being a kid and making those . . . movies on Super 8 [cameras]," he said of the formative childhood activity he shares in common with Spielberg, who famously shot his first films on 8mm as a young teenager.

"And working on the story as it developed over time, it was clear that it . . . fell under the umbrella of those kinds of [Amblin] movies . . . they all sort of share DNA. They're all about suburban American, sort of, ordinary people going through something that was hyperreal, whether it was otherworldly or supernatural or whatever it was."

Of course, successfully paying homage to those early Amblin films is about more than just following a prescribed formula but rather capturing the genuine humanity that made them so successful in the first place, and that, even more importantly, makes them endure in the popular imagination to this day.

"In these films, there was a big heart," he said. "There was just something about those movies where I would feel that they weren't afraid to combine that kind of spectacle and drama with emotion. And that to me was something that was really important. The ambition, at least, was that you feel something."

Amblin's early output also consisted of films that, unlike the mostly unoriginal, prepackaged event movies of today, actually felt inspired by something other than market value. Their trailers also held back—a marked contrast to the show-'em-everything-in-two-minutes advertising sensibility that unfortunately pervades the majority of mainstream film campaigns today.

"I just feel like you . . . see a trailer, and the trailer's over, and you feel like, 'I've just seen the movie,'" said Abrams when one journo brought up the relatively mysterious nature of Paramount's *Super 8* ad campaign. "So part of [the campaign here] was just about trying to allow people to have a sense of discovery the way . . .

at least in '79 [when] I went to the movies, I didn't feel like I'd seen every single detail of the film."

One key gift that Spielberg, a filmmaker Abrams obviously aspires to emulate in some way, has always possessed as a director is the level of on-screen naturalism he's able to coax out of his child actors—a gift that somehow seemed, either directly or indirectly, to extend to other early films in the Amblin canon (likely a product of the hands-on approach Spielberg was known to take with films he served as producer on). Much of this began in the casting process, with Spielberg notably preferring to cast children that lacked the "actor-y" mannerisms of more polished kiddie thesps—a quality that Abrams felt was important for the core group of young actors in *Super 8* as well.

"The truth [is] we saw thousands of kids over months and months and months, and Joel [Courtney] was great and Riley [Griffiths] as well because they weren't like professional people who were young enough to be that age and then acted that age; they were just those kids," said Abrams of casting two of the film's young leads. "They'd never been on the set on anything.

"So Joel, like the first . . . the week before we were shooting there was a script, and there were these, you know, when you make revisions you have the little asterisks on the side of the script to show you where the changes were," he continued.

"And I remember he looked . . . [and] was like, 'Are these stars for decoration on the side of the script?' And I was like, 'Oh, my God, no, no, no, no. These are lines you have to go memorize!' He didn't know what a boom was; he was scared of the boom, like, 'What the—?' And you know, the dolly tracks . . . nothing made sense [to him] at the beginning."

As for the monster, which has been carefully (and thankfully) concealed in the film's trailer, it was important to Abrams that it not exist merely for the purposes of showcasing state-of-the-art special effects but that it also hold some metaphorical heft as well.

"The idea of the creature was cool for me but just because [of] the idea that it would be a way to externalize and make physical this thing that this kid was going through internally, the idea of the loss of his mother," he said of Joe Lamb, the main boy in the film who is played by newcomer Courtney. "This creature sort of represented the thing that was the most frightening to him, which is the idea of never getting past it . . . the loss of this person.

"Physically and technically how to [realize the creature] is one thing, but I'm more interested in the idea of why there's something there, you know?" he continued. "Like what does it represent, or what does it mean for a character? I remember seeing *The Hunchback of Notre Dame* when I was a kid, the Charles Laughton version, and just, like, sobbing at this movie and realizing, 'Oh, my

God, they used makeup effects, and I was [also] completely into the story and heartsick over it.'"

Abrams's dedication to building *Super 8*'s more fantastical elements around a core of genuine human feeling was also evident in the way he described putting together the first-act train wreck, which is witnessed by the film's adolescent characters.

"All that stuff with the train, I tried to not have three shots go by before you were with the kids again," he said, "because it was very easy to go God's-eye, crazy-big wide, crazy shots, but . . . it was more important to me to do shots that connected the people to the event as much as possible than it was just [constructing] shots that you'd never seen before . . .

"I wanted it to be what [the kids] would remember the train crash being as opposed to, technically, how did the train crash—you know what I mean?—so that if they would tell the story of what the train crash was, that's what it looked like, as opposed to it being exactly that."

Speaking as someone who feels alienated by the majority of studio blockbusters today—films with technical merits to burn but no real heart—it's nice to know there are still a few action directors out there who genuinely care about infusing their effects-heavy films with a poignant human element.

In that regard, *Super 8* is an alluring jewel in a summer that stretches on ahead of us like a desert wasteland of Michael Bay sequels and soulless comic-book adaptations. Indeed, if there's any director right now who seems intent on bringing quality popcorn cinema to the masses, it's J. J. Abrams.

Near the end of the discussion, Abrams offered up a small-scale observation that felt rather off-hand at first, until I began to realize that he was actually summing up his sensibilities as a filmmaker. It's a simple idea, but nevertheless one that holds incredible value and is a testament to what, in my opinion, separates a film like *Transformers* from one like *E.T.*: "There's a stupid thing that I do sometimes when I'm doodling, which I'm always doing, which [is] I draw, like, a circle, and then I . . . shade it and draw a little horizon line so it goes from just being this circle to being a . . . three-dimensional [object]," he began.

"But then . . . whenever I draw a little figure next to it of a certain size, maybe very small, suddenly that circle . . . becomes this thing of scale. It's weird how suddenly . . . there's an importance to it, only because of the person, the figure that's standing there. There's a weird thing that happens when you connect a person to an event . . . Suddenly, the event has [a] different meaning."

J. J. Abrams Talks *Super 8*, Bad Robot, Lens Flares, *Lost*, Spielberg, and the Mystery Box

Peter Sciretta / 2011

From */Film*, June 10, 2011. Reprinted by permission.

A couple weeks back I got a chance to get on the phone with director J. J. Abrams about his new film *Super 8*. The interview is spoiler free, so feel free to check it out even if you haven't seen the movie yet. We talk more about the film's character-based storyline than the science fiction action, delving into the influences from his own childhood and why Hollywood doesn't make movies about kids anymore. We talk briefly about Steven Spielberg's involvement as a producer and what that really meant to the film. I get geeky with Abrams, talking about the Easter eggs in the film and even ask him if we'll ever see a movie about the Bad Robot in his production logo. Lastly, I had to ask him about *Lost* and find out how much he knew about the smoke monster while he was directing the pilot episode. We also talk about his use of lens flares and the infamous mystery box.

Peter Sciretta: Hey, J. J.
J. J. Abrams: Hey, how's it going?

Peter: Good. Loved *Super 8*.
J. J.: Thanks, man.

Peter: Your film focuses on a son and a father trying to recover from the death of their mother/wife. Spielberg drew the story of *E.T.* from divorce. I was wondering where this story sort of came from. What elements did you draw from your own childhood?
J. J.: Though I haven't lost a parent, the emotional lives of kids are so fraught and deep and complicated. I just remember being a kid and seeing friends whose parents were getting divorced left and right. My parents are still married. I watched

friends who lost parents or who had a single parent. I just remember the complexity of being a kid and all the types of fears that you had about "What if?" You know, what could be sort of the terror of the adult world. And that was the thing that was, for me, kind of the most compelling, which was being a kid and feeling . . . in a way you could almost kind of quantify the encroaching adult world and the reality that you would, at some point or another, be hit by the adult-world stick. So I didn't go through a particular story in that regard as Spielberg did with a divorced family—but the idea of loss and being without a parent. And the thing that I did experience was I had a father who, in a sort of typical 1970s way, was a little bit less involved than I think dads are now. So the idea in my life was if the mother is suddenly gone and this boy didn't have the greatest relationship with his dad, what is that relationship once she's gone? Part of the story was that. Like, what do you do when the primary parent goes away, and how do you reconcile that? How does the father reconcile it?

Peter: Definitely. You don't see movies like this anymore. You don't see movies about kids where it's not condescending or a family movie. This is a movie about kids dealing with complex issues, and it doesn't have the Rock as the focal point. Why is it that Hollywood can't make more movies like this?

J. J.: I have no idea why anything does or doesn't get made. But I feel like there was a kind of movie that I watched when I was younger, which was a movie that had believable characters that made you laugh, that made you comfortable, that then went through something insane and extraordinary and often faced with this genre. By the end of the movie, you didn't just go through something that made you scared and laugh and amazed but also made you emotional and perhaps even made you cry. There was something about those movies that were simultaneously moving and also fantastical.

Those were the kinds of movies that I loved. I'm not saying that you can't ever try them at all. But there was a kind of movie that I loved when I was a kid where I would be laughing one minute, crying the next minute. I would be amazed the next and scared the next. By the time the movie was over I felt like I had been through this sort of rollercoaster of various emotions, and it was a wonderful, satisfying thing. The goal of *Super 8* was to try to make a movie that was not just a comedy, not just a horror movie, not just a science fiction film, not just a love story, not just an emotional family trauma or a weird sort of paranoid thriller, but all of them.

Peter: I think you accomplished that because most action movies these days you don't care much about the characters. This movie, I could have seen a whole movie in an alternative reality where the train never crashes and it's just a *Stand by Me*–style drama following the kids, and I would have still loved it.

J. J.: I love that you said that. Thank you so much for that.

Peter: You got Steven Spielberg to come on to produce. Other than his name, what did he bring to the film? Do you have any examples of ideas or suggestions that Steven brought to the story?

J. J.: I've got to say this. One of the great things about Steven was his support in realizing *Super 8* the way it was intended, meaning if I had stopped talking with Steven, I'm sure I would have been much more self-conscious and reluctant to jump in and make a film that felt like the movies I loved so much as a kid. In a way, having the movie literally be a Steven Spielberg–Amblin film, it sort of allowed the movie to just embrace the DNA that was very actual to me as a kid that age in that year. So it was kind of a blessing to just work with him on this particular film for that reason alone, but he was also wildly helpful in the development of the story. He was wildly helpful in his opinions towards casting. He was in the editing room with me for hours and hours and just wonderful in that regard. He was a true collaborator and partner in this. It was a privilege to work with him for so many reasons. One of the largest was it allowed this film to genuinely be an Amblin film. It allowed us to sort of embrace that more and not feel like it was, in any way, apologetic for sharing the spirit of those early films.

Peter: In the movie I saw Kelvin, I saw Slusho, but I didn't see any Rocket Pop-peteers. So I'm wondering, are they in the movie?

J. J.: Oh, yeah, they're there. Jeff is wearing a commander shirt. There's a poster in Charles's room. We have a couple little other things hidden in there in the movie, but I'm glad that you caught Slusho.

Peter: It was all over that gas station scene.

J. J.: Some people don't see it at all.

Peter: This might be a strange question, but are we ever going to see a movie about the Bad Robot from your production company logo?

J. J.: Actually, the bad robot character originated as a children's book idea. My feeling is that I would want to start with that, probably, before we did anything else. We have some animation tests. There's a little maquette they sell.

Peter: Yeah, I own one of those. It's awesome.

J. J.: Yeah, they did a great job with that, I thought.

Peter: So many people wonder this, so I hope you don't think this is a negative question or anything, but why so many lens flares? What's your obsession with lens flares?

J. J.: Well, say that there's a . . . there's no question that I overuse lens flares on occasion. I know that there's a sort of . . .

Peter: It's funny because some scenes have none, but then other scenes are filled with them.

J. J.: Yeah, it's a weird thing. To me, it's a little bit like on a scene-for-scene or shot-for-shot basis where I'm looking for something like there's an opportunity to not necessarily put a . . . up in front of a light. The kneejerk reaction from the director of photography is usually . . . it's usually, "OK, we've got to flatten that light because it's going to flare." I think it's one of those things that you want to make sure that, obviously, it's . . . To me, it's such a cool, beautiful image, the light through the glass. There are times that I feel like it adds another kind of smart element, and it's hard to define. But it is a visual taste that I do like. I think there are a couple shots in *Super 8* where I just think I should definitely pull back here or there, but I can't help myself sometimes.

Peter: I have to ask you about *Lost*. I'm wondering—I'm a huge fan of *Lost*. I loved the finale. I loved everything from the first season that you were heavily involved with to everything. When you were working on the first season, did you know what the smoke monster was going to be?

J. J.: We had a lot of discussions about what the thing could be, and we knew that we had a few interesting ideas. It was everything from a creature that had been factored into a security system to . . . we discussed a bunch of things. All of them kind of had full possibilities, but we also felt like this was a . . . We wrote the pilot, shot it, edited it, and distributed it in twelve weeks. The whole process was so fast. And as we were writing it we discussed things, when we were shooting it we discussed things, when we were cutting it we discussed things, but we didn't have a bible written of what the show would be, like any series. Anyone who tells you otherwise is not being honest. You cannot know every single answer. You have big ideas that give you a roadmap, and you can have a willingness to take that leap of faith. You are going to find it, but we did not have, in any way, every answer. At the time, we knew specific things that we felt it was where the show needed to go, but when you think about things— like, Ben is not a character in the pilot; we didn't know he was going to show up. You think of how critical he was and what the others said and what his relationship was to the whole cast. It just shows you how the show, any show, evolves over time. So what Damon and Carlton and the others came up with as they worked on the show was never anything that we could have known after we did the pilot. But you go into it knowing as much as you can and believing that you've got a sense of what there's going to be. What it ends up being is always different—sometimes very close, sometimes as far away as you can imagine from those real ideas. You go into it with at least a bag of best ideas you've got, but you are well aware that as you travel down that path, if you are lucky enough to stay on the air, that bag of best ideas is going to shift, sometimes entirely.

Peter: I guess that's the great thing about a mystery box. What's inside it, until it's revealed, could be anything.

J. J.: That's exactly right. Often, you don't open that box until you have to, and other times you don't open the box ever. But in the case of *Lost*, I think that they brilliantly kind of balanced the promise of what it could be with answers about what things were. The end series allowed the show to be an emotional experience and not a kind of techno-babble mechanical one.

Peter: One last quick question, J. J. If the end of the world was happening and you knew it and you were in your office, would you open the mystery box?

J. J.: [laughs] I'd have to say . . . I think I'd rather go into the Rapture with the mystery box being closed.

Peter: Okay. Thank you very much today. I'm really a huge fan of yours.

J. J.: Peter, I really appreciate it. I love /Film, too, so thank you!

J. J. Abrams: The "Super" Career of a Movie-Crazed Kid

Terry Gross / 2011

Transcript of *Fresh Air* radio show, June 13, 2011. Published by permission of WHYY, Inc. *Fresh Air* with Terry Gross is produced at WHYY in Philadelphia and distributed by NPR. Podcasts are available at www.npr.org/podcasts and at iTunes.

This is *Fresh Air*. I'm Terry Gross. It is good to be back after a case of laryngitis and a sore throat that lasted way too long. I want to thank Dave Davies for hosting during most of my absence and for being so good-natured about taking on *Fresh Air* in addition to his other work here at WHYY. And thanks to David Bianculli for hosting last Tuesday.

Now, on to today's show, my guest, J. J. Abrams, cocreated the TV series *Lost*, *Felicity*, and *Fringe* and created the series *Alias*. He directed the films *Mission: Impossible III* and *Star Trek*. He wrote and directed the new film *Super 8*. It connects to his own childhood when he made horror films using a Super 8 camera, relying on family and friends as his actors and creating his own special effects. *Super 8* is set in 1979 in a small town in Ohio, where six friends, who are about fourteen years old, are making a zombie movie. They're about to shoot a scene at a train station where the husband is ready to depart but his wife wants him to stay. As they prepare to shoot, they hear a real train in the distance. The film's director starts shouting for everyone to hurry and get ready so that they can shoot the scene with an actual train speeding by. But as you'll hear, something shocking happens.

GROSS: Well, that's the sounds of the train exploding. Why and how it explodes introduces the science fiction part of the story. It should come as no surprise that there is a sci-fi dimension. This is, after all, a J. J. Abrams production and Steven Spielberg is one of the producers. J. J. Abrams, it's really a pleasure to have you on the show. Thank you so much for coming.

ABRAMS: I'm so happy to be here. Thank you.

GROSS: So, the kids in your movie are making a zombie movie shot with a Super 8 camera. Before we go any further, please describe the Super 8 camera you had when you were a kid.

ABRAMS: It was the camera that they are using in the film. It was a Eumig camera that was a sound camera, and my grandfather bought it for me when I was around thirteen. I really wanted to make sure that the camera the kids were using in the movie was the same one.

GROSS: So, why did you want to make a movie about kids shooting a Super 8 film who happen to witness and catch on film something very bizarre?

ABRAMS: The very first impulse here was just to do a movie about being a kid making movies, which is what I used to do. And before that idea was even formed that much, I picked up the phone and called Steven Spielberg, who I had gotten to know over the years, and I asked him, "Would you be interested in being a producer with me in a movie called *Super 8* about kids making movies?" I knew he had made films when he was a kid as well, and he said, "Yes," luckily. It was the beginning of the sort of process of figuring out what this movie might be, but that was the impulse.

GROSS: And, of course, there had to be a supernatural or extraterrestrial dimension.

ABRAMS: Well, you know, it didn't have to be, but it was one of those things where it started out—I actually thought it was going to be much more of a straight drama comedy, you know, much more of a—kind of a *Stand by Me*-type movie. As we worked on the story, I felt that there was something missing. I needed something in the movie that was going to be a physical manifestation of what the main character was going through, internally, the sort of struggle, having lost his mother and being left with a father he never really connected with.

So there was a kind of need that I had. Separately, I had an idea about the US Air Force moving Area 51 contents from Nevada to another destination and the train crashes and something escapes, but I didn't have more than that. But there was a premise, so I thought that's kind of a fun monster movie. The idea of connecting these two movies—suddenly, they started to answer each other's questions, and that was how that began.

GROSS: When you were making Super 8 movies, what were the movies that you made? Were they zombie films like in your movie *Super 8*?

ABRAMS: They were the worst. They were just these ridiculous, horrible—I mean, they were no good. I would take anyone who was available: my sister, my mother, any friends, and I would kill them in crazy ways. We would do makeup effects. And I wrote fan letters. When I was a kid I used to write fan letters to makeup artists whose special effect makeup stuff blew my mind like Dick Smith, Rick Baker, and Tom Savini, these guys who are sort of known for just incredible, —of course, as a kid when you're eleven, twelve, thirteen, you can't do that, but I would try. So, I would take the Karo syrup and food coloring and stuff from the kitchen, and I would make blood. I would ask my mom if I could borrow her makeup, which didn't trouble her because she knew that I was going to just kill someone basically with it. So, it was all ridiculous.

GROSS: What was the strangest way you killed people in your movies?

ABRAMS: Well, I remember there was this fight scene that I did where there were these two guys fighting on—I filmed this at UCLA—the parking structure, and there were these two guys fighting. One guy gets flipped over the railing on the fifth floor, and he's holding on to the railing. And these guys are fighting. The guy didn't die—I don't actually remember how that incredibly exciting cliffhanger ends. I remember my father watching this. I was editing the movie, and he came into my room. I was watching the scene, and he literally got angry at me that I would risk someone's life for a scene in the movie. Now, it was the greatest victory because it was a dummy, and I had rigged it with, like, wires so the legs were kicking and all this. He left the room really pissed, and I was so happy that he believed it. It literally speaks to that desperate desire as a little fat magician kid wanting your family to believe that that little foam yellow rabbit just disappeared from your hand or whatever. You know, it's that same thing—all you want is for people to believe it.

GROSS: Did you tell him finally that it was a dummy and that you weren't really risking someone's life?

ABRAMS: I did but then I think he got mad because he felt like he was embarrassed. You know, it was all good. It was one of those things where when I did finally tell him, he was like, "Well, okay," but it was great because it actually showed that these three cuts, by having the two guys on the ground floor and flipping over the side but then looking up to the fifth floor looked like they had flipped. It was all that kind of stuff that is pretty fundamental moviemaking stuff. It was those kinds of things. I had friends come over, and we'd make sets in rooms. I'd take all the furniture out of my room, and I would put black crepe paper on the wall and all this crazy stuff. My parents would come home, and all the furniture would be in the hallway. They'd be like, "What the hell's going on here?" It was always some ridiculous thing that we were doing.

GROSS: And the black crepe paper was for?

ABRAMS: I was making a film, Terry, called *The Attic*. It was just so good. There was a scene in it where one of the kids says, "Oh, an attic. I didn't even know we had an attic." And, actually, Greg Grunberg, who's one of my best friends since kindergarten—I've known him forever, he's been in a lot of TV shows that I've done, and he was on *Heroes*. He was in that movie. So what I did is I took all the furniture out—this is such a good story, you're not going to believe it, and I'm, of course, being sarcastic—all the furniture out of the room, put black crepe paper on the wall, and then put, like, contact paper to look like wood, like wood paneling—classic seventies, beautiful contact paper—and made it look like there was an attic basically in the room. There were the beams—the cross beams—and it was just this set, which actually for one angle functioned fairly well. But these were all just experiments of things to try and create an illusion of something that I wanted to do.

GROSS: My guest is J. J. Abrams, the cocreator of *Lost*. His new movie is called *Super 8*. Now there is an element—I'm trying not to give away a lot of the more supernatural or stop me if I'm making you real uncomfortable with what I'm giving away here, but I won't say much. Most of your stories have an element of either the supernatural, the inconceivable, aliens, all of the above. Is that just because of the influence of TV, movies, books that you loved? Or did you ever have the kind of experience that seemed impossible and only had a supernatural explanation?
ABRAMS: It's a funny thing. I remember as a kid just being in absolute tears over the Charles Laughton *Hunchback of Notre Dame* I had seen on TV.

GROSS: That is one of my favorite films ever made.
ABRAMS: Me too. It is literally this defining movie for me, and it just killed me. The idea of this misunderstood huge-hearted-seeming monster to strangers—it was the idea of that love story that was so profound, and I was aware . . .

GROSS: Because there was a Gypsy dancer who has compassion for him when everyone else just sees him as a deformed monstrosity.
ABRAMS: Exactly. The idea of not just that kind of love, but the idea that it was a movie that used makeup effects. It was a movie that used—there were visual effects. It was an incredible thing when they shot it at Universal Studios. But the idea of that movie was so profound to me, and I loved that notion that you could combine something that was a monstrous . . . I think as a kid, whether you're watching *Batman* and people are dressing up in costumes or you're watching cartoons or you go to see movies, there's something about monsters that I think kids always are drawn to and curious about. I always loved that idea of combining that kind of emotion with something that was so kind of like horrific or scary or literally an effect, a makeup effect. So whether it was that or *Frankenstein*—I mean, *The Elephant Man* years later, which I just . . .

GROSS: Oh, what a great film.

ABRAMS: . . . feel the same way.

GROSS: Yes.

ABRAMS: Oh, my God, so the idea of using visual effects, whether they be makeup effects or now, CG effects, to convey an emotional story was something that was really important to me. And *Super 8*, like anything, it's imperfect and there are things that don't work here and there as well as I would have liked, but you always look back and think, "Oh, I wish this. I wish that." But the thing that was most important to me, at least going in, the ambition was to create something that had—yes, it had a creature—but more important to me was that it was something that had feeling and had heart.

GROSS: You mentioned the creature; the creature is seen as very monstrous. It is very destructive, but it's also misunderstood. Like, in *The Hunchback of Notre Dame*, once you know what the story is, you have empathy for it.

ABRAMS: Yes.

GROSS: So, can we talk little about—without giving away too much—

ABRAMS: Sure.

GROSS: What you were up against in designing a creature?

ABRAMS: You know, the struggle [is] you look at one of the recent *Star Wars* movies, and you realize that every single creature in the history of time has been done. Like, there's just . . .

GROSS: Right.

ABRAMS: You can't—it's all been done and all the paradigm. What color is the creature? How many legs does the creature have? How many eyes; where are the eyes? You know, is it a biped, a quadruped? There are these kinds of categories, and they've all been completely covered. So working on this creature it is important to me that it be not just a sort of raving beast—chest thumping, scary thing—that it needed also be sentient and dexterous and thoughtful and nuanced and, yet, also just out and terrifying. So, it was this thing of trying to figure out what is something that could be hard to define for most of the movie so that you don't ever feel like, "Oh, I get it. I got it." The designer of the creature, Neville Page, did an amazing job, and I think he gave us something that took a ton of iterations. He really nailed it, and I'm really proud of how ILM brought it to life.

GROSS: If you're just joining us, my guest is J. J. Abrams, the cocreator of *Lost*. He directed *Mission: Impossible III*. He directed *Star Trek*, and now he's got a new movie, which is called *Super 8*. It's about a group of boys around what, twelve, thirteen years old?

ABRAMS: Fourteen. Fourteen.

GROSS: Fourteen-year-olds were making a Super 8 movie and accidentally capture this train crash on it, and the train has been carrying really mysterious stuff that leads to all kinds of mysterious and monstrous complications. So, one of the things you're famous for is trying to keep the story's plot, the plot twist a secret, particularly on things like *Lost*, but in this movie too. I read so much about how you're trying to keep everything a secret. How obsessive are you about that really?

ABRAMS: About fifteen years ago or so, I wrote a script for a *Superman* film, and it was leaked out of the studio at Warner Bros. Someone reviewed the script online in great detail, and it became this big thing. Ultimately, the film didn't get made. I'm sure not just because of the review, but because of any number of things, but it was one of those things where to have a script that is nowhere near the latest draft, let alone the final draft, being reviewed online, it frankly made me a little bit paranoid. I realized all they had to do was not give the script out to everyone. All they had to do was to take a few steps, and something that was very important to the studio and to the filmmakers wouldn't have been released prematurely. Of course, you never want a script to be reviewed before the movie even gets made. The point is, I guess, is that there are certain things that I think are important to kind of keep quiet, and, yet, I think, frankly, this whole secrecy thing has kind of been blown up a little bit out of proportion.

On *Star Trek* we had a lot of rabid fans we just were trying to kind of protect the experience for them. But I don't know how many times I've gone to the theater, to the movies, and seen a trailer and felt like, "All right, well, now I certainly don't have to see the movie anymore because I just saw everything." The experience of going to a film and seeing the movie and not knowing every plot twist, to me, is something that has been ruined and spoiled for moviegoers. I certainly don't want to be coy and be some kind of jerk and be withholding; it's not a Machiavellian sort of thing. It's literally wanting people to have a good time and to have a little bit of a surprising time. So, whenever I'm trying to keep things quiet, it is 100 percent an effort to make the experience of actually seeing the movie or the TV show more enjoyable for the viewers.

GROSS: Now, we talked before about how when you were a kid, you made Super 8 films, and you used special effects, makeup, and killed your characters off in all kinds of creative ways. One of the kids in the film loves making things blow up, and he always has firecrackers on him and stuff.

ABRAMS: Mm-hmm.

GROSS: Are you into pyrotechnics? And what was it like to direct this multiexplosion scene?

ABRAMS: As a kid, I would make models, and I would film them as I blew them up. I mean, that was—I wouldn't say a hobby—but it was one of the things I would try to do. Of course, you didn't have the lenses to get the shot quite right, and you didn't have slow motion. So when you watched the movie, it was always over in, like, four milliseconds. You're like, "What?!" You spent hours doing this whole thing, and you get back and you're watching it. It's like it's always over instantly. You just think that was the biggest waste of an afternoon. So, these kids, directing these kids in that experience, all I cared about was obviously that they were safe. Secondly, I wanted them to be scared. They have to pace themselves because they had to be just terrified out of their minds for days.

GROSS: Did you want the actual kids to be scared or the kids to look scared?

ABRAMS: Yes, well, I wanted the kids to look scared. I mean, I never wanted them actually to be scared.

GROSS: Okay.

ABRAMS: The whole thing for me with these kids was always that they feel safe so that they could be free to do the things that they might just do in the privacy of their room, like act out and do certain things. I needed them to feel like anything was okay. I never wanted to play tricks on them. It was funny. I was freaking out, just as a side bar, the first couple days of shooting. Frankly, I didn't know if it was going to work. We had Joel, the main kid, and Riley, and they were nervous. I mean, I was probably more nervous than they, but they were really nervous. And I just really . . .

GROSS: Because of the explosives?

ABRAMS: No. No. This was like school's out, and it was just early days of shooting . . .

GROSS: I see. Okay.

ABRAMS: It was before we were at the train crash. Sorry. And I really thought, "Oh, my God, this is—I don't know if this is going to work." I was in a panic. I called my wife. I'm like, "I don't know if this is going to work." I emailed Steven, and I'm like this: "I don't know. I'm terrified, and we did thirty takes of something." He sends me back an email, "Thirty's a lot." I remember I was just freaking out. I called Rob Reiner, who had directed *Stand by Me*. I called him. I said, "Rob, I'm working with these kids. I'm trying to be calm, working with these kids; it's all fine, but I just want to know do you have any advice, whatever?" He's like, "Well, do [you] trust them? Do they have good instincts?" "I think they do, you know. But can you just give me some advice? Just something? Can you just tell me something?" He was like, "I was an actor. We had three months of acting school. I worked with them." He wasn't helpful at all.

What he didn't say to me, though, was when he was filming the scene, the train scene, they wouldn't get riled up in *Stand by Me*. They wouldn't get to that place. And, finally, he yelled at them, and he just said, "You know, this whole crew, everyone here, they're working for you, and you can't—! You know, you're not able to get—!" And he literally got them to a place where they were crying. He just said that maybe sometimes you got to pull that out of your pocket and use that. I never had to use it, but the filming of the train crash in *Super 8* was really the most fun I think these kids ever had. Every time we'd do a shot, they would—immediately after I said, "Cut"—say, "Please, one more time. One more time. One more . . . ," and they were just so into running with these huge explosions happening hundreds of yards away from them.

GROSS: J. J. Abrams will be back on the second half of the show. He wrote and directed the new movie *Super 8* and cocreated the TV series *Lost*. I'm Terry Gross. And this is *Fresh Air*.

This is *Fresh Air*. I'm Terry Gross back with J. J. Abrams. He cocreated the TV series *Lost*, *Fringe*, and *Felicity*, and created *Alias*. He directed the films *Mission: Impossible III* and *Star Trek*. Abrams wrote and directed the new film *Super 8*. Set in 1979, it's about a group of kids making a Super 8 zombie movie, who witness a mysterious train explosion that leads to inexplicable phenomena. Part of the film was inspired by Abrams's experiences as a kid making Super 8 horror films.

Let me warn you, if you're squeamish or listening with young children, that Abrams is about to get a vivid description of a surgical procedure.

Right at the beginning of the movie, one of the main characters, one of the kid's mothers dies in an accident at work. And so, one of his friends, I think it's a friend who's actually directing the Super 8 movie—

ABRAMS: Mm-hmm.

GROSS: Some of the kids are talking to each other, and they're saying, "Will he really want to make a zombie movie now that his mother has died? Will that be right?" And, yes, he still wants to make the movie. But the zombie movie is about the living dead, and he has a mother who is now really dead. That led me to wonder when you were young and you were into all the special effects and blood and gore and stuff, had you witnessed real blood? Had you experienced real death?

ABRAMS: You know, as a kid I think because I didn't really go through anything like this, it was safe to play in that. It was something that was kind of terrifying and provocative and interesting. Because it wasn't real, it was something that was safe. So, as a kid, the idea that these horror films were as I just remember, seeing the most ridiculous, horrific, gruesome—sometimes horribly executed, by the way—deaths in movies. At the time it was sort of a way to kind of play with that idea of death. I remember—I think I was twelve, maybe I was fourteen—I came home one day, and there was a box, a little teeny box. It said, "Dick Smith from Larchmont, New York" on the postmark. I opened up the box, and it was a tongue in the box.

GROSS: Ha!

ABRAMS: And, it was from *The Exorcist*, which he had done. He had this little handwritten note—I still have it—that said, "Put a little dab of peanut butter in the tongue, and it will stick and it'll stay there." It was what Linda Blair wore in one of the scenes where she had to stick her tongue out. It had to be like four or five inches longer. My mom came home, and she was like, "What's that?" I'm like, "Oh, it's just a tongue that Dick Smith [sent]." She's like, "What man sent you a tongue? What's going on?" It didn't seem like a good thing for her kid to be doing. So the answer to the question, "Did I experience death?" Did I see death? I did not in that way. But it was all around me in all the stuff that I was interested in. I think as you get older it's far less fun, that kind of stuff. I mean, I am no longer, in any way, a fan of those kinds of movies. Actually, I have not seen, for I don't even know how many years, movies that are of that genre—that kind of, like, that sort of torture porn, horrific, ultraviolent movie. I used to love those movies as a kid. Now, of course, having three kids, those films are repulsive to me; yet, I'm amazed and applaud the work of the artists who create the illusions of those movies.

GROSS: But let me ask you this: When you passed a car accident when you were young, would you look or not look?

ABRAMS: It's a funny thing. I've always been interested in that kind of stuff. But, I think when you're actually confronted with the real deal, it changes everything. I wrote this movie years ago. It was called *Regarding Henry*, and there was a character who gets shot in the head and survives. I was actually interested in seeing a brain surgery, and I called a cousin in our family who is a doctor. I asked him if he knew of any way I could get in to see an operation, a brain surgery. He said, "Well, let me see." Anyway, five years later, I swear to God, he calls me. He's like, "Still want to see a brain surgery?" I'm like, "What?" I was like, "Oh, yeah, yeah,

yeah. Sure." That next morning, 5 a.m., I go down to USC, and there was a woman who had a tumor on her pituitary gland and it was being removed. We are in this operating room and right there, watching this woman. The anesthesiologist comes over, and he puts the mask over her face. They're talking to her, and she's going under. Literally, the promise of what was to come turned my stomach. Even the promise of what was going to come next.

It was an interesting thing because this was the kind of thing that I had been obsessed with as a kid and would put derma wax on my sister's face and then cut it with a little wooden dowel and put blood inside. I would do these kinds of cuts all the time. I left the room for a minute. I was like, "Holy—, like, this is really—," you know, and I went back inside. I watched as they did this amazing thing—once she was under they opened her mouth, and they cut above her gum line and above her teeth, her upper teeth, and they did this insane thing, which was just directly out of any of those makeup magazines that I would have read as a kid. They pulled her mouth open past the nasal cavity, and they went into the nasal cavity to remove this tumor, which they did. They sewed her up and—but it was an amazing thing to watch. Again, obviously being privileged to be witness to a miracle like that to see what doctors can do is incredible. It was an amazing thing to see for real something that had been play for essentially my whole childhood.

GROSS: And does that have an effect on you in terms of showing gore?

ABRAMS: Doing a movie that was a truly gory movie hasn't really interested me. It's not that I'm opposed to it, and I'm a big fan of directors like David Cronenberg and some of the work that they've done in showing just crazy horrific things. I love, for example, John Carpenter's *The Thing*; the work that Rob Bottin did on the effects of that movie are just amazing. But the idea of doing a horror film or a slasher movie or something that's too overtly gory doesn't appeal to me. I remember when we were doing the pilot for *Lost*, there's this big plane crash, and I knew there was one moment I really wanted to have an impact, which was when they were pulling the guy out from this engine cowling and you see his leg and how bloody it is. So, what occurred to me was to have no red at all in the scene. I didn't want the plane to have any red in its logo. I didn't want to have any red on the wardrobe. There was a little bit of blood here and there, but I wanted to keep it really about dirt and sand and just the mess of this crash so that when they pull him out and you see blood, it really has an impact and it really stands out. It's interesting. I've seen the pilot, at least years ago, with full audiences at a couple of screenings and the reaction that they've had; it's like the communal immediate repulsive reaction to the blood. All it really was, was blood, fake blood poured on the guy. You weren't seeing bones stick [out]; it wasn't anything crazy, but it was such an interesting thing. I think it spoke of how we become desensitized to that stuff. So, a little bit to me is a far more effective tool, and it doesn't feel disgusting and gratuitous. I just have no interest in that stuff.

GROSS: Okay. While we're on the subject of the pilot of *Lost*, the first episode, so that scene you're describing, it's not—it doesn't look just like blood. It looks kind of like something you'd see in a butcher shop, you know. And . . .
ABRAMS: Yes. It's probably because it was on his clothes, too—on his pants.

GROSS: And then, like within just a few seconds, you see that leg, and then a woman is kind of crawling to the shore, shrieking because she's like nine months pregnant, and she's starting to have contractions. And one guy is sucked into one of the jet engines of the crashed plane, and he's kind of totally . . .
ABRAMS: Yes.

GROSS: . . . sucked into it, and that makes the whole engine explode.
ABRAMS: Yes.

GROSS: And this is all in a few seconds. It's . . .
ABRAMS: Right.

GROSS: It's so much. It almost verges on funny; it's so much.
ABRAMS: First of all, it's exactly right. And the idea of that guy getting sucked into the engine though it was never meant to be like a laugh, it was meant to be a kind of "Oh, my God, this is insane" kind of feeling.

GROSS: Right.
ABRAMS: Where it was almost like a circus of horrors. The idea of the subjective experience of that character, Matthew Fox was playing Jack, and his experience in that was really about just how this guy needs to be ten places at once. Then, of course, the engine gag was really about just how frightening this airplane—that it was the monster that had fallen but hadn't died yet and that there was still some danger left in it. It just was about what would you do if you were surrounded by that kind of madness, and that was the reason we went so far.

J. J. Abrams and his new film is called *Super 8*. He also cocreated *Lost*. He made the films, *Star Trek* and *Mission: Impossible III*. He created *Felicity*. So, let's take a short break here, then we'll talk some more. This is *Fresh Air*.

GROSS: My guest is writer, producer, and director J. J. Abrams. He cocreated *Lost*. His new movie is called *Super 8*. It's about a small group of kids—about fourteen years old who are making their own Super 8 movie. This is set in 1979. And while they're making a movie, they witness, and their camera records, a very mysterious train explosion, which kind of sets the plot in motion. Although the film *Super 8* is set in a small town in Ohio, you grew up in Manhattan?

ABRAMS: Yes. I was born in New York, but I was raised in LA.

GROSS: Okay. In fact, your father was a producer of several movies and TV shows.

ABRAMS: Yes. He still actually produces TV movies, and my mother actually produced a couple as well.

GROSS: So, you got to spend some time on the set at Paramount, was it?

ABRAMS: He had an office at Paramount, but there were any number of TV movies that were being filmed. And I would visit the set. I was very lucky to get to, as a kid, watch the process and see how movies got made, and it was enormously informative.

GROSS: So, what's one of the things you learned watching on the set of one of the films that your father got you into as a child?

ABRAMS: One of the biggest lessons actually came from a movie that he didn't have anything to do with. One night I was, I guess I was like fifteen years old, and my dad said, "I want to take you somewhere." We drove to Paramount Studios where he had an office, and we got to the small theater at Paramount. We get there, and there are probably twenty people there, twenty people in this theater. I would recognize one of the people there, John Carpenter, and he's a director who had done *Halloween* and *The Fog* and . . .

GROSS: *Escape from New York.*

ABRAMS: Well, this was the movie he was going to show.

GROSS: Oh.

ABRAMS: He announced that what we're about to see is an incredibly rough cut of *Escape from New York* with none of the visual effects at all, no special effects, with a lot of the sound missing. He's like, "I'm going to be reading a lot of the lines that aren't on the soundtrack." I was stunned. My mouth hit the floor. I couldn't believe that I was in this small theater with this director who my father knew I admired so much. So, I'm sitting there in this theater, and John Carpenter starts this film. There was a whole opening sequence where the main character, Snake Plissken, is robbing a bank and he ends up getting caught, and the movie plays. The whole thing, it was magical; it was amazing. The movie was over, and John Carpenter said, "Okay, I want to talk about the movie."

And what I learned was just by watching him be open to any criticism. It was just incredible watching him take notes that were sometimes easy and understandable, other times huge. He knew he had a movie that at the time was problematic in certain ways, and he was trying to fix it. I remember my dad raised his hand. I was like, "Oh, God. What? Just don't . . ." He said, "Yes." My dad said, "Cut the opening from the movie." I thought, "I'm leaving. I am out, so mad that I'm here. I am so humiliated." John Carpenter said, "What do you mean?" My dad said, "Snake Plissken is a more imposing character. He's more of a mythic character if you don't see him get caught, but when you meet him he's already held." I thought, "This is just the dumbest thing I've ever heard. God, I wish he hadn't said that." In the final movie John Carpenter cut it out and that whole sequence is not in the film. The other thing that was interesting is I remember I finally had the guts to raise my hand. He said, "Yes, you husky, husky kid in the back, . . ." and I said I couldn't tell that this one character that Adrienne Barbeau, who was his wife at the time, played—I couldn't tell that she had died in this crash on the bridge. He said, "Oh, interesting. That's interesting."

Anyway, years later, I see the movie—the movie had come out later that year and not only was that opening scene gone, but there was a shot of Adrienne Barbeau dead on the ground after she was killed. I said, "Oh, my God, that's cool they put that in." Years later, I was working for Steven Spielberg—doing a couple weeks' work on a script for this movie they were doing. Dean Cundey was the DP, and he was also the director of photography of *Escape from New York*. I went up to him, and I said, "Excuse me, Mr. Cundey, my name is J. J. Abrams." I said, "I'm a big fan. You know, it's funny 'cause I was at the screening of *Escape from New York* at Paramount years ago." I was describing it, he said, "Oh, no, no, no. I totally remember that night. I remember a kid in the back saying that." He said, "The next night, we went out onto John Carpenter's driveway and shot Adrienne Barbeau dead on the ground because we realized people needed to see that she had actually been killed. So that was hopefully not the last time I collaborated with John Carpenter, but certainly the first.

GROSS: One more thing: One of the things you're famous for is the mystery box. You gave a great TED lecture, and those TED lectures are of incredibly creative, genius people. So yours is like . . .

ABRAMS: And me.

GROSS: And, you, right. Yours is really funny and entertaining and very kind of informative about your process of thinking through movies. One of the centerpieces of it is you talking about this mystery box that you bought at this magic shop in Manhattan. It was, like, a $15 box in which you were supposed to get $50 worth of magic stuff. But you never—you've had the box for decades, and you've never, ever opened it because what you love is the mystery. You didn't want to open it and see what was really inside. So, I imagine it's still unopened.

ABRAMS: It's unopened. Yes.

GROSS: Yes. Now, for me things like that are always about disappointment because if you open them what they've given you is actually probably really disappointing. It just reminds me this is really different. But when you bought Cracker Jacks back in the old days and there'd be a surprise inside, the surprise would always be this cheap little piece of junkie thing.

ABRAMS: Paper. Nothing. Yes.

GROSS: It would be like nothing.

ABRAMS: Yes. Yes.

GROSS: A lot of those surprise mystery kind of things, if you do open it, it's just going to be a disappointment. So, are you protecting yourself from disappointment or just in love with the mystery that if it was solved might be disappointing?

ABRAMS: I think it's a great question. I think the answer is a sort of combination of things. Clearly, I know, having gone through my share of Cracker Jacks, and when I tell you—that I know that I open that magic mystery box, and there's no way it's going to be something that is satisfying. In fact, I will tell you that is the key to magic itself. The magic mystery box for me, of course, I know that whatever it is inside can't be the end all. But there's something about, first of all, the box remaining closed that— even just aesthetically, I love that box; there was a really cool question mark on it—but for me the thing is that box. With it closed, the potential for what is inside is endless, the possibility of what might be in that box. It's not a literal thing where I actually feel like, "Well, maybe it's this great—" It's not—it's all kind of this metaphor. For me the thing that I love, and I've talked about this as well—in a movie like *Jaws*, famously, the shark wasn't working so they couldn't show it very much. So, your imagination is going crazy, sort of imagining where it might be, what exactly does it look like. In a movie like *The Graduate*, Ben and Elaine had their first real date, and they're sitting at a restaurant eating in his convertible car. People are being very loud, and they put the top up. They're having this conversation. You can't hear it, but you're watching it. So, you get to sort of fill in the blanks, and I think there is almost a reflexive reaction that we have to fill the blanks in when there's something of some substance and pieces are missing. You sort of fill it in. I think there's something about the unseen and the unknown that has real value in moments, but I do think that you can't apply a magic- box approach to everything. If you go to see a movie or if you watch a show, you better have something of substance that you're building to. The whole thing in itself can't be a magic box. The magic box is a great device to enhance a moment to make something more frightening or romantic or mysterious. But, as an end, it must be serving something of value and of substance.

GROSS: Well, I want to thank you so much for talking with us, J. J. Abrams. Thank you. It's been really fun.

ABRAMS: It has been such a pleasure. It's been a blast. Thank you so much, Terry.

GROSS: J. J. Abrams wrote and directed the new film *Super 8*. He's the producer of two upcoming TV pilots: *Alcatraz* on Fox TV and *Person of Interest* on CBS.

J. J. Abrams

Charlie Rose / 2011

Transcript from *Charlie Rose*, June 15, 2011. Published by permission of Rosemary Guerin, coordinating producer, *Charlie Rose*.

Charlie Rose: J. J. Abrams is here. He has written and directed and produced some of the most successful television shows and films in recent memory.

Perhaps the best job of his life came when he was just a teenager at fifteen. He and a childhood friend were offered a job cutting together the great Steven Spielberg's 8mm home movies. Now, nearly thirty years later, Abrams and Spielberg are collaborating for real. Their new film *Super 8* is written and directed by Abrams with Steven Spielberg producing.

Super 8 opened in theaters on June 11. I'm pleased to have J. J. Abrams back at this table. Welcome.

J. J. Abrams: Great to be back, thank you.

Charlie Rose: Abrams and Spielberg.

J. J. Abrams: Crazy.

Charlie Rose: More than that. A dream?

J. J. Abrams: It is a dream. It's a privilege to work with someone who was a hero of mine as a kid, is still a hero of mine now, and to get to work with him and have it exceed expectations is unbelievable.

Charlie Rose: It exceeded expectations?

J. J. Abrams: It did because it was impossible. The idea of getting passed that notion of working with Steven Spielberg, I couldn't go into it being a sycophant. I had to go into it being a filmmaker.

Charlie Rose: And he would want no less.

J. J. Abrams: That's true. What was wonderful was just the energy working with him was all about making the movie better. He has so many ideas. He has no ego that the latest idea may not be the right idea, might not fit. He knows he's got another one right behind it.

Charlie Rose: But you two had developing ideas that had some overlap.

J. J. Abrams: I had a notion about a movie called *Super 8* about a group of kids making movies on Super 8 film the way I did when I was a kid, the way I knew he did when he was a kid. I called him instantly, and I said, "Would you be interested in doing a movie called *Super 8*?" And he said, "Yes," before there was any sense of story. That was the beginnings of it. He said he had always wanted to put the idea of kids making movies into a film, but he hadn't figured out the way to do it. So that's the beginning of the story.

Charlie Rose: He said, "I'll produce, and you direct"? First you need a script.

J. J. Abrams: I said, "Would you want to produce this with me?" I started meeting with writers to see if there was somebody who wanted to take this on, and, frankly, the more I did it the more I started to feel like that's not what the movie wants to be and combined the idea with another thing I thought of which is something escaping from a crashed Air Force train. It was more of a monster movie, and I thought that idea allows me to make physical the internal struggle that this kid, the main character, is having.

Charlie Rose: Joel.

J. J. Abrams: Joel, yes. All of a sudden, it started to make sense to me, and I called Steven and I said, "Listen, I think I want to take a crack at writing this. I think I know what this movie could be."

Charlie Rose: He said, "You made my day."

J. J. Abrams: Luckily, he said, "OK."

Charlie Rose: First of all, you have the idea for *Super 8*, and you have something for the kids to be making, right? So, therefore, you've got to create in your script what happens to them.

J. J. Abrams: The movie they're making or the thing that happens to them in the story.

Charlie Rose: The idea is to have kids making a movie, right, in *Super 8*?

J. J. Abrams: Yes.

Charlie Rose: Then you have something for them [to] want to do.

J. J. Abrams: Part of the idea was that they're making a zombie movie, and they witness this train crash and something escapes from the train. But the story—

Charlie Rose: That's something Steven can identify with.

J. J. Abrams: He loves that stuff. It was great fun working on that aspect. The thing that mattered to me more than that was the heart of the movie, the main kid, because this is a kid who's recently lost his mother. He's left with a father with whom he never really had much of a relationship. This is a kid who has no hope, no joy. The world is dark. The idea is that in the course of the movie he has to find his voice and fight for what he believes in and deal with his dad and save the girl. It was a story of this kid going from boy to man. That's why I set it in '79, the end of an era; it's all about that last moment of true childhood and encroaching adulthood. So, there were a lot of issues I cared about far more than the spectacle, but the spectacle was fun.

Charlie Rose: How much of this, as Steven has said, is your first real movie?

J. J. Abrams: This was, from the very beginning, a very much autobiographical idea, which is those kids making movies. That's exactly what I used to do when I was a kid. Clearly, what happens in the story is fantastical and nuts, but the origin was incredibly relatable to me, to a point that it was almost surreal when we were shooting. Being on the set and seeing the details the set dressers would leave, like the *TV Guides*, and I remember reading that very issue cover to cover thirty years ago. It was really bizarre seeing those models and posters and games and books and things. That was sort of the way in. What ends up happening was something that never happened to me as a kid because it's crazy.

Charlie Rose: We can't give it away. In fact, you're so obsessive about secrecy of plot.

J. J. Abrams: Charlie, what is this?

Charlie Rose: Am I right or wrong?

J. J. Abrams: Here's the thing. Two things. One is, years ago, I wrote a script, and it was reviewed online. The whole script was just torn apart and attacked. The movie never got made, and it made me a little paranoid, I have to admit. So, I just thought we should be more careful, but the truth is I go to the movies, I'll see a trailer and the trailer will end, and I feel like—

Charlie Rose: I've seen the movie.

J. J. Abrams: Why do I have to go see the movie? It's done. What's amazing is this: everyone feels so entitled with instant information whenever you want it in your hand that the idea of something you aren't being told you feel a sense of entitlement, like, I want to know why that is. When they're not told they analyze why they're not being told. My feeling is, it's just a movie; that's all it is. It's entertainment. Go to the theater; be surprised; have fun. If you don't want to go, don't go.

Charlie Rose: So, do you recommend people not read reviews before they go to see a film? I have friends that don't read reviews of books or reviews of films. I read everything.

J. J. Abrams: You do?

Charlie Rose: Yes.

J. J. Abrams: But there are also people who read the last chapter of a book before—there are all types. My feeling is—here's the thing, I like to go in knowing as little as possible. My wife and I just saw the Woody Allen movie. I knew nothing. I didn't want to know anything about it—

Charlie Rose: Midnight in Paris.

J. J. Abrams: *Midnight in Paris* and it was fun. I enjoyed not knowing anything about it. But then there are movies where I will read reviews because I'm curious, I'm on the fence, and I want to know what they think. So I think it depends.

Charlie Rose: Do you also go back if you like a movie; do you like to go back with your analytical brain?

J. J. Abrams: To watch the film again?

Charlie Rose: Sure.

J. J. Abrams: I'm sure everyone has this. If it's what you do, to go to see a movie, and you're a filmmaker you can't help but be aware of process, but at the same time the greatest movies you just get lost in, which to me is why the idea of 3-D, though it can be very cool, is beside the point. The great movies suck you in far more than 3-D does.

Charlie Rose: It's the story.

J. J. Abrams: Yes, it's the story.

Charlie Rose: Do you care about the medium? What's the common denominator of everything you do, storytelling?

J. J. Abrams: I can tell you what it should be, and I wish it were always. It's one of those things that I'm determined to do always, is it's got to be something that I desperately love and that I would truly want to see myself because there are times when you work on something and you think the audience will love this, and you are doomed. It's like if you think you know—it's never going to work. And if it does, which it could I guess, it's a hollow victory because it wasn't really what you loved. It was a guess and a lucky shot in the dark.

Charlie Rose: Okay, *Lost* is what you wanted to do?

J. J. Abrams: *Lost*, at the very beginning was. To be fair, when you mention *Lost*, as you did earlier, that show was run for six years by Damon Lindelof and Carlton Cuse while I was off doing *Mission: Impossible* and I was off doing *Star Trek*. So, just to be fair, that show—the beginning, I wrote it with Damon; I directed it. But that show went on for a hundred-plus episodes more, and that was really Damon and Carlton.

Charlie Rose: Give credit where credit's due. *Mission: Impossible*, would you like to direct another one?

J. J. Abrams: It was fun. I feel like I don't direct movie after movie after movie. So, I'd probably want to try something else.

Charlie Rose: When I saw that and realized you had done it—and got great reviews, as I remember—my sense was that you just wanted to show you could do it.

J. J. Abrams: The fact you're considering me at all in any moment—you've made my day. You have no idea. But the thing is this: I'd never directed a movie before. Out of nowhere and I'm saying this—it blindsided me. I got a phone call that Tom Cruise wanted me to direct this movie, *Mission: Impossible III*, which was insane to me. I thought maybe he'd want to talk about helping on the script but the idea that he was asking me to direct the movie was absolutely preposterous. So, of course, I did it because it was a chance not just to play in a genre and—*Mission: Impossible* the TV series, in many ways, inspired the show, *Alias*, that I had done—so, in a way, it was kind of coming back to the thing that really inspired that series. It was just an incredible chance that Tom gave me that no one else would have.

Charlie Rose: And you never for a moment thought of not trying to do it?

J. J. Abrams: No, as soon as I knew it was an opportunity, I thought, "Oh, my God." I just knew it was the right thing, which is, by the way, how I felt about *Star Trek* although I was never a *Star Trek* fan. I just knew this was an opportunity that was right for me, for some reason.

Charlie Rose: Will you do another *Star Trek*?

J. J. Abrams: We're working on the story right now, so, hopefully—

Charlie Rose: *Mission: Impossible* breeds *Mission: Impossible*. *Star Trek* breeds *Star Trek*. What does this breed? Is this a series, a television series?

J. J. Abrams: Super 16? No, it will end after *Super 8*. It's a one-off.

Charlie Rose: Because knowing your sense of not everything wanting to be known and wanting people to come in with fresh eyes and enjoy the experience being in the theater, seeing this. You want me to show some clips or—

J. J. Abrams: Whatever you want to do. I'm having so much fun talking to you. If showing clips means I get to talk to you less, then, no, let's not show it. Whatever you want to do; show the clips.

Charlie Rose: No. Let's just see this. This is just an example of what this man does so well. First clip.

You watched that intently.

J. J. Abrams: Well, it was just fun watching the kids.

Charlie Rose: You said when we started—

J. J. Abrams: The kids were great. A couple of those kids had never been on the set of anything before, and, suddenly, they are in starring roles in a movie. It was just amazing watching them handle it. I remember this scene was shot over a number of days, and it was an incredible thing to watch these kids who, a few weeks earlier had never been on a set, suddenly understand blocking and being sweet to each other and the crew. It was like making movies when I was a kid again.

Charlie Rose: How do you explain it, just that?

J. J. Abrams: The kids in the movie were real kids; they weren't those Hollywood kids acting their age. They were actually their age.

Charlie Rose: And how did you find them?

J. J. Abrams: We had great casting directors, April Webster and Alyssa Weisberg. They had to look through thousands of kids. Then, what was great was while we were shooting the movie, we had this great guy, Jay Scully, who is an acting teacher; he would run lines with them so that by the time they came to set, they were ready to go, like they never came to set having forgotten their lines. They were ready to go so that was a really wonderful thing.

Charlie Rose: Do you want to act at all?

J. J. Abrams: I wouldn't do that to people. No, I did a little bit just to figure it out, but I feel like, you know, I honestly—

Charlie Rose: You can't imagine yourself putting yourself in one of your movies?

J. J. Abrams: No, I would never do that. If a friend of mine said—

Charlie Rose: If Spielberg said—

J. J. Abrams: If he said, "J. J., please, star in *Lincoln*."

Charlie Rose: Is that what he's making next, *Lincoln*?

J. J. Abrams: The man is unstoppable, and Daniel Day Lewis is—

Charlie Rose: That will be unbelievable.

J. J. Abrams: It's over right now.

Charlie Rose: Anyone else who is competing that year—

J. J. Abrams: Forget it. You should just not make a movie that year.

Charlie Rose: Daniel Day Lewis is perfect.

J. J. Abrams: Delay your movie for one year.

Charlie Rose: Can we see one more scene? I want to see Joel, played by Joel Courtney. Role tape.

It almost makes you feel like you're their age.

J. J. Abrams: That's great. That's fantastic. Well, that was them. They're amazing.

Charlie Rose: Back to Spielberg.

J. J. Abrams: Yes.

Charlie Rose: What did you learn from this experience with him?

J. J. Abrams: Oh, my God, first of all, it really was an education working with him. Part of it was learning to trust my instincts. There's a moment we were outlining the script after a number of, I don't know how many, meetings, and finally he just said, "J. J., go write the script," because I'd been trying to figure it out so much. And at a certain point it was—stop thinking—

Charlie Rose: Go write.

J. J. Abrams: Just go do the thing. Stop talking about it. I was like, "Okay."

Charlie Rose: That's a good principle for life.

J. J. Abrams: It is, exactly, but it was every step of the production—here's the thing about the magic about Steven, and it's true in his movies and it's true with him, he sees the best version of things.

Charlie Rose: So, in his mind he knows how good it can be.

J. J. Abrams: Exactly. When I showed him the first cut, he got emotional in the scenes that eventually people get emotional watching. He laughed in scenes that eventually when people started laughing—when the edit was approved and we got the rhythm. My point is he saw what the movie was going to be, and he saw it in the very beginning before I did. But he saw it when I first showed him the rough cut. It was the thing where he just knew. He's just so—he's just incredibly wise about so many things, but about story and film that he was able to make me relax and just keep going because I knew he believed in it. He knew that it was going okay, and it was that belief that gave me comfort.

Charlie Rose: The idea to be able to visualize what is really good and to know that in your brain so you know if you're not there and how much better it can be is a huge gift.

J. J. Abrams: It is a gift and, by the way, it's his heart. That's the amazing thing about Steven. If you watch his movies, it's the same thing, that even the darkest of his stories that he's told there was always a sense of being in the hands of someone who is humane and who was going to take care of you. There was a safety in it that never felt sadistic or that there was some kind of overpowering darkness. It was an optimism in everything that he's done. I feel like in working with him it is—after working for someone as long as we have on this, you really get to know who that person is. He's just been remarkable.

Charlie Rose: And might you work together again?

J. J. Abrams: I would hope so. I would love it.

Charlie Rose: Is it in part homage to him because you both have this 8mm experience and thought it would be nice to have a film based on kids like we were making a movie.

J. J. Abrams: *Super 8* was, without question, inspired by the movies of that time and a lot of those movies that had an influence on me were Amblin Films; that's his production company. This movie is literally an Amblin production. The fact that Steven put his stamp on it and allowed us to collaborate freed me completely to embrace that DNA of what Amblin movies are. Often those films involve young characters or empowerment of kids and families that are broken, for some reason, that need to be fixed, and some other spectacular, other-worldly supernatural element, and heart. By the end of those movies, even if they didn't always do it, their ambition was to make you feel so that you'd leave the movie having laughed more that you thought you would, gasped more, shrieked more, and cried. That, to me, if you can go through a movie and have all the feelings—it's the perfect date movie and the perfect movie if you're a kid, if you're an adult. Those are the movies Steven, in large part, was responsible for.

Charlie Rose: How much of your filmmaking essence is something that is essentially you?

J. J. Abrams: When I was eight years old, I knew I wanted to make movies. It was crystal clear to me, to a point where, even in elementary school when I would talk to friends and they wouldn't know what they wanted to do, I would think, "Really?" It was so clear to me—I didn't know if I would ever be allowed to make movies [or] be able to make a living doing it, I just knew it was what I wanted. We are all, obviously, a result of our experiences and who we were at birth and this weird combo of things, but it was clear to me at a very, very young age what my goal was. As soon as I went to Universal Studios with my grandfather and saw how movies got made and—I loved magic when I was a kid and it was my obsession, as much as secrecy. I just knew that movies were it because movies are magic tricks. Movies are all about the illusion that anything is happening and that you can practically apply magic to a form of entertainment. It was an exciting idea.

Charlie Rose: You know how lucky we all are to do what we most want to do and probably what we should do.

J. J. Abrams: It is the luckiest thing in the world. It's an amazing thing to me that I was able to—

Charlie Rose: David Brooks wrote a recent column in the *New York Times*, which I found appealing, which he basically said everybody looks to find themselves, to find their identity. He said the best thing that can happen to you when you're young is to lose your identity in something that's larger than you are—for you, for example, losing your identity and wanting to make films, that kind of thing and the doing of the thing. In this film, *Super 8*, the love story is central, the most important element. It is the fantasy of making a movie and the love story.

J. J. Abrams: It is. Yes. The love story's always the most important thing to me in the movie. And it can be between friends; it can be a familial thing.

Charlie Rose: A buddy movie, if necessary.

J. J. Abrams: It could be anything, of course. In this movie, what's fun about it is there's a scene where the kid who makes the movies is talking to the main character about how, in this zombie movie they're making, this kid desperately needs the main character in this movie to have a love interest; otherwise, you won't care about the main character. Now, as he's talking to the main character of our movie, all he's talking about is, "I can't believe you talked to Alice Dainard. I can't believe you talked to that girl," meaning that in the scene we're discussing how stories work and how love stories are important. All we're doing is talking about the love story of *Super 8*. That is to say that I think it would be hard for me to make a movie that I really cared about where there wasn't a romantic, rooting interest or where there wasn't—that to me has always been the most important.

Charlie Rose: Rooting for love. You are a romantic, aren't you?

J. J. Abrams: I guess I am. I think so. I feel this kid in the beginning, when you meet him, he's alone; he's lost his mother; he's devastated. The story—I always feel like a movie is the dream that the main character goes through to become enlightened in some way and more fully realized. So, the dream that this kid is having during the film is one where he goes from follower to leader, he's got to find his own voice, and he discovers that the world can be happy again. There can be love; there can be joy. He has to confront the father with whom he never really had a connection. The friends that he used to follow around are now suddenly following him. You've got to confront the thing that scares you the most. He does that. In this case, it's this creature that represents this pain.

Charlie Rose: As you laid that out, did you say to yourself these are the elements I need in my movie?

J. J. Abrams: No. It was in retrospect. I realized that this is what I was doing. There were certain things I knew. For example, I knew the creature represented the mourning, the loss of his mom. This creature wasn't just a monster, but it was about this thing that he needed to, inevitably, confront in order to get passed it, move on, and live. In fact, when he does, he says words to this thing that, literally, he needs to hear. It's what lets him survive and go the distance.

Charlie Rose: In your films, what role do heroes play? He becomes a hero.

J. J. Abrams: He does. But the funny thing about heroes is they're usually the most beaten up character; they're usually characters that are just getting their asses kicked again and again and again, but they don't stop.

Charlie Rose: Because of the dream.

J. J. Abrams: Because of the dream. Because of what they need to go through to come out the other side. A lot of times, heroes—people think the hero is always the guy beating up—no, he's the guy who's getting beaten up. He's the guy who keeps coming back again and again. The character who gets beaten up is the character you are interested in.

Charlie Rose: Why is that?
J. J. Abrams: Everyone relates to the—

Charlie Rose: Underdog?
J. J. Abrams: Yes. The guy who walks in, and everyone's like immediately in that scenario—

Charlie Rose: They say in America—this is said by people who look at these kinds of things we love—in America you can always have a second chance. We love the idea of a comeback. We do. Maybe it's true in other cultures, too. Maybe it's true in Europe and Asia.
J. J. Abrams: It's very much what you just said—hits the nail on the head. This movie is about a second chance. This movie is about having gone through this tragedy and realizing you can live another day and actually be stronger than you were before.

Charlie Rose: A montage of Spielberg before we go. Roll tape. Here it is.
     What did we just see?
J. J. Abrams: Come on. Magic.

Charlie Rose: Magic.
J. J. Abrams: Unbelievable.

Charlie Rose: Genius and magic. You wanted to tell a story real quick.
J. J. Abrams: The *Jaws* thing, real quick. Steven has the scripts in his office at home that are the original scripts from the shoot of his movies. One day, we were working, and I saw that he had these scripts. I said, "Can I look at one?" He said, "Sure," so I pulled down the *Jaws* script. It was the original script from the set.

Charlie Rose: Written by Peter Benchley?
J. J. Abrams: Peter Benchley wrote the book. The screenplay was written by a number of people. John Milius wrote some scenes. Steven wrote stuff. Robert Shaw did work too. But anyway, there were all these multicolored pens and liquid paper and some of the storyboards. It was the original script—just that alone was cool. I open to the middle of the script just to a random page, and what I saw was that scene you just showed. What was amazing was there were three speeches in

the middle, short speeches, that had all been crossed out with a red pen. In its place was written "Brody—we need to get a bigger boat." And what it said to me was—Steven told me the story about how he just came up with that and the lines that were crossed out were not memorable lines. "We have to get help." "What are we going to do?"

Charlie Rose: Brody. Bigger boat.
J. J. Abrams: Maybe the classic line of that film was just a kind of capricious moment that Steven wrote the line, and it's film history. It's just another great reminder you don't know where the lasting moment's going to come from. You have to follow your bliss.

Charlie Rose: It's the doing of the thing, too.
J. J. Abrams: It is.

Charlie Rose: Congratulations, one more time.
J. J. Abrams: Thank you very much.

Charlie Rose: *Super 8* opened in theaters on June 11. It's doing quite well. If you want to celebrate what movies are about, here's a good chance to do it.

J. J. Abrams Interview

Abbie Bernstein / 2011

From BuzzyMag.com, December 27, 2011. Reprinted by permission.

The fight for the title of busiest man in show business is always in motion, but there's a good case to be made that it should at present go to writer-director-producer J. J. Abrams. Abrams, cocreator of the epic series *Lost* and creator of *Alias* and *Felicity* on TV and producer-director-cowriter of the 2009 film that rebooted the cinematic *Star Trek* franchise, has not exactly sat idle this year.

On the big screen, Abrams produced (with Steven Spielberg), wrote, and directed *Super 8*, a film about kids making a zombie movie in 1979 while a large extraterrestrial is decimating their town. He's also the executive producer on *Mission: Impossible—Ghost Protocol*. On television, *Fringe*, which Abrams created with frequent collaborators Roberto Orci and Alex Kurtzman, is enjoying its fourth season on Fox. Abrams's new thriller series *Person of Interest*, created by Jonathan Nolan, is a hit for its network CBS, and he's also producing *Alcatraz*, which debuts on Fox early in 2012.

Abrams arrives at a party thrown by CBS, Showtime, and the CW for their actors, creative personnel, and the press. All he has to do is stand in one place and people encircle him, eager to hear what he has to say. The peripatetic film- and television-maker explains why he was absent during the press conferences held earlier in the day. "I had to go to Houston today to pick up my son from camp. So I'm back."

In addition to being an actual father, how hard is it to parent three television shows simultaneously, with one on CBS and the other two on Fox? "It might be harder if they were on three separate networks," Abrams replies. He makes a comparison. "You know, you have friends who have kids who go to three different schools, with all the different parent meetings? I can imagine, if [one of the shows] were on another network, it might be a harder thing. Because Fox is so great and we love working with them, it kind of makes it easy doing two shows with them.

CBS has been extraordinary. I couldn't imagine it being better right now, so it's been kind of wildly lucky-good."

How did *Person of Interest* come about? "Jonah [Jonathan Nolan's nickname] pitched an amazing story, and I just found myself like a kid at a campfire, wanting to hear more," Abrams explains. "We were actually talking about a movie at the time. Then he pitched this idea for a TV show, and I screamed and grabbed the people who are repping me on TV to hear this idea. Then he wrote a great script."

Asked how much of his fingerprint is on the day-to-day production of *Person of Interest*, Abrams quips, "I was wearing gloves. At the beginning, it's a lot more about making specific notes and [setting the] tone, and then when things come in and they're not quite working right, you jump in and try to help. The kind of crazy luck at the moment we have on that show is Jonah and Greg Plageman are literally writing episodes that are better than the pilot, and it's that thing that you cannot believe, that it's working so well. So all I can tell you is, when a fire needs to be put out, when there are issues about a story or a character, obviously, I'll be more involved. But when things are working and the scripts are as entertaining, it feels more like, 'Get out of the way; they're doing good work.' So my day-to-day— I read every script; I give notes to the scripts, watch dailies, watch the cuts, give notes on the cuts. It's more about responding to what they're doing. When you have someone like Jonah Nolan, Greg Plageman, David Semel [who directed the pilot], a director like Richard Lewis, on *Alcatraz*, Liz Sarnoff and Jennifer Johnson, we've got Jack Bender to be a directing producer on that show, who did the greatest work ever on *Lost*, directed the best episodes of that show—again, we just work with very good people. If you cast things really well, either as a director or as a producer, and you crew it really well, half your job is really just finding those people who want to and can do such great work. Then the big thing is to just get out of their way as much as you can. This was a show that, basically, Jonah came in and said, 'Here's an idea for a show.' Then he wrote the script that was better than the pitch, and it was done. It was just done in a way that I knew that I would want to watch it, so that is me being like, 'Just do your thing.'"

Despite loving the networks, Abrams adds that he'd love to do something for cable in the future as well. "I have a vague idea for something, but I don't think it would work on a network. You know, some of the shows that I've done that ended up on networks, I've been proven right," he laughs, "so I'd love to try it."

Among network shows—not just Abrams's—*Person of Interest* has a unique viewpoint, which is that all the technology used to intrude on our privacy can conceivably be used for good rather than evil. Is that how Abrams feels about it? "This is a weird thing," he responds, "because my gut says, 'Probably not,' and, yet, I'd like to think that I'm more of an optimist, that people are generally good and not bad.

"The thing that Jonah did is to pitch this great idea of kind of a super-heroic duo"—*Person of Interest*'s leads are Jim Caviezel as Reese and Michael Emerson as Finch—"these two guys who work really well together to do good but have a lot of suspicions about each other, and each [character] has kind of a great mystery. Whenever you're walking around town, certainly driving, and just start counting cameras, it's insane. It's crazy. It's like when you see people who are the centers of documentaries, you think, 'Why are they doing that in front of the camera?' You realize, they forget there's a camera. To the subjects of documentaries, cameras just disappear for them because they become so accustomed to it, and they become immune to the idea of being on camera. We're all the subject right now of a documentary, all of us. [The cameras are] there for a reason. It's not just traffic cameras. It's everywhere, including our phones. So the idea that Jonah pitched was answering that question—who's behind those cameras? I think that's what happens with all of us because you think, 'No one's watching that camera.' They're not there not to be watched. So the question is, who's behind those cameras? Jonah pitched a story that answered that question in a way that was actually heartening—definitely wish fulfillment, but heartening. So I don't know what the answer is ultimately, but I love the idea that Finch and Reese are behind those cameras and that they're the ones who are able to hack into a cell phone [instead of] people who are going to manipulate and destroy."

Person of Interest star Emerson won a Supporting Actor Emmy for his previous collaboration with producer Abrams, back when Emerson was playing the chameleon-like Benjamin Linus on *Lost*. Terry O'Quinn also earned a Supporting Actor Emmy for his work as John Locke on the same series. Abrams has a sense of pride about both. "To see those guys—I had worked with Terry on *Alias* and loved him for years. He had a rather small role in that show, and I always felt like, 'God, [he's good.]' He was one of the first people we cast in *Lost*. To see him become John Locke, to see him embody that character and then be rewarded for it—I could not have been happier. He's a wonderful guy. We were actually in talks to do something with Emerson and Terry O'Quinn—another show—and when that didn't pan out Michael Emerson was a free agent. I know he was being approached by everyone, but we had this, I thought, amazing script [for *Person of Interest*]. I called and said, 'Listen, would you mind reading this thing?' and he read it and called us and said, 'I'm in.'"

The series is developing in a way that Abrams is very enthusiastic about. "When you see these episodes that are coming up—because it's that weird thing, again—when you look at the trajectory of a show, the pilot is that first point. That next episode is kind of huge because that next episode [on most series] is lower, even in terms of quality, but when I saw [the second episode of *Person of Interst*], it was like, 'What the . . . !' It was better than the pilot. We're seeing where it goes, and it feels like it's really got that conflict. There's a mystery of the week thing, which is also this great thing of, who are these guys that are working so well together? And they're not quite trusting each other completely. It's really fun."

Abrams also completed his very personal project *Super 8* this year. "Doing *Super 8* was a thrill," he reports. "Working with those kids was a blast. They're so wonderful. It was reinvigorating. It wasn't like a conscious thing; it wasn't like I thought, 'I want to do something that's going to be a kind of change of pace or a sorbet between courses,' or anything. It was just kind of like, 'I want to do that movie,' and Paramount was gracious enough to let me do it. So I do feel like, if *Trek* happens as we hope it will, it will be a fun return to that group of people, because it's an amazing group."

Since Abrams has brought it up, how is he feeling about the next *Star Trek* film? "I'm excited." Does he think that the *Star Trek* franchise, which has gone from the small screen to the big screen, back to television, and now back to feature films, may one day wind up returning to its broadcast-series roots? And, if it does, might Abrams be involved? "I don't know. It's never really come up. Depending on what that would be and how it would be done, I'd be open to the idea of it, but right now, we're just sort of focusing on making a movie that's worth people's time."

With its cast of young budding filmmaker characters set in the late seventies, does Abrams think that *Super 8* might work as a television series? "I think that there are things about the kids in that world," he says. "There are elements that I think would work. It would obviously have to be [different]—it wouldn't be literally that movie. It would have to be something else. There's definitely something about those kids that occurred to me."

On the other hand, Abrams isn't anxious to adapt any of the TV series he's created as feature films. "I think that people can probably come up with better ideas for movies than rehashing my old TV shows," he laughs.

As for Abrams's new series *Alcatraz*, which premieres on Fox in January, he explains how it developed. "There was a script that was written. We needed to do some work on it. Liz Sarnoff came in and wrote what I think was an amazing script, but the idea was just the simplest thing, really, which was, what if when Alcatraz closed, it wasn't because of budget reasons. It was because everyone on the island disappeared, and what if they were coming back [in the present]? I just liked that Spidey-sense thing of, 'Ch-ching! I love that idea. I want to watch that show. Oh, my God.' That stupid little kid [inside us all], you want to get home to turn the TV on to see that episode. I just felt that, and I thought, 'Why has no one done this? That's not a book already?' It feels right and familiar and, yet, new. It was a weird thing. So Liz wrote a great script, and we were just lucky to set it up and cast it with these amazing actors. And it was very exciting."

Since Abrams tends to do very well with genre television shows—*Lost* has eternal iconic status—it was something of a surprise when his romantic spy comedy *Undercovers* didn't make it through a full season. He explains why he feels it didn't work. "I've got to say, I didn't feel the problem with that show was my being overextended. I thought the problem with that show was, I made bad choices. I wasn't as respectful as the audience or the characters—I didn't give people anything of substance. The thing that's fun about fluff is, it needs to be contextualized; it needs to be fun and fluffy within something of meaning. It was kind of fluff on top of fluff, as opposed to something more substantial. Josh Reims [who cocreated the series with Abrams], who I would work with again, kind of took my lead on that in a big way, and I just honestly wrote it into mediocrity. I feel guilty because I love the actors, I love the idea of the show, I love the idea of a couple that loves each other, but, ultimately, if you don't have great conflict, what do you have?"

The conversation circles back to *Person of Interst* and why Abrams feels it's doing something different. "I was interested in that idea of surveillance and the spy genre stuff. I've always loved that kind of thing, and, on the way in, you think, 'Oh, it's just a TV show. It's just kind of stretching [the surveillance concept].' But it's in that area where it's not insane, and it's not so far away from what could be done that you think, 'This is silly or preposterous.' It's just far enough where you think, 'It may or may not be happening right now.' That's all you need, that feeling of, 'It could be happening,' that's the value of the show. It's definitely wish fulfillment. They're almost like superheroes without capes. As Jonah was pitching it—because it was Jonah. I know him and, obviously, I know his brother." Nolan's brother Christopher is the director of the *Batman: Dark Knight* film trilogy; the brothers wrote *The Dark Knight* and the upcoming *The Dark Knight Rises* together. "I was seeing Gotham City in my head as he was pitching it. He was describing this city and the villains in it and the bad guys, and it also was a tapestry of good versus evil. So I literally was imagining the amazing cinematography of Wally Pfister in *Dark Knight*. Of course, it's a very different kind of show, but there's a sort of DNA that I think is connected to the work he's done on the *Batman* films."

Finally, there's the new big-screen spy thriller, *Mission: Impossible—Ghost Protocol*, which Abrams produced (he directed and cowrote the previous installment, 2006's *Mission: Impossible III*). The project has some sequences actually shot in the IMAX format by director Brad Bird. Asked exactly how much IMAX is in the film, producer Abrams says, "It's a lot. It's insane, and it's really cool. [Bird] just did some amazing work. I cannot wait for you to see the movie."

Interview: J. J. Abrams—*Star Trek: Into Darkness*

lamag.co / 2013

From lamag.co, May 2013. Reprinted by permission.

Abrams grew up in Los Angeles and has been working in the entertainment business since he was sixteen when he wrote the music for the film, *Nightbeast*. He is now regarded as one of the most prodigiously talented filmmakers working today.

As a director, his film credits include *Mission: Impossible III*, *Star Trek*, and *Super 8*. On television, Abrams created the hit series *Felicity*, *Alias*, and *Lost*, amongst others, and has directed several episodes of each of them.

Don't miss this interview with J.J Abrams about *Star Trek: Into Darkness*.

Q: What do you hope that audiences will get from this film?
J. J. Abrams: Well, this is a far bigger film than the last one in every way, I think. The story was paramount for me. You don't have to have seen the other film but if you did, then great, because you will understand how they all came together. The story is full of intrigue, incredibly dramatic and wonderfully complex. The moral dilemma is 'How far are you willing to go to protect the ones you love?' That's something that's being played out on both sides.

Q: Does it stand alone as a story?
J. J. Abrams: Yes. A lot of sequels, I think, fall into the trap of assuming that you care about the characters and assume you love them and are connected to them. Sometimes I see a sequel and the movie is starting, and it assumes that I've just watched the other movie. So we tried to come at this from a stand-alone point of view. You don't have to have seen the other film but if you did, great, and you'll understand how they all came together, but you don't need to. These characters have grown to love each other and that means the stakes are immediately higher. And in *Star Trek: Into Darkness* they are up against a formidable adversary.

Q: Why Benedict Cumberbatch for the role of John Harrison?

J. J. Abrams: People have asked me why I choose Benedict for this, and I would answer that by saying, "Why not Benedict for everything?' He is so crazy good. I loved working with him. He brings exactly the respect and intelligence and depth and also humor to every scene as I was hoping he would. When I saw his work in Sherlock, like so many others, I was impressed by his seemingly effortless dexterity and his ability. It was almost like watching an Olympic gymnast go from incredible position to incredible position. He really is an exceptional talent and in addition to being the great actor he is, he was an absolute joy to spend some time with.

Q: There have been some memorable villains portrayed by British actors down the years. Did that give you pause for thought?

J. J. Abrams: I didn't have qualms about any nationality, but I had qualms about not having the best possible actor. He is someone who just elevated everything and while you don't want the classic, clichéd British villain, which we've all seen a million times, my guess is that we've seen just as many American villains. I think Benedict is one of the best actors alive. So the real question is 'Why did he accept the movie?' I think he is so good, and seeing him in Sherlock just blew my mind. I had that feeling that he would be great for almost anything. He exceeded all my expectations.

Q: What was it like when you first walked out on to the *Enterprise* set for *Star Trek: Into Darkness*?

J. J. Abrams: I remember walking on to the set for the first movie, and that really was a magical moment. This time we had an even bigger set, and it was the same feeling when I first walked on to the bridge of the *Enterprise*. It's a magical feeling, and it's almost like there's some power coming from that set and all of the people on it. It was like returning to your favorite place—a place that you hadn't been to for a few years.

Q: Is it important to create a balance between the existing *Star Trek*–universe with creating something new?

J. J. Abrams: Well, it was important to us that we acknowledged the importance of the existing fans and the existing series because we wouldn't be doing this if it weren't for them and for what Gene Roddenberry created. Having said that, I was never a *Star Trek* fan. I never cared about *Star Trek* in the same way that some of my friends did, so I didn't have that sense of reverence for this story. When they asked if I wanted to be involved in it and I heard myself say, "yes," I thought, "This is so curious because I never really cared about this group . . ." But it helped me, in part, tell the story from the point of view of a moviegoer not a *Star Trek* fan. So for me the question was always, "How do we tell a story that, if you're not a *Star Trek* fan, you will love and, if you are a *Star Trek* fan, you love it too?"

Q: Have other films influenced *Star Trek: Into Darkness*?

J. J. Abrams: Everything has something it borrows from and certainly with the opening of this movie we were aware of a kind of nod to the opening of *Raiders of the Lost Ark*. But really the spirit of the movie is that it's about a group of characters that I hope you like, that make you laugh, and that you cheer for. If you are going to a place as intense as some of this stuff is in our movie, I think you need balance. There are moments that are pretty dark and crazy, but those sequences won't matter to you. You won't care about them, if you haven't been laughing along the way and rooting for these characters who you feel for.

Q: Is it true that you were reluctant to use 3D at first?

J. J. Abrams: Frankly, the decision to do it in 3D was made for me. The studio said, "If you want to do this movie, we have to do it in 3D," and I was against it because I was not really a fan of 3D. But then, I was also never really a fan of *Star Trek* to begin with, so the idea of working on something that is not necessarily your favorite thing or your forte can actually help because it forces you to engage with something in a way that an outsider can appreciate. My initial feeling was that I didn't like 3D, but it was very helpful in some ways because we worked with the 3D crew in a way that didn't assume that we loved the technology.

Q: Why didn't you like 3D before?

J. J. Abrams: I have trouble with 3D sometimes—I can't see it quite right, I get a headache, I hate the glasses, and it annoys me. So I approached it cynically. The fact is that we have been using techniques that haven't been used in 3D before. They have made enough movies in 3D now that they can understand ways to eliminate some of these problems. We shot the movie with anamorphic lens so it had the same look and feel as the first movie, but because we were converting it to 3D later, we have so much more creative opportunities and ability to do things, push certain things and limit certain things. It actually allows you to be able to fine-tune it, and the audience gets to see something that is, I think, really fun and dynamic. The key for me overall is I got to make my 2D movie, that I really wanted to make, just the way I wanted to, and it gets to be augmented in 3D. But it doesn't detract from the 2D.

Q: You've got a big ensemble, and you've got new characters in *Star Trek: Into Darkness*. Is it hard to find moments for all of them to develop their characters?

J. J. Abrams: The first movie was easier in a way because it was introducing all of these people. It was easier to give these characters moments to be introduced because they would be introduced to each other and to the movie. The key to this one was not just how do we introduce them again to the audience but how do we give them moments so that the story couldn't take place unless they were all there? If you take out anyone of them, it would fold like a house of cards. We knew that in the first film when we introduced these great characters to the audience. They each had their part to play. We needed to do the same thing on this, and it was really important that every single character has a moment and without that the story just wouldn't have worked. Part of the multilayered process of developing the script was making sure that every single character had not just their moment, but their thread, their story line.

Q: You talked about how special a moment it was when you first walked out on to the bridge of your *Enterprise* set. You must have had quite a few special moments making these two films?

J. J. Abrams: I remember meeting William Shatner and Leonard Nimoy separately, and just hearing their stories about what *Star Trek* was like back in the day was wonderful. The first screening of the movie we had with an audience was the premier at the Sydney Opera House, and that was an incredible evening. It was so big that I couldn't tell if they hated the movie or not. I couldn't tell what the reaction was. I was fairly certain that they didn't like it because it was such a big place and you couldn't hear the audience the way that you can in a normal movie theater, and then when it was over they gave it a two-minute standing ovation. It was just this crazy relief of "Oh, okay, they didn't hate it." That was really nice.

J. J. Abrams interview for *Star Trek: Into Darkness*

John Hiscock / 2013

From the *Telegraph*, May 8, 2013. © Telegraph Media Group Limited.
Reprinted by permission.

J. J. Abrams has revived *Star Trek* and aims to do the same for *Star Wars*, but don't call him a rebooter, he tells John Hiscock.

He has brought new life to three near-moribund film franchises, but J. J. Abrams is quick to reject the sobriquet that some people have hung on him.

"The last thing anybody wants to be known as is 'The Rebooter,'" he said. "As a storyteller you have to love the characters and feel the passion that comes with the story. The opportunity to do something cool and to feel in my gut that it could be something special is what excites me."

That is why, at Tom Cruise's request, he directed *Mission: Impossible III*, and then four years ago he rebooted Gene Rodenberry's long-running *Star Trek* space series. With a new cast and fresh ideas, he breathed renewed life into the film franchise, which had ended in 2002 with *Star Trek: Nemesis*, and planted the seed for a new generation of Trekkies.

His next task will be creating a new story and characters for the *Star Wars* series, but first he has brought his crew of the Starship *Enterprise* together for a second time for *Star Trek: Into Darkness*. Zachary Quinto, who plays Spock, says, "It was like coming back to school again after a long summer holiday."

The excitable and garrulous J. J. Abrams (the initials stand for Jeffrey Jacob), who created the television series *Alias*, *Lost*, and *Fringe*, has come up with a spectacularly visual adventure that includes romance and humor, as well as explosive action and a grim theme of terrorism. It depicts devastating attacks on futuristic London and San Francisco with more scenes on Earth than the previous one had.

"It's intended as entertainment—it's not meant to be a preachy polemic, but it comments on relevant issues," he said.

Early reviews have been favorable, but in this paper Robbie Collin's review of *Star Trek: Into Darkness* said the movie seemed to have reverted to the style of the earlier films in the series. As producer and director, Abrams says he had to walk a fine line between creating fresh, new *Star Treks* for the twenty-first century, while avoiding alienating diehard Trekkies who still revere the old series as an icon of modern pop culture.

"I wanted to do the fans proud and make sure the story is something that touches people," he said. "The goal was to try to tell a story which can be seen and enjoyed if you haven't seen the previous one or know anything about the original series. Having said that, there are those fans of *Star Trek* who are very vocal and like things the way they were—we've all met them, and I love and respect them because we wouldn't be doing this if it wasn't for them—but we couldn't make a movie just for those fans."

His first *Star Trek*, released in 2009, followed the rebellious young James Kirk (Chris Pine), whose father sacrificed himself at the helm of a spaceship, and Spock (Zachary Quinto) the troubled half-human, half-Vulcan, as they enlisted in the Starfleet Academy and joined the Starship *Enterprise*. "The first one was the story of Kirk getting the captain's seat, and this one is the story of him earning it," says thirty-two-year-old Pine, whose father was a regular on the *CHiPS* television series. "The crew is tested, and the tests are cruel ones."

A newcomer to the cast is Benedict Cumberbatch, who plays a new galactic bad guy, the mysterious John Harrison, whom the crew of the Starship *Enterprise* pursue into Klingon-controlled space territory after he lays waste to a top-secret Starfleet intelligence facility in a terror bombing.

It is a change of pace for the thirty-six-year-old actor, best known for his stage performance in *Frankenstein* and his television roles as Sherlock Holmes and in the Tom Stoppard–scripted series *Parade's End*. He freely admits that when he was growing up he much preferred the *Star Wars* movies to *Star Trek*.

"I didn't realize the impact of *Star Trek* until I saw J. J.'s reboot of it," he says. "The Trekkie world is phenomenally rich and entertaining, but at its core it's about humans and being human and how to aspire to a greater democracy than we have. It's beautiful stuff. Emotions are ramped up, and men cry in this film.

"J. J. is extremely talented. He's a polymath and a genius, and I don't use those words very often. He's very funny, extremely warm, and exceptionally talented. He's like a ten-year-old boy, with infectious enthusiasms."

For Zachary Quinto, who alternates between New York– stage roles and Hollywood movies, donning Spock's pointed ears again was a defining moment. "The ears were a moment of magnitude," he said. "I knew when I was putting them on I was getting back into it in a real way.

"Spock is a lot more emotional in this movie, and although it is pure entertainment and has a summer blockbuster feel about it, it is also reflective of the violent times we are living in."

Spock and Lt. Uhura, played by Zoe Saldana, supply the movie's romantic moments, and the actress believes the problematic romance will continue to blossom in future movies. "It is particularly challenging for them because they are not of the same species," laughs Saldana, who had to learn to speak in Klingon for her role.

Chris Pine, who spent a year at Leeds University and was a virtual unknown when he landed the Captain Kirk role, will soon be seen in another franchise when he stars as Jack Ryan in a prequel to the film versions of Tom Clancy's novels. But he expects to return as Kirk in the next *Star Trek*, too.

"I find Kirk very endearing, and I love his spirit of adventure," says Pine. "He goes at things like a bull in a china shop, which is his strength and also part of his weakness. This film is a very emotional journey for him. In the first film he was very self-assured and confident, but now he's racked with self-doubt. I think it's wonderful to have heroes who are not that heroic."

Abrams, who is expected to produce, but not direct, a third *Star Trek* film, is already at work on *Star Wars*, although it is not something he wants to discuss yet. "I can't wait to talk about it because there's so much I want to share, but it's premature," he said. "The only thing I can say at the moment is that it's wildly exciting to be involved in it."

Pine, for one, will miss Abrams's hand on the tiller of the next *Star Trek* voyage. "I'm very disappointed that he won't be directing, but I am not worried about *Star Trek*'s future because J. J. and his team are in love with this story. I know that no matter what happens and who is in charge on a day-to-day basis, they will protect and care for it."

Meet the Author: Jonathan Tropper, J. J. Abrams, and Doug Dorst

Jonathan Tropper / 2013

From "Events at the Apple Store—J. J. Abrams and Doug Dorst," November 22, 2013, at the Apple Store, Soho: apple.com/jjabramspodcast. Reprinted by permission.

Jonathan Tropper: Hi, everybody.

J. J. Abrams: Hello.

JT: Thank you for being here. We're going to spend a little time talking about *S.* before we get you guys involved. J. J., I'm going to start with you for a second. The first kernel of an idea for this book happened in your brain about fifteen years ago when you were in the airport and you found a discarded Ludlum paperback. And there was a note in there from the last reader addressing it to whoever the next reader would be. Could you give us the CliffsNotes version of how you got from that—fifteen years is a lot of development time, even by Hollywood standards—what the evolution was from that idea to getting to this place?

JJA: Sure. First of all, thank you all for coming tonight. Yay, all of you! Well, essentially what happened was I was at the airport, and I found this book, like you said, someone had written, "To whomever finds this book, please read it, take it somewhere, and leave it for someone else to find it." It reminded me of being in college and seeing what people had written in the margins of books that you check out and sometimes seeing what they would highlight and wondering about the life that this book had before I picked it up. It stayed with me for a long time and many, many years later—this is now three or four years ago—I mentioned this to Lindsey Weber, and Lindsey runs our Feature Department at Bad Robot. Lindsey thought the idea had some promise, and she found a genius who is sitting to my right named Doug Dorst. Doug came in to have a meeting and talk about this idea, and all I really knew—and this is not the CliffsNotes version—I wanted to try and create a book that was a novel that had two people who didn't know each other. The idea was that someone left a novel, that they had written all these notes in, in the library;, someone else had found it, read some of the book, read some of the notes, responded to the notes, and left the book back where it was found. The original person found the book, responded to those notes, and this conversation would begin. The book itself would become a vessel of communication between two people. Lindsey and I pitched this idea to Doug, who miraculously lit up and started making the idea better instantly, and that was how the collaboration began.

JT: Doug, let's talk to you for a minute. If you guys could show what the inside of the book looks like for a second. You bit off a mammoth undertaking. I didn't understand it until I opened up the book. You know, most writers, myself included, would not even try to do what you did here. You basically created three books within one: you have a 460-or-so-page historical novel; you have a fictitious editor annotating the book who may or may not actually be the fictitious author, who is a man of mystery, and through his annotations you're starting to learn about a separate life of mystery that surrounded this fictitious author; and then on a third level you have a disgraced grad student, Eric, and this undergrad, Jen, passing the book back and forth, scribbling all their notes, and uncovering both a larger, contemporary conspiracy surrounding them and, at the same time, falling in love. So, you wrote three books within one, and I guess the first question that occurred to me as both a writer and a reader is how do you accomplish that process-wise? Did you write all three at once? Did you first write the novel and then write the other two? I don't even know how you sat down at your desk that first day.

Doug Dorst: I think the thing that made it easy to sit down was that I had no idea that it would turn out to be this complicated, this difficult. I'm a notoriously poor planner, and, so far as I knew, it might well have been notes in the margins of a sensible, tight, compact collection of haiku, which probably would have been a good strategy, actually. So, I sat down; I knew that *The Ship of Theseus*, the inner novel, I had to get some of that done first and then figure out how the margin notes might work in it. We did the foreword and chapter one, which is what we took out to publishers, with both the inner novel and the margin novels in place. After that, I wrote *The Ship of Theseus* straight through because we thought that it was essential that the inner novel work well, and once we all felt comfortable with it, that's when we dove in and got started with the margin story.

JJA: Just to also speak to Doug's brilliance, insanity, and ambition, in the original idea, it wasn't even clear that the novel had to be an original idea. We had thought maybe there was even an existing novel that we can sort of play this game with and have a play on top of a book, but Doug had this, I think, brilliant conceit about using the authorship conspiracy idea. Who is this author? The book had to be an original book and had to be great writing so that all of it made sense because it's such a gimmick otherwise, and I think what Doug did was say, "Not only do I want to write the novel because it needs to be the central idea and, within the novel, in addition, are all these pieces of ephemera. There's an obituary; there are notes, letters, postcards, pictures; there's a map drawn on a napkin. When you get the book, it's in a slipcase, so when you open it, you see that there's these things stuck inside—this book, this document of this relationship and this love story that exists between the undergrad student and the grad student.

JT: J. J., you're a director, you're a screenwriter, you're a producer, and, from what I've seen about you, that keeps you pretty busy. What compelled you to want to write a book?

JJA: The idea was a book; I just felt like if we didn't do this—and, look, there have been other examples of things in the past that have—it's not the first time to be experimental with a novel like this. But, in this particular way, I think, it is pretty unique, and when I talked about this with Lindsey, the thought was, "Someone is going to do this, and if it's not us, I'm going to kill myself." I just really wanted to see this thing and, the truth is, that not only did Doug go above and beyond what anyone could have imagined, in terms of the quality of the writing and in the imagination of it, but then Mulholland Books and Melcher Media created the physical object. The book itself is incredible. I know we're here to talk about the iBook, digital version, which in some ways is great because you can actually remove, as you might have seen, some of the handwriting to make the reading of the novel easier because it is pretty clean. But, to have the physical object, whether it's the actual thing or the facsimile, it's an incredible thing that they did; the design was amazing. I just thought that was the goal, not to make a movie or a show.

JT: So, Doug, this is for you. Let's talk about *The Ship of Theseus* for a minute, which is the novel within the book. Forgetting everything else that's going on in these pages, that's a fully wrought novel. That is *Treasure Island*. That's four hundred and sixty or so pages, and it's very compelling.

DD: Thanks, that's great to hear.

JT: My question is: you're basically ghost writing for a fictional author. So, it's a two-fold question. First is, and I think I heard you talking about this in the green room, there a bit of method acting for you as a writer where you actually put yourself into this fictional writer? And, the second part is, did you really feel when you finished this book, because now that you've told us that you actually wrote that book all the way through, did you feel you had a fully realized novel that you were proud of on its own before you went into the second part and third part and fourth part?

DD: Second question first, because that's the one I remember right now, and you're gonna have to remind me of the first. Yes, when I got to the end of *The Ship of Theseus*, I did feel when we got it to a place that we felt it was working—I definitely felt some sort of accomplishment. I knew there was more to do, but I'm actually really proud of the underlying novel. Wait, was that actually the question?

JT: Yes, and you weren't doing anything in that novel that was going to feed anything to come later, or you were?

DD: No, I wasn't. I tend to work really improvisationally, and so I thought, "Let's let the novel unfold as it does, and I trusted that there would be ample opportunity for the story between these two readers to find its way, to find the right places in the margins for it. So, yes, it was me trusting the process, mostly because I didn't feel like I could plan it. Oh, the first question was about method acting.

JT: Yes.

DD: It would be a great answer. Like, I imagine myself stomping around my office like a furious revolutionary, possible assassin, but no, I didn't. There was something I was well aware of: how freeing and exciting it was to write as someone who was explicitly not me. And part of that was being able to say, "Oh, I have this idea," and, "Wait a minute, that's ludicrous and a terrible idea!" Then I thought, "Well, wait a minute, I'm not me. This writer might have followed that idea." So I did, and, actually, some of those things worked out really nicely, I think.

JT: Great. J. J., a number of articles I read have likened your role in this to a showrunner—you know, the way a showrunner runs a series or contributes creatively or runs a show while other writers sit in a room and hammer out the episodes. I wonder if you accept that comparison or don't accept that comparison and how you would compare your role in this book to your role overseeing a show like *Lost*.

JJA: Well, in fairness, as you well know, a showrunner typically writes, rewrites most episodes, or, at least, oversees, in incredible detail, what scripts get written for that show. That's not what I did here at all. I had the original idea, and then we collaborated. I gave notes, and Lindsey did an extraordinary amount of notes on the book, developing it. But Doug did the heavy lifting and the writing. I would liken it more to being a producer of a movie where you have an idea, a conceit for this thing that could be and then collaborated with writers and storytellers—in that case, like *Cloverfield* or something, which is this monster movie we did. I'm also a big fan of *Gone With the Wind*—I have nothing to do with that. When we did *Cloverfield*, it was: someone directed that film, someone wrote that film, I was a producer on the film. It was an idea I had, but other people did all the hard work—and, yes, I give notes. I collaborate with these incredible storytellers. That was the case here, so showrunner would be giving me far too much credit but producer does feel right even though it's a weird thing to say, "I produced a book." But I do feel that is kind of what I was doing with Lindsey and Doug.

JT: This is for both of you, and you can chime in with each other. Reading this book requires a level of commitment and energy. This is not a book that you just grab and jump out into the back yard for twenty minutes. This is a book that requires attention. Did you worry that it might require too much of the reader, were you concerned that maybe taking it as—realizing it as fully as you did, you might be asking the reader for more of a commitment than readers generally give a book.

DD: I knew it would be demanding. On some level, I knew there was something slightly insane about it as a project. There was too much to worry about in writing it, and just trying to get the stories out and telling them as well as I could, I kind of thought, "I'll worry about the other stuff later." If I make too big a mess for a reader to deal with, we'll figure out a way to clean it up, but I freed myself from worrying about it in the writing.

JJA: The goal was to create something that wasn't just a typical book. Whether that's wonderful or better or infuriating and frustrating or worse, it'll depend on how different people accept it and take it. I remember when I was a kid, there was this series of books written by this British author, Dennis Wheatley, and these were these great mysteries—murder mysteries often. There would be these documents that would talk about the case as if it were real. Inside, there would be these little wax paper envelopes that would have a stamp that was a piece of evidence or a lock of hair or a photograph that had been ripped into four pieces or something. You'd read all these letters and things, and it wasn't a novel. It was really this presentation of a situation, and you would have to read through all this stuff, figure out what you thought. Then, when you were ready, you could open up the seal on the back and read this essay that basically explained what really happened and why. It was asking something of you that was not a casual "beach read," necessarily, but I do think this wasn't quite that. It was not your typical novel either. There were definitely times where I thought, "This is going to be a confusing moment." But I think Doug did an extraordinary job and, one of the things I love is, just like with any great author, just when you're feeling, "Oh, I don't quite get it," soon enough it happens: information is given to you and you go, "Oh!" The book is somewhat an analog interactive experience you can find your answers to if you want to. I think that the romance, the flirtation, the fun between Jen and Eric is wonderful and current. The book itself, *The Ship of Theseus*, alone is good entertainment, so I think there are a lot of ways you can approach it.

JT: As soon as I got the book, I opened it up and cracked the seal; the first I did was I called Lindsey and said, "How do I read this?" We talked about it for a little while and, ultimately, I discovered my own way that I enjoyed reading it. I wondered if each of you wanted to tell readers how you think it is best read— if you have a way that you think it is best read, I'd love to hear what you each think of that.

DD: I don't think there is a best way to do it. I think it entirely depends upon on how best you process information or the most exciting way there is for you to get involved in the story. I think I would be inclined to read *The Ship of Theseus* all the way through and then go back and tackle the margin story.

JT: That's exactly how I am not reading it.

DD: You're doing it perfectly simultaneously?

JT: No, I read about ten pages, and then I go back and read—but that's a tribute to you because I don't want to leave Jen and Eric behind.

DD: Oh, that's nice.

JJA: Aww. I think that my guess is I would probably read a chapter and then go back and read the chapter with the notes. It is definitely a little bit distracting sometimes, and I can't hold myself completely. It's a weird thing when we first read Doug's early drafts. They were written, and it was his handwriting. It was an amazing thing to see what Melcher Media did in finding people to actually play Jen and play Eric in the handwriting because it was almost like watching an actor come in. We had to choose the handwriting, the people who—whose handwriting would be Eric or Jen's. It was a very different kind of book experience, I would guess, from any typical one.

DD: Which ended up being a really cool thing because handwriting is such an intimate thing. The casting they did with the writers really helped shape the characterizations. The voices feel differently in the different handwriting options that we saw.

JT: That actually brings me to the next thing I wanted to ask you. You took the old-fashioned epistolary novel, which are novels written in letters back and forth. You created an epistolary novel through margin notes, and, yet, I found it super impressive that Jen and Eric both emerge with fully formed personalities. You could see the feelings going back and forth; you could see the thing becoming a love affair and the same time you use them to communicate this threat and this danger and this mystery growing around them so that there is actually a completely effective novel written purely in margin form. That might not be the right way to say it. I guess the question I have for you is: That was a tremendous limitation that you exploited to a very artistic endpoint. Did you feel frustrated by that limitation you had set for yourself, or did you ultimately feel that it showed you had to write their story?

DD: I don't think I was frustrated by it. I think that was part of the attraction to the project, was trying to tell an interesting story with this challenging constraint. It was really difficult—I was probably halfway through it when I thought, "Wait a minute. I'm going to have a lot of trouble narrating action in it. Action will be very, very difficult to do without it sounding horribly expository and fake and lame." There were some moments where we had to figure out, "How do you have this thing happen but have it feel like it's emerging organically in this conversation?" The voices of Jen and Eric were probably the trickiest part of the book. For all the formal stuff going on, for all the layers, really getting Jen and Eric right was the most difficult part. And, actually, Lindsey was a tremendous help there. Jen and Eric were very much the last thing to fall into place. The whole thing depends on them. I think I had to write my way in pretty deeply and have a little help before they really took shape.

JT: I think you did an incredible job. I think it's my favorite part of the book, watching that relationship grow.

DD: Thank you, Lindsey.

JT: Thanks, Lindsey. Okay, J. J. *Lost*, *Alias*, *Fringe*, *Believe*, which is shooing now, what these shows have in common is the sense of shadow world of greater conspiracies that exist—the truth beneath the truth beneath the truth. And with *S.*, as well, there's both that mythology and that sense of a shadow world, which are two separate things that you've married together. I don't want to pathologize this too much, but I was just wondering what it is about that sort of universal well that you feel drawn to or that you feel that readers and viewers are drawn to as well.

JJA: I think that without sort of analyzing any of the stuff that I've done because you're scaring me. I think that truth is that when I was a kid, I remember looking at the world in a way that I thought anything was possible, which was an exciting feeling that everyone seems to share when you're a kid. As I got older, I remember feeling like, "Maybe not everything is possible," but appreciating that feeling that there is that door on the side of a building. And, what if, behind that door, there was a really dark corridor with a red light at the end with a staircase going down and, what if, you went down there and there was a door that had a keypad—I would always imagine things like that. When I would drive with my parents, we'd be in the middle of nowhere. There would be a shack with a field. What if you opened the door to that shack, and there was this bunker. What is in that bunker? I was always drawn to that: the idea that there's always something behind the things that seem normal. I think that the idea of a show like *Alias*, the natural playground for an espionage series is "things aren't what they seem; people aren't who they appear to be." *Lost*, one of the first ideas that came to me, not knowing who or what would be in there, was this idea of this hatch on this island. That this island wasn't just an island. You know, *Fringe* is a place; there's a lab beneath Harvard where crazy, fringe science is done. I am drawn to that kind of idea. It's funny because none of that was imposed upon Doug at all. Doug, in his insanity, came to this kind of stuff on his own, but it was my favorite kind of thing. It felt like the notion of identity, the whole question of *The Ship of Theseus*, if you keep replacing the pieces of a ship, is it still the same ship? That notion applies to the author, Straka, it applies to the main character, it applies to Jen and Eric, it applies to the editor of the book, as you mentioned. So, the idea of identity, that things not being what they seem at first glance, is sort of a theme of the book. It admittedly felt very comfortable for us.

JT: Well, congratulations to both of you. I really do think it's a tremendous accomplishment, this book.

JJA: Thank you.

JT: Let's turn it over to questions from our audience. There should be some guys running around with mics.

Question: This is a question for both of you. J. J., you talked about this earlier, about influences, but I was wondering if there were any other influences from your past works in film, in writing books, or in any other types of literature that you guys might have read that influenced you more for this book?

DD: I think there have to be influences. I don't think any writer can write without influences showing through. I went out of my way to try to avoid having anything look like too much of an influence. I was trying to resist really obvious influence because, in part, I'm writing as this writer who is, sixty years later, thought of as this singular writer. I have to be really careful about exposing influences. I have always loved storytellers who have approached telling stories from odd angles and odd structures. So, Donald Barthlemay is a huge influence, one of my old teachers, Gilbert Sorrentino, who is just this genius of rule-breaking. That's always appealed to me, and I think that's why this project was appealing to begin with. Here's this notion, this crazy conceit: what are you going to do; how are you going to tell a good story with that? I just lit up because that's fun, that kind of challenge.

JJA: We both have our different influences, but, like I said before, for this particular project, I was most influenced by those Wheatley books and that woman, Janet, who wrote that note in the book and left it at the airport.

Question: This question is for J. J. Creative people tend to struggle with giving up ownership of their ideas and be very territorial over something that is theirs, that they view in their world. It seems like from your history that is something that isn't a factor for you. That you tend to think that the more people collaborate together and work together, the better the process can be. Can you talk about your view on that and, if that is accurate, why you feel that way?

JJA: It's incredibly nice of you to say that, thank you. The truth is if the master you are serving is the project, is the idea, is the book, in this case, being territorial or not being willing to share this idea, I'd be nowhere near this room right now, and I would not be talking to you. The whole point of it is: if there is an idea that's worth doing, and if you think you can do it yourself, great, you should do it. But no movie gets made with one person; no television show does. While a lot of books do, I knew that this book wouldn't, just by myself. The collaboration was really something that was born out of discussion with Lindsey Weber and, in talking about it with her, the idea that, "Well, let's find someone who can collaborate on this thing." My name is on the book. I'm already getting too much credit as it is; the truth is that Doug is the author of record for this book. My involvement, yes, I had the original idea, but it was easier to go out and sell the book if I was part of that. The experience of doing it was such a wonderful experience; the collaboration was so great, and anytime I'm sure you felt this if you've ever collaborated with people in this way. When someone is better than you are at something, and they inspire you, your ideas get better. Then you say, "How about this? We've never thought about this." I will say, I'm working right now with Lawrence Kasdan on a script and working with him has been such a joy because he will throw out ideas that in a million years I would never have thought of that are patently better than any idea I would have had that day. All of a sudden, he up's my game because he is so good. I felt the same exact thing working with Doug. He brought to me and to Lindsey a world that took a notion that could have gone any direction and just elevated it completely. So, I embrace the collaboration. I don't care who has the best idea when working on a movie. I always tell the crew, whoever has the best idea, if there is a moment that could make this moment better, more authentic, funny, scary, or interesting, please share it. Don't be at the wrap party saying, "You know, on day 34, I should have said this. Oh, my God, that would have made this better." Tell me now when we can actually do it and that was certainly the experience working with Doug.

JT: Is that unusual, that experience; have most people had that?

JJA: I work with a lot of people who have that. I feel like it is. I'll tell this very quick story—I'm talking too much anyway. When I was fourteen years old or something, fourteen, fifteen, my father was a TV movie producer and took me to Paramount Studios one night. I was like, "Where are we going?" We lived in Los Angeles. He goes, "I'm taking you somewhere, and I can't tell you where." So I get to Paramount; it's at night. We go into this small screening room, like thirty seats and there fifteen, eighteen people there. I see that one of the people is John Carpenter. He's right there. John Carpenter, ladies and gentlemen. John Carpenter, who was one of my favorite directors at the time, and I still adore him. I'm freaking out. I had loved *Halloween* and I loved *The Fog*, and I'm like, "God, it's John Carpenter!" He was going to screen for the first time a cut for his new movie *Escape from New York*. So, my head is exploding; I can't believe it. I'm sitting there watching this movie, which, during the screening the projector broke, they had to change the thing, put the film back in. He had to read dialogue that wasn't recorded yet. I was watching this whole thing, and this movie is over. And John says, "So, what did you think?" The reason I'm telling you this is that I got to watch someone with a completely open mind embrace any idea that he heard, and it was this unbelievable education in the notes that came after the movie to see how someone who clearly is nervous, clearly vulnerable, but was asking these people. It turned out, my father knew the DP and that was why we were invited. It was an amazing thing to watch someone, at that age to watch someone that I admired, watch them be so open to the better idea, no matter where it came from. It was an inspiring thing to see and it occurred to me now.

Question: Hi, this is for both of you, but specifically for J. J. You mentioned earlier about the history and how it started with a note from Janet, or whatever her name is in the airport, and I kind of wanted to know, where are you and Janet now? Because, obviously, the story didn't end there with the book coming out and everything. Have you met Janet since then? Do you know her? Have you heard from Janet?

JJA: Janet and I . . . I really don't want to talk about it. No, I don't know who the hell Janet is. But I'm grateful to Janet, and I still have the book. I have yet to read the book. I will read it, and I will leave it for someone to find. Janet, if you're out there, let me know.

Question: This question is for both of you. I'm glad, myself being a book reader and technically challenged; I like the feel. Growing up, like you said, with decoder books and the duality of the book is what's intriguing me now, that there's two stories going on, with two doors opening and closing. Do you envision these two characters, eventually, being in a book by themselves, to continue the conspiracy?

DD: I think they could. I like them, and I like their world. I really haven't had a problem thinking of fun things to do with them and this world. So much so, that it was really the deadline that got me to stop and, then, only reluctantly. They certainly could. I'm not planning to sit down on Monday and start it, but I like to think they could keep going.

JJA: Doug's answer.

Question: This question is for both of you as well. One thing that I've noticed is that there's been a fairly recent trend—even when I was growing up—movies can inspire people at middle-school age, to go back and read the book before seeing the movie. In this case, with your involvement J. J., it seems like you're creating a book experience for the sake of reading, for re-creating that joy of reading for people my age, younger, or older. My question is do you see this as maybe becoming a new trend where more people start to jump in for the sake of creating these book experiences where people aren't just trying to read a book for the sake of being in the know, so that way they have no surprise of the movie, but they actually want to read the book to read the book?

JJA: Well, I would say that it's probably more practical and realistic rather than cynical to imagine that many books are written to become something else, but it's sort of an unfortunate thought that books don't exist for books to exist. That's what this is. It's funny, a lot of people have said to me because of what my day job is, "Oh, so where are you going to develop this? When is this going to be a movie?" That's not what we're doing, and that was never the goal. This is the end game. This was always the goal. But, if you're asking if this book might inspire other people to do more interesting things in terms of the physical book itself, I will say that there have been a few authors that we've spoken to both here and in Europe who have said that they're so interested in what can be done, having seen what the publishers did with *S.* that they're looking to push the limits a bit as to what their books look and feel like. I think that's an exciting thing.

DD: I don't have anything to add.

Question: Hi, guys. Oh, this is cool. Hey, J. J., what you do is really big. You undertake these huge projects, *Star Trek*, *Star Wars*, that's crazy, and this book, too. I've never seen anything like it. Not only are you doing them and doing them well, you're making pieces that will last forever, really. My question is where do you find the courage, the ambition, the tenacity, and inspiration to do these huge things?

JJA: Okay, I love you. Clearly, I paid him to say nice things. Very kind of you, thank you very much. But it also terrifies me because the idea of things outside of the project themselves, to look at the context in which you are making something, it's important, you gotta know who your audience is; you have to know what's out there. You have to understand if you're writing something to make sure you're not spending the year of your life working on something that is right there already, and no one is going to want another version of that. At the same time, you know, working on things from the inside out, which we always try to do, and you can have an ambition that doesn't always work. For me the closest thing for me that I know as a litmus test is whether something is going to work for anyone else. A lot of time, writers are working on something else, "I'm working on this thing, but I don't know if anyone is going to like it. This feels like this boring thing that I love." It's amazing how often that boring thing that you love becomes a sensation. I think the key is to do that. Once you start working on something, say, "Oh, they'll like this. This will be something for them." Literally, we were working on this book, and we're like, "This is insane, and it's never going to happen!" And "We'll see." To approach something with that kind of excitement that is shared in this weird way where you just know what makes you happy and then to see it on the *New*

York Times Bestseller list, we're like, "Oh, my God! That's nuts! We would never have dreamed it." It's really a result of having an idea that stayed with me and I loved but that Lindsey felt like this could be something. Finding Doug, who took it and said, "Oh, my God, what about this?!" At each stage, we were sort of turned on by what it could be but never thinking, "Oh, this is going to work really well," because, actually, we were thinking, "Oh, my God. No publisher is ever going to be able to pull this off"—you know, which Little, Brown and Mulholland Books totally did—"and, even if they do, who's going to want it?" and have it received warmly and very unexpectedly, frankly. But the answer is just work stuff you care about whenever you can and try not and think too hard about what it's going to be like in the world. Thank you again for your kind words.

Question: I really liked your speech at TED where you talked about the mystery box, and when I read the book, when I started opening the book and looking at it, I immediately thought of the mystery box. I was wondering, while you were making the book, or putting it together, if you thought of the mystery box at all?

JJA: Okay, you're a genius. You should be at the Genius Bar right now. Thank you for watching the TED Talk and making that connection. Clearly, the fact that it comes in a box, which was a practical matter that came later, was only a result of all the things that were in the pages, and if we didn't have a box, there would be nothing in the pages. It's a funny thing, when you look at the thing, you have this black, kind of cool, sporty box that just has this *S* on it. I think that it does have a little bit of a sense of, "Ooh, what's inside there?" That's an example of the design work they did that was gorgeous, but the thing about the mystery box that was a talk at TED that I did, it was just about how the potential of what something can be is an incredibly powerful thing. Anyone of us who have read that compels us that has many moments as the story goes on where you go, "Ooh, I want to know the answer to that." I promise you there isn't a story you've read where you ask that question because it has to be liked. It has to be something that drives you in. The key to something like this working is that what's inside the box has to be great. You can't just have fluff and mystery and promise; it's nothing. That's what this book would have been with Doug Dorst. What this became—it became a great read and not just a cool box. So, I love the box, and I love the *S* on it. I open it up, and it's sort of a keepsake. But the reason I think it's worthy of people's time, I would hope so, is because I think what Doug has done is written an extraordinary book with an extraordinary play happening on top of it. So all the gimmicks and all the fun stuff, I think, are transcended by the contents of the box, and that's thanks to Doug.

JT: Ok, thank you all very much. That's all the time we have. You've been a great audience. Thank you, Doug and J. J. for coming out, and, if you haven't yet, you should pick up *S.* because it's really something you'll remember for the rest of your lives. Thank you.

J. J. Abrams: Hollywood's Renaissance Man

Horatia Harrod / 2014

From the *Telegraph*, January 25, 2014. © Telegraph Media Group Limited.
Reprinted by permission.

Sci-fi visionary J. J. Abrams tells Horatia Harrod about publishing his first novel and breathing new life into *Star Wars*.

J. J. Abrams is not an easy man to pin down. When you're the busiest man in Hollywood, it takes the combined efforts of a publicist, a personal assistant, and a scheduling assistant to carve out even half an hour from your day.

Aside from the novel, the television programs (he's producing three that are currently airing in the United States) and the children (he's coproduced three of those, too, with his wife, Katie McGrath, and likes to be around to take them to school every day), there's the minor matter of the three sprawling film franchises he's overseeing, one of which also doubles up as his next directorial duty: *Star Wars*.

I've just broached that daunting subject, down the line to Abrams in Los Angeles, when he arrives at the offices of his production company, Bad Robot. Abrams is a voluble man, as you'd expect from someone who sold his first script when he was still an English student at Sarah Lawrence College, had a multipicture deal when he was in his early twenties, and whose first feature film, *Mission: Impossible III*, had a budget of $150 million.

Suddenly, though, the line goes quiet. A moment later Abrams laughs incredulously. "Are you kidding me? My God. My office . . . I'm working on the *Star Wars* script today, and the people in my office have covered up all my windows with black paper. I guess they wanted to make sure no one could see what I was doing." He seems lost for words, for the first and last time in our conversation. "It seems rather extreme."

There is something old-fashioned about J. J. Abrams. He's polite and self-deprecating, for one thing, but his interests are also strangely antiquated. "I'm drawn to typewriters and printing and paper craft, and the idea of actual bookbinding and box-making," he says.

"I do think there's something about the digital age that is increasingly dehumanizing us. We're in this very weird place where we're being pulled into experiences that aren't really experiences at all. When you're printing something on a Chandler & Price letterpress, even though it might take a long time and it's imperfect, isn't that the point?"

Abrams is a classic geek, then, a tinkerer—something that should hearten those who are hoping for a return to the rough, space-Western feel of the original *Star Wars* trilogy.

Born in 1966, he came of age in the era before the internet. "We're living in a moment of instant information and a sense of entitlement to that information," he says. "But I think it's nice to remember that there's nothing wrong with a sense of anticipation."

Late last year, Abrams found time to publish a novel. *S.* is not just a book, of course, but a J. J. Abrams production, complete with an enigmatic online trailer and teasing back story (as Abrams tells it, the idea for it came to him fifteen years ago, when he found an abandoned novel at Los Angeles airport signed by a mysterious Janet).

The book wasn't actually written by Abrams: that job was given to a writer named Doug Dorst, who batted ideas back and forth with Abrams chapter by chapter. "It was not unlike working on a film," says Abrams, "where you could be working on your own idea, or a writer's idea, or a preexisting storyline—something along the lines of *Star Wars*, where obviously you are inheriting something that is bigger than all of us."

In truth, *S.* is an extraordinary creation, a beguiling fake artifact: the main text is a book apparently printed in 1949, the pages lovingly yellowed and foxed. In the margins, a love story plays out in the alternating annotations of two American college students, and there are also editorial interventions in the footnotes that point to a shadowy global plot centered on the author of the novel. Then there are the ephemera: notes on napkins, telegrams, photographs, photocopies, all perfectly reproduced and inserted between the pages.

These are Abrams's obsessions—with craftsmanship, with puzzles, with esoteric conspiracies—played out in print. *S.* is that rare novel that comes with a code wheel. "For me, the fun of something like *S.* was taking something that we all know very well," he says, "that incredibly analog, simple, and ubiquitous object, which is the novel, and saying, 'What would happen if the novel had another dimension to it?'"

Maybe it's because he grew up in Los Angeles, where both parents worked in television, that the line between reality and fiction seems so thin in the Abrams universe. What starts on screen almost always ends up down some real-world rabbit hole. In the darkest recesses of the internet there are probably still people trying to figure out what happened in *Lost*, the confounding program that made Abrams famous.

As a child, Abrams loved magic; he has often spoken about a black box he bought as a teenager from Tannen's magic shop in Manhattan. He's had it for more than thirty years and has never opened it. It represents, he says, "infinite possibility." "Magic is something that's informed what I've done," he says. "The magic that works, to me, is the magic that feels completely grounded and real and tangible, and movies and television are extensions of that."

That's why Abrams doesn't like to fumble his big reveal, which takes us back to *Star Wars*. The film won't be released for almost two year; yet, as Abrams's blacked-out windows attest, it's already the subject of feverish attention. When we spoke, Abrams was discussing the idea of shooting the films in 3D, a technology about which he seems fairly skeptical. "Yeah, I'm not, like, a 3D fanatic," he says. "I did feel pressure to do it on *Star Trek: Into Darkness*, but, ultimately, I understood why it was important to the studio. I was actually really glad in the long run that we did it that way, and I think it worked all right."

Before the release of last year's *Star Trek: Into Darkness*, Abrams tried to keep secret the identity of the villain played by Benedict Cumberbatch—something he now regrets. "We were trying to preserve the unexpected for the audience, but it came across as if we were trying to be too clever," he says.

"*Star Wars* is in every way a different animal. It's always been a more open, fan-engaged universe than I've been used to, so I'm sure there'll be some sort of compromise. But it feels to me like there's a purity in not knowing every little thing."

Believe: J. J. Abrams Interview

UKTV / 2014

From UKTV, March 2014. Reprinted by permission.

UKTV: When did you first meet Alfonso Cuarón?

J. J. Abrams: I met Alfonso over twenty years ago, and I've wanted to work with him desperately ever since. I was a huge fan of every movie that he made, and each one made me more and more desperate to try and figure this out.

UKTV: And how did *Believe* come about?

J. J. Abrams: It wasn't until Alfonso, through some magical moment, called and said, "I have an idea for a TV show," that it gave this opportunity to me and to Bad Robot. When he pitched the idea, it didn't have to come from Alfonso to be something that was compelling and something that felt like I had to see that on television. We were all desperate to be involved, but, of course, because it was Alfonso, it was even more so. So, it was one of those things that was an opportunity too great, too exciting to pass up.

UKTV: You have so many different projects on the go. How hands-on were you for *Believe*?

J. J. Abrams: I was very hands-on in the pilot. I was hands-on in putting that together and in getting the team and everything. The key is to be available when you're needed and help get the thing on its feet and be there when it's necessary to help with decisions or help fix problems when they arise. The goal is to get and find and encourage the right people to do their job.

UKTV: Do you think we will see a season two of *Believe*?

J. J. Abrams: I think it definitely has a chance. I feel like it's one of those things where, as series go, creatively you always find yourself finding your footing eight or nine episodes in. You just begin to do it. Usually, the first season you get it, fingers crossed that we're able to continue that in season two.

UKTV: If you had supernatural powers, what would you do?

J. J. Abrams: It's hard to answer that question without being corny, but I would try and make people blind to people's differences so that they wouldn't see people as Other, but we'd all see each other as one.

Interview with J. J. Abrams

Andrew Fish / 2015

From *American Cinematographer,* February 2016. Reprinted courtesy of *American Cinematographer* magazine.

Shortly before the release of *Star Wars: The Force Awakens*, J. J. Abrams spoke to *AC* about his collaborative efforts with cinematographer Dan Mindel, ASC, BSC, and the creative team at Lucasfilm to give the *Star Wars* universe a modern upgrade, while keeping the saga firmly rooted in its hallowed history.

American Cinematographer: Tell us about the importance of having a noncynical perspective when taking on a project like *The Force Awakens*.

J. J. Abrams: Since I was eleven years old, when I saw *Star Wars* for the first time, what it had at its core was a sense of possibility, optimism, and hope, so the approach had to be in that spirit, in an authentic, and not in a Pollyannaish, way. From the very beginning, working with Lawrence Kasdan, one of the [saga's] original storytellers, this was about embracing a spirit that we love so desperately.

AC: You have collaborated on three other films with Dan Mindel, two *Star Trek* films and *Mission: Impossible III*. What draws you to work with him?

Abrams: One of the things that I love about Dan, [beyond] his versatility, is his love of film itself and his appreciation for the look of anamorphic lenses. There's a kind of aesthetic that he and I both get excited about. I learned so much from Dan on *M:i:III*, which was my first movie. He was the first cinematographer I worked with on a feature, and his generosity and patience with me were sort of stunning—and something for which I am still so grateful. He was an amazing collaborator from the very beginning, and we immediately found ourselves laughing more often than not and celebrating a great shot. We found ourselves in such sync. Dan is someone who I consider to be not just an incredible genius and a brilliant cinematographer, but also a dear friend.

AC: How did you set out to create the look of *The Force Awakens*?

Abrams: What I really wanted to do was embrace a feeling more than a particular aesthetic. [It was] the feeling that I felt when I saw *Star Wars* for the first time; there was a scope and a scale and an authenticity to those early movies. When you looked at the gorgeous lighting in *Empire* [*Strikes Back*] or the scenes in the ice fields of Hoth or in the desert with the diffusion on Threepio when they shot in Tunisia for Tatooine or if you looked at the forest of Endor, you knew you were in real places. It gave you license, as a viewer, to let go and be in a real place, and it made all the other locations feel real. For example, when you're in some of the ice caves in Hoth, I suppose you could scrutinize those sets and say, 'That looks a little like a set,' but you believe it 100 percent because you were just outside in what you knew was a legitimate location. Aesthetically, that was the most important thing for me. I wanted people to feel like they really were in these places. Dan and I talked a lot about what lenses we could get that were closest to, if not the actual, original lenses that were used on a particular original *Star Wars* movie. We knew shooting on film was essential. It was really a question of trying to serve the feeling more than it was trying to copy a certain aesthetic.

AC: How did you and Dan go about creating that realism?

Abrams: Part of it was location shooting, making sure that we were on actual sets and builds and locations wherever possible. The ability to shoot actual locations—in Abu Dhabi or in the forests of Wales or on [Skellig Michael] in Ireland or getting plates in Iceland—was enormous and something we're really grateful for on this movie. Part of it was embracing and encouraging the unexpected. Whether it's atmosphere or natural light, it's embracing the things that you sometimes desperately try to re-create in post, where you can spend a lot of time trying to make something that nature is often giving you for free. This was more about the approach and not just to the photography of the movie, but to the creatures and the props. For the lightsaber battles, we were very lucky to actually have sabers that were practical, that could light up incredibly brightly. While [the prop itself] certainly doesn't make a scene with a lightsaber work or not, it's certainly a visually stunning thing to see how much interactive light actually occurs when [you're holding] something in your hand that's that bright and colorful. That was just one of many things that allowed us to take advantage of whatever resources were available to us and apply each when necessary.

AC: Lucasfilm President Kathleen Kennedy explained to us that concept art would be brought into story brainstorming sessions and that it sometimes inspired an idea that would take the story in a different direction. Can you elaborate?

Abrams: There were times when certain images came in that we felt could be applicable to certain scenes. One of the great opportunities on this movie was working with Rick Carter and Darren Gilford, our production designers. I brought Rick into the story process at the very beginning, probably because I knew how inspiring Ralph McQuarrie's designs were to George Lucas when he was working on the original films. Rather than write the script and then hand it off to a designer and ask him to design everything that was written, it felt like we had such a brain trust—and I should also say a soul trust—in Rick and Darren. Rick is such a dreamer and such a glorious connection maker, with a capability to hear what we were talking about and then go work on something and bring it in and show us. It might have been a detail we would have forgotten or overlooked, but Rick visualized it and brought it to life. Or he'd bring in something that we hadn't thought of. It was an inspiring thing to see the work of such extraordinary conceptual artists and designers. To begin to identify which images could apply to the movie, just because you knew it and you felt it was right, was as informative to how our story was going to unfold as anything. All we're saying is that the best idea wins. The sooner you have smart people helping and working on something from any angle, the better.

AC: How was this film influenced by the work of original-trilogy concept artists Ralph McQuarrie and Joe Johnston?

Abrams: I knew this movie needed to feel like it was part of a continuum, and part of it was a gut feeling of what makes a *Star Wars* movie a *Star Wars* movie. Films have been trying to do what George did since *Star Wars* came out, and this was an incredible opportunity because we were actually inheriting the legacy of *Star Wars*. The question became, "What do we embrace, and what do we let go of?" For certain elements—like the *Millennium Falcon*, an X-wing, a TIE fighter, or a Star Destroyer—that were so gloriously associated with this world, it felt criminal to not use them. When you look at what Ralph McQuarrie did, and certainly Joe Johnston and others, there was a kind of unbelievable simplicity. When you look at a triangular Star Destroyer or the sphere and two planes of a TIE fighter or the literal *X* of an X-wing, there was such a primary-color approach to some of these things, which were then rendered and executed in such incredible detail. The wear and tear and the sense of practicality to these fanciful designs were really inspiring. So we knew that going forward we needed to embrace these iconic pieces of the puzzle, and yet we needed to adjust them in ways that made them new again. Sometimes the feeling you wanted to [evoke] wouldn't be effective if [you were] literally re-creating it as it was. Some things needed to be embellished; you want to see some adjustments, some changes, some advances for things to be believable in a story taking place nearly forty years after the first movie. With [costume designer] Michael Kaplan, there was an enormous amount of work to be done on costumes for characters that no one had ever seen before. Of course, they all needed to be unique and stand out and be different from each other. The design of the movie—from locations to set design to props and wardrobe—all of it, even the casting of it, was about, "What feels right? What feels like it is the *Star Wars* movie that's relevant for now?"

AC: Were there any sets that made you particularly nervous, where you asked yourself, "Will this really work?"

Abrams: Probably because I was so obsessively critical of the process, I think every set had a little bit of that. I guess for me, the thing that was the most surprising was working on the set of the *Falcon*. Because it was a set that I knew so well as a fan and I'd seen some of my favorite scenes on that set, what I found myself feeling was that the scenes we were shooting needed to be as good as the set was. It wasn't so much that I was concerned that the set might or might not work, but the set itself challenged the scenes!

AC: When we spoke with Kathleen Kennedy, she mentioned that it was almost three years to the day since you and she sat down and talked about whether you would take on this project. What do you feel today that you didn't feel then?

Abrams: Gratitude for the work that everyone did on this movie. It is one thing to theorize and anticipate and hope for and expect a certain kind of commitment and passion from a cast and a crew, and it is quite another thing to get to know those people and watch them constantly exceed expectations. I feel more grateful to everyone, from Kathy Kennedy to the original cast, and I feel gratitude toward the film community in London. Given that the work that so many have done is so good, I'm actually—not theoretically, but actually—excited for people to see the movie. Maybe it's an obvious thing to say, but it's nice to have come through this and not just feel overwhelmed by it, beaten down by it, or exhausted by it. I'm a little bit of all those things, but I'm mostly excited for people to see the movie.

AC: The overriding theme of *Star Wars* is the balance between good and evil, light and dark. Lucas, in fact, once said, "Do unto others" is the philosophy that permeates his work. What are your thoughts on those ideas?

Abrams: The idea of good vs. evil, light vs. dark, is certainly the core of *Star Wars*. There's the temptation of power and greed—the Dark Side—and the sacrifice and nobility of fighting for justice, [which is] the light. These are the tenets of the *Star Wars* universe, and all the props and gizmos and spaceships are incredibly cool, but the core and heart of the story is family and which path you're going to take. The beauty of working on this movie was getting to play in this incredible sandbox that George Lucas created. Everyone who worked on this film approached it from a place of reverence, but everyone was also determined to do it proud and to tell that story of good vs. evil. The main characters of the film, we worked hard to make sure that the Dark Side gets its ass kicked!

J. J. Abrams: *The Force Awakens* Interview

Tara Salinas / 2015

From TrippinwithTara.com, December 18, 2015. Reprinted by permission.

Tara Salinas: Director, producer, writer, actor, and composer. Unlike the new faces of relatively unknown actors in *Star Wars: The Force Awakens*, J. J. Abrams's list of credits is long, being that he wrote and/or produced many feature films such as *Regarding Henry*, *Forever Young*, and *Armageddon*. He is also heavily credited for drama series he created or cocreated, including *Felicity* (cocreator), *Alias* (creator), *Lost* (cocreator), and *Fringe* (cocreator).

As far as a director, J. J. Abrams directed *Star Trek* and its sequel *Star Trek: Into Darkness*, *Mission: Impossible III*, and *Super 8*. Most importantly, he directed and cowrote *Star Wars: The Force Awakens*, the kick off film in the *Star Wars* sequel trilogy. The man is brilliant and is rounding up a week of incredible interviews and excitement around the release that has long been awaited.

You were just eleven when your love of *Star Wars* began. Did that influence the way that you approach producing this film?

J. J. Abrams: Of course it did because it was something that meant so much to me for so long. The thing is that it's because it's been ingrained in sort of all of our conscientiousness for so long that it's become a birthright to just know *Star Wars*. You're sort of born, you know what a light saber is, Darth Vader, you understand that. At three years old, kids talk about *Star Wars* in a way that is so eerie 'cause you think, "How could you possibly know so much?" Somehow they do, and even those kids who haven't played the games have seen the shows. I don't know how it is that they understand *Star Wars* immediately.

But my job wasn't to be a fan boy or an eleven-year-old kid. It was to be a nearly fifty-year-old movie director, so I tried to approach this thing from a point of view of obviously acknowledging how much I love what George Lucas created but understand that being a fan doesn't make the story work. Being a fan doesn't make the scene any good. Being a fan is great, but we all had to be storytellers and filmmakers.

I was surrounded by people like Lawrence Kasdan, who'd written, obviously, the original *Empire Strikes Back* and the *Return of the Jedi*, and actors who had been there from the beginning, all the way through visual effects and sound too—of course, John Williams, who—collaborating with him is like cheating 'cause he speaks to our soul with music in a way that I think is super-human. The whole process was really about trying to love it but also be hard on it so that the story meant something and was emotional and not just a fan film.

TS: It was reported that you had collaborated with Lin Manuel Miranda for the music, and I was wondering, how did that relationship come about.

JJA: Our seventeen- year-old son and I went to see *Hamilton*, which if you haven't seen it is one of the great experiences of all time, which cannot be oversold. You hear crazy hyperbolic language being used about it, and then you go to see it and it's better than anyone described it and gets better as it goes, which is impossible.

At intermission I was thinking, "It can't possibly continue at this level," and it just gets better. Then I was distracted at intermission by a tap on my shoulder, and I turned around. It was Lin Manuel Miranda, who normally stars in this thing he wrote the songs for, but this night it was his understudy. And he said, "Hi." I was like, "Oh, my God. Do you understand what you've done?" He's like "Yes." I was just essentially fawning over him, and he said in this jokey, off-hand way, "If you need music for the cantina I'm happy to do it." It was so weird because a couple weeks earlier, John Williams had said to me he really wanted to focus on the score. There's a lot of music in the movie.

He said this one scene in the film, which is, essentially—if we have a version of a kind of cantina scene, if, like, someone I work with said, "*Star Wars* is a Western, there's a sort of a saloon in every Western, and this was our saloon"—John said, "I'd rather not work on this music because I have so much other score to do, and this is really source music." I was like, "Alright." I thought, "Crap, what are we gonna do?" I started working on something as a sort of a hobbyist musician my-self, so I was working on a piece of music. Anyway, Miranda says this to me. I can't believe it, so I email Lin and I say, "Listen, I know you were joking, but the truth is we sort of have a need for some music in the scene, if you're serious." He emails back. He's like, "I'll drop everything." I'm like, "Oh, my God. You're kidding me," so we started collaborating on this music. We both use the same music software, we have Dropbox, and we would send files back and forth. We came up with this piece of music, actually two pieces of music, for this sequence and to get to work with him was preposterously fun.

I got to hang out with him subsequently, and if you haven't seen his appear-ance on Jimmy Fallon, it's one of the greatest things you've ever seen because it's freestyle rap, which is actually, truly, unprepared in any way, and staggering. He is amazing.

TS: Can you tell us about how it all started for Episode VII, who asked you to be involved, and how that felt for you to be asked?

JJA: Yes, it was Kathleen Kennedy, whom I've known for a long time, and she called and asked if I was interested in working on *Star Wars*. Of course, it was a very surreal question, and it was very flattering. My answer was, "No," partly because Katie, my wife, and I, had plans to take our kids away. I'd been working on a lot of back-to-back projects for a while partly because I'd worked on a number of sequels and it felt like enough is enough and partly because I care about *Star Wars* so much that the idea of taking it on felt like a kind of a thing that I couldn't imagine, and intimidating.

So I said, "No, thank you," and she said, "Can we get together?" I said, "Yes," and, when Kathy Kennedy and you get together, she'll convince you of whatever it is she wants you to do. She just was amazing and basically said this was going to be an opportunity to continue the story since *Return of the Jedi*. As we were talking, I realized this is thirty-some years after the fact; the main characters would have been born ten to fifteen years after that movie. They'd be looking back on what we know of the story that would be ancient history for kids who were nineteen, twenty years old. What do they know? What do they believe? What do they believe in? The idea of finding these young people who exist in a *Star Wars* universe was so compelling to me, and that feeling of rediscovering a world and a feeling that was so powerful for growing up was undeniable. After the meeting, I went downstairs and found Katie, my wife, and I just said, "I think I really want to do this." And she said, "Really." I said, "Yes." She said, "This is definitely a once in a lifetime opportunity; you really need to consider it if this is something you want to do." I did, and it wasn't easy for us, for our family, for my company, Bad Robot.

There were a lot of issues that came with it, and yet I knew that as challenging as it would be, if we could all get our sea legs and do it right, that it could be an extraordinary situation and an amazing experience in every category from prep and figuring out the story to writing the script with Lawrence Kasdan and designing the movie and shooting it and editing it and doing post and scoring it. Literally through the 3D pass, the reviews that we've had, and I'm not always the biggest 3D fan, but I will tell you there are things in this movie that I actually felt were shockingly better in 3D because there are literally shots that I couldn't believe I saw things in in 3D that I hadn't seen in 2D. It was so strange, and I know this might sound like I'm selling the 3D—and to anyone who doesn't really care, see it in 2D; don't see it in 3D. It's okay. I was amazed at how great that looked. Every stage has been as gratifying as it was challenging, and it's all because of the unparalleled and unbelievable work that everyone did at every turn. I'm very grateful.

TS: I have a question about the characters that are puppets, which is kind of a different thing for nowadays, to use actual puppets. Can you talk about your choice in that?

JJA: Yes. Well, I remember seeing *Star Wars* and *Empire* and *Jedi*, and, of course, that was before there was such a thing as a CG character. The use of puppetry was so brilliant, and it reminded me—this is so strange because when we were shooting the scene that I was referring to, the Mos Eisley Cantina, there were a number of creatures there, as well as other sequences, but a lot in that one scene. I remember looking around, and there were just puppeteers under every table and poking through things. There were just all these people; they were basically invisible, but they were performing these characters that Neal and his team created. I remember feeling like, "Oh, my God. It's like we're on the set of a Muppet movie." It was so cool, and I realized Frank Oz—and this Venn diagram of what Jim Henson and his workshop—did and what George Lucas did, not only to overlap obviously in Yoda, but that there was a kind of creative, home spun, do-it-yourself genius that was, when the Muppets were brought to life, of course, they were playing these sort of often plush, comedic characters.

George Lucas used the same technology to create what appeared to be living, breathing flesh and blood characters. It was so wonderful to have that, and as the shoot continued, the biggest advantage was in BB-8, who is our new droid, who in scenes with the other actors, Daisy and John and Harrison—this droid was alive, was expressive, was passionate, curious, helpful, afraid, daring.

He was literally on camera in scenes doing everything that you could have ever dreamed of. We could have worked with our extraordinary computer graphics department at ILM and made that work, but it never would have looked quite as good, quite as real. Daisy (Ridley), who is now starring in her first movie, she is fearless and sweet and vulnerable and tough and a revelation in this movie.

To have her interact with BB-8, performed by Brian and David—Brian always right there next to him, so off and on camera, David with the remote control off camera. We use CG for BB-8 not to bring BB-8 into the shot but to remove the puppeteers. We use CG quite a bit to actually get rid of legs poking out from the bottom of a creature—wires, rigs, arms, and stuff like that—but it was really an amazing thing to have all those creatures and BB-8, the most important one, live and present and in the frame and in the shot so that when there where CG creatures, when there were things that we couldn't do physically, there was a standard to match, which was actually captured on film.

At this time the PR rep from Disney lets us know "Last question," and to that J. J. responds, "We can do a couple more, right? Let's do, like, two more questions."

TS: I have one about BB-8. I wondered—everyone's fallen in love with BB-8 already, and so how did the idea come about? I know you worked with Sphero, but how did that all . . .

JJA: Well, Sphero actually came later. What happened was we were working on the story, trying to figure out. We knew we had a droid that was gonna be a critical piece of the puzzle, but we didn't know if he was going to be sort of bipedal like C-3PO or roll around like R2-D2 or some other thing. I just had this idea that if we had a sphere and then a semisphere on top, you could get quite a bit of expression without a face.

So I drew a sketch of BB-8, and I had the eye and little antenna and everything. It didn't have a color pattern—it didn't have all the critical details that Neal and his team brought in—but I sent that to Neal Scanlan, and he began to come up with designs that would sort of follow that. It was amazing how quickly it looked like it could work, and I didn't know if they would be able to create something that could be performed on camera, which I knew was going to be important. They did, and I will never forget the first day that we came to their offices to see BB-8 being performed after we'd agreed on design, et cetera, and scale and everything. We walked in, and Brian, the puppeteer, came out and wheeled out BB-8 on his rig. Literally, within seconds, Brian disappeared—he was right there—but it was like he wasn't there, and this thing was looking around curious. You could feel the soul because Brian was imbuing him with life. Daisy said at one point earlier today, "Every time we weren't shooting, we were on a break, and BB-8 was just sort of sitting there and not being performed, it was heartbreaking because he was this inert thing, and you were like, 'Where is he?' Then Brian would get him; you'd be like, 'There he is.'" It was this very odd and very important thing, but it was a result of Neil Scanlan and his amazing team.

TS: Being here to help relaunch this saga for a new generation of families, and you're kind of passing the torch to future directors that are going to be exploring this in different offshoots and what not, will you be able to really sit back and enjoy it as a fan now without thinking of what your creative stamp would be as the saga continues?

JJA: Well, I will say that I knew getting involved in this project that it was an honor to be asked, and I knew that my role would be as temporary guardian of this saga. I knew also as I was working on it that if the movie works, what a great time to step down. If the movie doesn't work, who wants me to work on the next one anyway? So it was win-win.

I'm really looking forward to telling original stories—I've been sort of wonderfully and happily sidetracked with the movies I've been working on—but I do look forward to working on something that doesn't need to have a number in the title. I cannot wait to see what the directors who are named and being discussed will do in this universe coming up because there's some really talented people that I know are doing extraordinary things. So it's very exciting, and to get to work with Larry Kasdan to begin what we knew was the start of a trilogy, was a rare thing in a movie, which is to start a story that you know needs to be satisfying, in and of itself, but also is the beginning of a larger tale. So that was really cool to get to do.

TS: How do you find the balance between the preservation of what *Star Wars* is and integrating the new technology and new things?

JJA: It's a great question. This whole process has been going backwards to go forwards; it's the next chapter in what happened in IV, V, and VI. This is VII. It needs to feel like the continuum, but the important thing was recognizing what are the tenants of *Star Wars* and the things that make *Star Wars* specifically *Star Wars* and not one of the many attempts to rip off what George Lucas created.

The beauty of what we had was we actually inherited *Star Wars*. We could actually put TIE fighters and lightsabers and Star Destroyers in our movie and it feel essential as opposed to derivative. But this was all about telling a new story, so the brilliant luck of having Lawrence Kasdan along for the ride is, he knew having written *Empire* and *Jedi*, having lived with it for decades, about that world and where it might have gone.

So discussions with him were informed discussions. The most important thing was always, Well, why are we doing this? What's the point of trying a new *Star Wars* story? What do we want people to feel? Who are the main characters? That was the most exciting part, finding this young woman, Rey, this character who from the beginning was a central role and character and voice in the story; to find this character Finn, who we started to fall in love with very early on; and to realize that their story of discovering what their role is in this universe, and not just any universe but the *Star Wars* universe, that was thrilling.

All of that was happening before we were even really talking about what the original characters were gonna do. That was why we started getting excited. We realized there was a story that was working, not because it was a nostalgic trip and that we were relying on things that came before, but because there was a pulse to the story now; they could use the fabric of what had come before to tell that story. In terms of technology we had at our disposal kind of everything, and it was great to be able to, like we're saying, use practical, tangible puppets where necessary, to use CG when required, when better.

Finally, you know, I think you'll see that BB-8 has a slightly better hologram that R2-D2 does. There are things that happen that you go, "Oh, I see how there have been advancements," but it feels—I think, in testament to the amazing work of the design team, it feels of the DNA of the movies we've seen before.

TS: So, I want to thank you for the diverse cast for a new generation. I love the idea that you've come up with the first female villain. So, how did that come about?

JJA: It was really important when we began working on this script that this movie feel and look a little bit more like the world than one might have thought. When I say, "one might have thought," I don't know who that one is, but I'm sure that person's out there because when people say, "Thank you for this," it sort of means that they haven't seen it like this before on some level. I know that looking at the story from the very beginning, Rey was— and she wasn't always named Rey—but Rey was always at the center of this story.

We knew Leia was going to be in the movie from the beginning, of course. This character of Maz Kanata that is played just beautifully by Lupita Nyong'o was always a character and somehow always named Maz Kanata, who was part of this world. Phasma came about because we were trying to figure out the look of the— of Kylo Ren and this amazing design was presented, and we just were floored. It was the coolest thing we'd ever seen.

We knew it didn't make sense for Kylo Ren. But it was really great, so we started coming up with this character that was inspired by this, that was the head of all the Stormtroopers, and working on that character. The idea, we knew we wanted to have female Stormtroopers—and there are in the movie—but we knew we wanted to have the head of the Stormtroopers be an important character. We thought, "Well, why not have her be female? Gwendoline Christie's name came up, and I was already a fan, but just thought, "Oh, my God. That would be unbelievable if that was possible."

Somehow she was available; our British casting director, Nina Gold, also cast *Game of Thrones*, and so luckily there was a connection there already. Gwendoline came in and is as lovely as you'd ever want someone to be and was such a *Star Wars* fan, and she got exactly what it needed to be instantly and was just an utter joy to work with. So we have good guys and bad guys who are not guys. We have female humans and nonhumans.

In casting Finn, for example, we had no idea what he looked like. We had no idea what Rey would look like. We just started casting knowing you needed to be inclusive. We ended up finding Daisy Ridley, who was like a prayer answered. We ended up finding, John Boyega, whose work I was an enormous fan of from *Attack the Block*; Oscar Isaac, who couldn't be better; Adam Driver, who was Kathy

Kennedy's idea, the only name ever mentioned for this part. We'd say, "Okay, so who should we cast for Kylo Ren?" She's like, "How about Adam Driver?" I'm grateful to Judd Apatow and Lena Dunham, who actually had to do a crazy, sort of sneaky, work to get him available to us because they had him as first position on their show, *Girls*, and contorted things somehow to allow him to be in this movie. So I'm enormously grateful to them.

Anyway, I will tell you that the experience of working on this movie really has been nothing short of shocking to me because it kept living up to its potential in a way that didn't really feel like it would. I kept waiting for the other shoe to drop—and it's never too late, I guess, for that to happen—but regardless of what the reception is or what the result of the movie is, I know for a fact that when you see the movie, you will be seeing truly extraordinary work by thousands of people. It is something I will be grateful for forever, and to you guys for being here today and staying so late, so thank you so much.

It was a very long day for us, and especially for J. J. Abrams. He gave us his time, answered all of our questions. When you have someone of that caliber that gives you their time, when they really didn't have to, it says a lot about their character.

It's hard to believe I am wrapping up my coverage of the #StarWarsEvent with this being my last post covering my interviews. It was truly one of the most memorable experiences I've had in all my Disney Entertainment adventures. I don't know how to stress how much I loved *Star Wars: The Force Awakens*. I appreciate all the thought and love that went into making Episode VII. J. J., Katherine, Daisy, John, Lupita, Oscar, and the rest of the team—Congratulations. I feel so honored to have had this opportunity to be part of something so huge!

J. J. Abrams Talks 10 *Cloverfield Lane*, the "Clover-Verse," *Cannibal Airlines*, and More

Peter Sciretta / 2016

From */Film*, March 10, 2016. Reprinted by permission.

J. J. Abrams is a busy man. Not only did he direct, produce, and cowrite *Star Wars: The Force Awakens,* but he still found some time left over in his day to produce a follow-up to Matt Reeves's POV monster movie *Cloverfield.*

Dan Trachtenberg's *10 Cloverfield Lane* might not be a sequel (although Abrams seems to suggest one could still happen one day), so how does it connect to the original *Cloverfield* movie? Will *God Particle* be the third film in the "Clover-verse"? And might *Cannibal Airlines* actually become a real movie? We also learn how Abrams found director Dan Trachtenberg, discuss the cleverly minimal marketing campaign, and get the details on Bear McCreary's masterful score. The best thing is this interview is entirely spoiler-free, so don't be afraid to start reading now.

Peter Sciretta: In what aspects is *10 Cloverfield Lane* a *Cloverfield* movie?
J. J. Abrams: Well, there are a number of connections, some obvious, some not, things that I want people to sort of find on their own. Some are thematic, some are genre. But what defines a *Cloverfield* movie is part of a kind of bigger idea we had. This is sort of part anthology and part a larger idea. The fun of having a movie that is connected to *Cloverfield*—but not a literal *Cloverfield 2,* which is of course what we would have called it had it been a literal sequel; it would have been a more obviously titled sequel—this is something that hopefully if we get a shot to continue this idea that we have, we can have a lot of fun with and come clearer to what constitutes a *Cloverfield* movie.

Peter: If this does as well as you hope it does, is *God Particle* the next one, or is *Cannibal Airlines* in the movie the next one?

J. J. Abrams: Well, that remains to be seen, but the *Cannibal Airlines* thing is a very funny little reference. It's sort of something that is part of another conceit, but we'll see if that comes to light. It'd be fun if it did.

Peter: I was kind of expecting it to show up in the A.R.G., like a fake trailer for it or something.

J. J. Abrams: [laughs.]

Peter: I feel like even though this film isn't shot in POV like *Cloverfield*, it feels— there's a lot of moments in it that you get the same POV feeling that *Cloverfield* had. Is that one of the connections? Is that something that you're gonna bring on, hopefully, to other movies?

J. J. Abrams: I think that because the premise of this movie is so strong, meaning it is so singular in point of view, I feel like one of the many cool things that Dan did was allow the audience to vicariously experience moment-to-moment what Michelle is going through and, partly, because Mary Elizabeth Winstead is so good. There's no strategy behind that other than I think Dan telling a story very well.

Peter: How did you find Dan because, I mean, this is a big movie to give to a first-time director?

J. J. Abrams: Well, Lindsey Weber, who produced *10 Cloverfield Lane* with me, knew Dan beforehand. When we were searching for the director, she brought him in. What I was mostly impressed by was the clarity and strength of his vision for how he would do this movie. He had a confidence that I think is apparent in the film, a strong sense of tension and focus, and he did this really beautiful work with the actors, with the camera, with modulation. I think that the tension of the movie—it's not just creepy and scary, but there's a great sense of tension to the movie that I think is really all about what Dan brought to it. So I would credit Lindsey for finding him and credit Dan for what the movie is.

Peter: During the making of this film, you were off filming your own . . . small indie movie; you were probably busy with that. How involved were you in this film?

J. J. Abrams: I was involved in the script stage. I was involved in what dailies were sent in, notes, or suggestions, or trying to help whenever I could be of help to Dan and Lindsey, who was on set all the time. In post, I was, like, more involved in helping wherever Dan needed it. But again, this was something that really was Dan's vision, and I was just trying to do what a producer does, which is help out.

Peter: What can you tell me about the music in this film because I loved the score?

J. J. Abrams: So do I; I'm so glad you said that. First of all, Bear McCreary, with whom I've never worked and that Dan had never worked—I think Bear did an extraordinary job. He brought to the movie something that Dan really wanted, which was a bit of a Bernard Herrmann feel but brought to the modern age. I think that there's a very sweet sort of sad but, ultimately, really beautiful theme for Michelle and a creepy theme for Howard, Goodman's character. He provided the movie with incredibly solid emotional foundation. For a movie that takes place a great deal in this bunker, I think he gives the movie a scope and a scale that is really important emotionally. I really can't say enough about working with him. He was a terrific collaborator, wonderful in meetings and open to adjustments. He brought a very strong point of view himself. I think his orchestrations were terrific. I just think he did a great job.

Peter: One other thing I wanted to ask you: it's amazing how you were able to keep a lot of the footage out of the marketing for *Force Awakens*. And I believe that helped the experience. I feel like this film, it's the same thing. You are not showing much. How does that work? Do you have a contract with the studios to have control over the marketing? It feels like a lot of other filmmakers and producers feel the same way you do but are unable to make it happen.

J. J. Abrams: I can only speak for our experience with Bad Robot and the marketing department, the films we worked on. What's been great is there's a relationship we have in the marketing departments that feel like it's about mutual understanding and respect and strategy. We get together very early on to discuss how we're gonna approach what I think it is. Obviously, it's a hugely important thing, how you announce and reveal and, hopefully, pique interest in a story. We made a very specific decision early on to not announce this movie a year in advance, six months in advance. We thought let's break the template and try something new in an age of people knowing most everything about every stage of the prep, production, post, and release of a movie—the fun of saying, "Here comes a movie. It will be in theaters in two months or three months," not give people much time to conclude, to pass judgment on a movie that they could already feel that they know everything about, but rather have some fun with a movie that I think is a fun movie worth having fun with and then surprise the audience.

Peter: Okay, I have one last question for you. *Cloverfield* felt like the beginning of a new thing . . . Is there anything you wish you could have done with the original *Cloverfield* but didn't have the chance at that time?

J. J. Abrams: Well, not really. That was Matt's movie—Matt Reeves— and, obviously, you'd have to ask him, but I think he did an incredible job telling a familiar story, a giant monster in the city, in a way that you've never seen before, in a way that was unique in its found-footage style, but also in its comedy. Given the budget of that movie, given the constraints of the style of camerawork, I think he told an incredible and wild story in a very unique way. What more could you ask for?

Peter: Yes, I think that has certainly resonated with a lot of people, and that's why everybody's looking for a sequel ever since.

J. J. Abrams: It would be fun to do a sequel, but we just want to make sure it's more than what people expect, that it's got something really worth people's time.

Peter: So a sequel isn't out of the question, eventually?

Publicist: Sorry, that's all we have time for.

Peter: Okay, no problem.

J. J. Abrams: I appreciate your questions though, man, and thank you for your time.

Peter: Thank you, J. J.

J. J. Abrams: No. Thank you.

J. J. Abrams Interview

Erik Nagel / 2017

From *It's Erik Nagel*, July 15, 2017. Transcribed and published by permission.

Erik Nagel: [I'm] here with J. J. Abrams. I'm so excited. I met you on another show that I used to work on, but this is the first time you and I are getting a chance to talk one-on-one—

J. J. Abrams: I'm thrilled to be here.

EN:—and I do appreciate your taking the time to do this. Let's get down to business, and then we can get all the fan questions and stuff out of the way. *The Play That Went Wrong*—amazing—

JJA: Oh, I'm so glad.

EN: The story I heard, and correct me if I'm wrong, is that this was some down time while you were shooting *Star Wars* over in England.

JJA: That's right.

EN: And you happened to see this play on the West End.

JJA: It was a weekend. I looked to see what was playing. There was a play called *The Play That Goes Wrong* and I thought, "That sounds interesting." I bought a ticket, went to go see it, and [I] hadn't laughed that hard since I could remember. The audience was going insane. I went to the producer and asked when it was going to Broadway, and he said, "Well, we're just getting it up and running here." I said if I could ever be of service and help to bring the thing to Broadway, I would love to. It was so funny and so irreverent and inventive and just a wonderful escape from whatever it is at the time. The stress of working on the *Star Wars* movie—anything to get me out of that head for a second was a helpful thing. It's been such fun to work with this incredible group of people.

EN: When I heard about you going backstage—I had to ask because we had the writers and the cast. When you do Broadway and the West End stuff, you get a lot of celebrities that do want to come and meet the cast because they appreciate the work that you've done and the art and the craft of everything. Sometimes, they all say, "Oh, if I can ever help you out, let me know." That's just a nice gesture, but it never really comes to fruition.

JJA: And that's how I meant it, and then they forced me to actually do something.

EN: So, I said, "When J. J. comes in and actually says this to you, what goes through your head?" "We thought it was very nice, but we didn't believe any of it." And then, all of a sudden, your people were calling and talking about "How do we make this happen? How do we bring it over here?" Then, all of a sudden, it started to come together. They said this is the first time they've ever seen that really, actually come together.

JJA: I will say that being welcomed backstage, getting to meet these people, they are such a great group. Then the cast that's on Broadway now is that original cast, and they are the creators of this thing; three of them are the writers but they all originated these roles. So, while they're there until September, this is the time to go see them, that original group. My interest in this thing was only sincere, and it was completely self-serving because I just thought it was so funny to get to be a part of that fully-formed, Olivier Award–winning comedy. It wasn't like it was in workshop; it was a finished thing. It was a completely selfish act, so there was nothing altruistic about my interest in that play.

EN: Real quick, just proof that I actually went and saw it.

JJA: Dear God, you're holding up a playbill. You're holding up a playbill.

EN: You're going to have to sign this, my friend.

JJA: I am not going to do it.

EN: I'm throwing it away. It's such a great thing that somebody in a position of power and influence that likes somebody's works says, "I would like to help you do what you do" and that it actually comes to fruition. Somebody actually is kind enough to go and say, "Look I have some influence. I want to get this done. I believe in your project, and here we go. We're about to do all this."

JJA: I hear you, and having been the recipient of that kind of kindness or interest in the past and getting to work with people that are simply inspiring, it's something that I'm grateful for. And I'm grateful to have the chance to do again.

EN: You've had a long career of writing, directing, producing, all these different things. One of the most recent things that I've really admired you for is you're go-ing in that Steven Spielberg route where you're presenting. Where you believe in another project and say, "This thing may not get done if I don't help it," or "I really like this idea, and it's not going to get through a lot of the red tape unless I throw my name on it." Are you looking to do more like that? In the nineties, he helped get animation and video games and all these other genres to where they are now because he took the time to present that.

JJA: It isn't a conscious idea to do that. Every project, every step of the way, there's a conscious decision to get involved in something that feels exciting, that I want to see. So, I'm sure that when Steven did, for example, *Animaniacs*, in the eighties that was the thing that was exciting to him. He obviously was a huge fan of *Looney Tunes*, of Chuck Jones, of that world, so getting involved in that was a passion for him. I know that when he did *Amazing Stories*, he loved those kinds of stories, and it was a passion for him. The movies he produced over the years, the stuff that Amblin did—I get why he was involved in those things. Something like *The Play That Goes Wrong* doesn't fall into any kind of category—it was simply a brilliant night at the theater, and I've never heard a crowd laugh that hard. My involvement in that was in no way a strategy, other than this is really funny, people will enjoy this, they won't forget it, and you can be ten years old; you can be ninety years old. I've seen this range—but ninety-one you can't go, [only] up until ninety. But it's amazing to see this comedy work. To have been at all a part of it, at all a help, is something that I feel lucky that I get to do as opposed to, like, I'm doing some kind of service. I'm the one who's selfish and benefitting from the involvement in this amazing group of people's work.

EN: I've talked to some people who are not on Broadway now but had done theater in college, or some sort of theater, and have seen this production. They said they take things that are just utter nightmares for those who act in plays and theater and made it part of the show—like, "If this happened, oh, my God, in front of the audience, what do you do?" That's now written into the performance. Every-thing, the stage collapsing, the lighting going out, somebody almost falling off the stage—all these things that are just nightmares for professionally trained actors, let's just take that and make it what we're purposefully going to do.

JJA: I remember when I first saw *The Play That Goes Wrong* and, somewhere in the second act, realizing that they had clearly gathered all of the worst-case-scenario things and it didn't feel like a list. They somehow found a way to incorporate these things: someone who forgets their lines all the time, an actor who says the line at the wrong place that creates this loop where you go back to the beginning of the sequence.

EN: Which, by the way, brilliant. That sequence, it's like, "How long are they going to keep going? Alright, it's funny; it's funny; it's getting very uncomfortable. Oh, my God, they've got to stop this. Oh, wait, now it's becoming funny again." And it goes in this loop, and it's still going.

JJA: It's exactly that. The things that they exploit in this are those unbearably painful mistakes that, even if you have nothing to do with theater, if you don't care or like theater, you can appreciate what it must be like. There's a sense of a kind of vicarious, cautionary tale. Oh, my God, it's like a nightmare; if I were on stage and that happened, what the hell would I do? What's incredible is seeing how much has to go right for everything to go wrong. The amount of precision and discipline and timing—

EN: It's all choreography.

JJA: But it's invisible. It almost looks sloppy and haphazard, and none of it is. They reminded me when I first saw them, a bit, of *Monty Python* in their irreverence. It just makes you appreciate when you see what they do, what they have to go through, even in rehearsals. It makes you appreciate the math and the mechanics of what looks like just pure silliness.

EN: The fact they've been doing this so long that it's just second nature to them, I guess if you didn't know something screwed up in the performance, you wouldn't know, as an audience member, because everything is meant to screw up in this thing. They know it, but they're not going to let you know it. The fact that they can just get out of bed, hop on stage, and run through everything flawlessly is amazing.

JJA: It's funny, the other night one of the actresses got sick during the performance, in the first act, and literally had to step out and the understudy had to step in for the second half. I don't know if the audience realized that wasn't part of the joke necessarily because everything is just constantly—

EN: "She just got knocked out; of course, the understudy is going to come in."

JJA: It's the perfect show for something to go wrong, but the dedication that these actors have, you're right, the fact that they can go in and do it that well. By the way, they rehearse every day. There's always something that they're working on even after years of doing the show; they're still fine-tuning things and perfecting.

EN: I told Henry Lewis, who is probably my favorite in that performance—and the weird thing is, too, that they're actors who are playing actors who are playing actors, so they have actor names but, in the play, they have different names. There's a whole tier of lunacy going on. One of the funniest moments in that whole performance was not something that was supposed to get a big laugh, but I caught it and I couldn't stop laughing. He was having a series of incidents on the second floor when the ceiling is caving in. He gets back out the door and makes a wrong turn, so while you're focusing on the stage, while all the other characters are talking, he falls through the window set and just goes, "Oh, no," and you just hear this big thud. I don't know why, of all the hilarious stuff in there, but that caught my eye. That is one of the funniest things because he just fell passed the window, "Oh, no." This wasn't supposed to happen.

JJA: There are so many things like that, and, having seen the play as many times as I have, there are still things that I pick up on. What you realize is there is the central focus of what the moment is, but if you're looking in the periphery, if you're watching—one of the gags of the show is that there is a guy named Trevor, who is the stage manager. You can watch him in his box, but you're usually not watching him until there are moments when you're supposed to. But if you happen to look up at him, he's as entertaining as what's going on the main stage. There are things to look at constantly that, for me, are wonderful little discoveries, but it all speaks to the amazing attention to detail and the way that these people have so precisely created, choreographed, directed, written, and performed this thing. Anyway, I can't stress enough, while the original cast from the UK are here, to go see them before they leave.

EN: Right, they're done in September, and they told me it's because of their visa restrictions, which is why they're done in September.

JJA: I hear that the new cast that is coming in is fantastic, but it's a chance to see the people who created this play.

EN: Right, and to really appreciate it for the guys who wrote it and brought this thing to life. One other thing on that and then we'll move on to some other stuff: get there early because the play has already started, and you don't even know it. There's stuff going on as people are funneling in to get to their seats, if they're out in the lobby area. There's stuff always going on, and at intermission—you think it's just a simple intermission, you go to the bar to get a drink or something, and there's people interacting there, too—the thing never stops until the very end.

JJA: By the way, one of my favorite things is in the preshow. It's a little thing and

I don't want to ruin it, but it's this little thing that happens that just kills me. It's something that is so subtle and small, but if you are there early enough and you happen to see it, it's like a microcosm of what the whole play is. It's a little thrown away gag that never comes back, but it just says to you in the audience, "We are so aware of what we're doing that we're going to do a fairly elaborate little thing as a throw away," and there's just something genius about that for me.

EN: Go to BroadwayGoesWrong.com for tickets. Again, see the original cast by September because that's when their visas are up and they're heading back over to the UK. Please, definitely check that out. You mentioned *Monty Python*; are you a big British comedy fan?

JJA: Yes, very much so. *Monty Python* specifically—growing up with their albums and loving them. In fact, it's funny that when I got older we would play some of their routines and albums for our kids, and I realized how many things that have always killed me I didn't even understand. As a kid, I was laughing at the rhythm of their comedy maybe—

EN: Like Spam?

JJA: Spam, sure. But they're all sorts of, like, specific references and things within scenes that I didn't even pick up on what they were referring to. I just knew it was funny. It's a very weird thing to realize, so many years later, just how brilliant they are, and I was getting them but on a more sophomoric level.

EN: I agree. As you get older and keep revisiting Monty Python's work, you start to learn more things that you didn't notice the last time you made a serious attempt at going through all their stuff. "Oh, I know what that means now. I know who this reference is about. I know that artwork that Terry Gilliam is using."

JJA: They did a show at the 02, a live show.

EN: I know. That was huge.

JJA: I got to see it. It was amazing.

EN: I got to watch it online.

JJA: It was just amazing to see them live doing it. "The Argument Clinic"—

EN: "The Argument Clinic," of course, a classic, but the over-the-top production from *The Meaning of Life* when they did "Every Sperm Is Sacred." Canons, Irish step dance, it just kept going, and Eric Idle is just like, "What else can we throw into this thing?"

JJA: Isn't it amazing?

EN: Then he comes out and takes the bow in front of everybody, which is what you don't do in theater. You're supposed to be in line with everyone taking the credit—he went right in front. I'm like, "Of course he did; this is perfect."
JJA: So good.

EN: Were you a fan of *Fry and Laurie*?
JJA: Yes, but I don't know their stuff as well. I have a lot of British friends who like to talk about them in this way like the early Dudley Moore–Peter Cook stuff—

EN: Rowan Atkinson—
JJA: Of course, it's amazing stuff, but I wasn't as well-versed. I can't quote them the way I can with *Python*.

EN: *Star Wars*, got to throw that in there, was it hard to walk away from that franchise, or do you feel that it's in good hands and you did the absolute best to get this new generation of the franchise going?
JJA: I could not feel luckier to have been involved in that. I love *Star Wars*. I was worried—my biggest, selfish concern was that after having been involved in it I wouldn't love it. The idea that it was somehow—ruin this thing that was so—

EN: You had been a fan for so long and now that you're in the grind maybe, "I don't like this anymore."
JJA: Yes, is it getting too close to the thing? I will say, it's different because of the experience. But I love it as much, and I'm incredibly grateful and nothing more. In terms of what comes next, I'm executive producer of VIII and IX. Rian [Johnson] has just done an extraordinary job. I can't wait to see what comes next.

EN: I didn't think about this, but I saw a lot on the internet about the title of the next movie, *The Last Jedi*, that maybe it was one particular person, like Rey or something like that. But Jedi is plural so it's the last Jedi, meaning the whole religion of the whole thing.
JJA: That's true.

EN: Is there anything to that?
JJA: There could be.

EN: Too direct, okay, I figured—just thought I'd throw it out there and see if anything would come from that. A lot of people are like, "It means this. It means this." If you look at it from a broader spectrum, it means a lot of things. So, the title can be misleading or could be dead on accurate. I guess you don't know until you see the movie.

JJA: There's no question that they didn't name the movie without a lot of consideration.

EN: Right.

JJA: So, clearly, it's meant to raise these kinds of questions. What are you pulling out of your bag? What is that?

EN: I wanted to ask you about this. I guess this was a character that was being developed but, I guess, was cut out of the movie. Constable Zuvio?

JJA: There he is. Black Series.

EN: What can you tell me about this because I know the product line is done way in advance, so they put it out but he wound up getting cut from the movie so he's not technically in the story.

JJA: The movie was originally called *Star Wars: Constable Zuvio*.

EN: It was five minutes.

JJA: Does anyone understand what that is? This was a character, and there are many of them, that was created to populate Jakku. It was really an amazing thing working with Neil Scanlon in the creature department, working with the production designers on the movie, working with the special effects–visual effects in creating the characters. There were so many different worlds and places—when you think about what had to be on Jakku to make you feel like, "Okay, that was a place that had a diverse enough group of species in characters," that you would feel like you'd get the vibe of it. Meanwhile we also had things like going to Maz Kanata's castle where you had to have a completely different and motley group of people. It had to feel like, maybe there's some overlap; this is a different place. So, this is one of the characters that we developed that was for Jakku that was just featured in it. There was no dialog for this particular character, but once we chose characters we love, we would talk about where they were from, what they might be, and it's the thing that I think, for me as a ten-year-old, I remember, made *Star Wars*, the very first one, so powerful—that you heard about things but you didn't necessarily see them or you got a glimpse of them but didn't necessarily understand all the details but you could feel that they were so deeply considered. Even though at the time, who knows exactly what George Lucas knew about the Clone Wars or what the Senate really looked like or who the Emperor might have been. These are things you didn't really see but are referenced. As a viewer, there's that feeling you have when you see Boba Fett for the first time—you don't really get to know much about that character unless you start reading expanded universe stuff. That character is one of the characters that we wanted to have in the movie. But, in truth, we had so many bigger concerns, and there were so many more important things that we were dealing with. So we have these characters, and we will bring them up if and when it feels right to. Captain Phasma is a character that we all just loved from the beginning—we loved the look, we loved the feel, we loved that she was female—

EN: Shiny.

JJA: Shiny, but, obviously, there wasn't an enormous amount of room for that character to do a lot, but part of the mission of *The Force Awakens* was to plant a bunch of seeds of things that in the moment we had ideas about and answers for but knew that they were potentially worthy of exploration and that character was just one of those.

EN: It's understandable that things get cut, either for time or things just don't work as the story evolves, but did you run into much interference for things you wanted to put in the movie but had to be taken out? Or was it, you know, what you're doing and go see what you can do with it?

JJA: Kathy Kennedy, Larry Kasdan, and I, at the very beginning, it was pretty clear that they were really open to what we wanted to do. The truth is that they've got a big job overseeing not just what the movies are but what will happen in all mediums and that toy line. That toy you just held up, they've got to be thinking about all of this stuff, and that's a big job—and really a good question for Kathy—but they were completely open to the story we wanted to tell. I know that, as it continues and Kathy's leading this charge, I'm sure she's juggling a whole bunch of things as it goes, but there's no one better qualified for that job than Kathy.

EN: One little sidebar about *Star Wars* and then I want to get into *Cloverfield*, if we could.

JJA: Sure.

EN: Are you aware in the original *Muppet Show*, there's a scene with Mark Hamill and Kermit the Frog, and they're singing "When You Wish Upon a Star"? It's amazing foreshadowing that all of those properties eventually become part of Disney way in the future.

JJA: That's really interesting. I didn't know that, but I'm sure I saw it because as you were saying it I was having this weird sense-memory of having seen it. But, if I have, it was probably when it first aired.

EN: No Easter egg, no one knew back then—it was just a bizarre coincidence. You just get chills seeing that.

JJA: Wouldn't it be weird if Winnie the Pooh was walking in the background.

EN: This was a long con; they had this planned forever.

JJA: That was where their strategy comes from: they just watch the *Muppet Show*, and they buy whatever's there.

EN: *Cloverfield.*

JJA: Yes.

EN: I'm a huge fan of the original, and I really adored the second one.

JJA: Oh, cool. Thank you.

EN: I had a question about the second one: it's one movie all the way up until, maybe, the last five minutes, and then it seems to turn into something completely different. Was that the original concept, or is that just pasting two ideas together?

JJA: The original idea was—

EN: Because John Goodman is terrifying in that movie.

JJA: I know. There's certainly a version in which that's all that movie ends up being, and I'm sure, for a lot of people, that probably is the better, smarter, faster movie. The idea was always to do a movie that was a science fiction movie that you're being told the whole time is a science fiction movie but that it doesn't become that 'til the very end. The idea was having this kind of crazy, compressed space that the main character's in for the whole movie—no flashbacks, no nothing. You're just in that space.

EN: It's a hostage movie.

JJA: It is and at the end of the movie, burst out and have it be insane, just madness. The idea that it was terrifying in there but infinitely safer than out here, that once she's out there the idea that by the end of it that whole experience that Michelle, the character, goes through in the movie is the thing that galvanizes her to not run away anymore. At the end of the movie the idea that she's driving towards the problem and that it's this crazy, terrifying, massive alien thing. It was meant to be a kind of origin story for the female character who has this on-going story, but it starts off in the most unlikely way.

EN: Any rumor to the first movie where TJ Miller's on the Brooklyn Bridge, he's got the camera, and he runs into another guy who is taping it. Was there any rumor that there was going to be another movie of the same scenario but from a different perspective?

JJA: Yes, that was something we talked about and thought it was funny.

EN: Because that's never been done. It's like you doing the same movie but from the other side of what was going on.

JJA: By the way, there are a couple bizarre little things that were planted in that film that were discussed as ideas that might literally be sequels. The issue with doing a literal sequel to that movie, and we discussed that quite a bit, was the idea that beyond it just being a kind of repetitive thing and doing something it's like a classic in an old-fashioned sequel, which is to say the same thing but different. It felt to us like there is a more interesting way of taking the spirit of what *Cloverfield* was, what it was born out of, which was this idea of doing a genre movie but in a slightly different way and telling a story that felt like this is a great date night, scary, bizarre, weird experience.

EN: It was like doing a *Godzilla* movie without using Godzilla.

JJA: Yes, have you ever seen a *Godzilla* [movie] specifically from the perspective of those people running in the streets? Usually, it's the military; usually, it's the scientists.

EN: And that overhead shot of him walking through the city—

JJA: Yes, and the only overhead shot you have in *Cloverfield* is when they're literally in the helicopter flying passed it and you see this thing wreaking havoc. That was the fun, the conceit of it, and Matt Reeves, who, by the way, did an extraordinary job on *War of the Planet of the Apes*, if you haven't seen it—Matt directed that movie with a kind of intimacy and specificity that makes it so special.

EN: Unfortunately, we've run out of time. Of course, I wanted to talk to you about *Westworld*, but congratulations. Twenty-two Emmy nominations for the series and it comes back in January 2018? Later?

JJA: We haven't made the announcement yet. We just started shooting.

EN: But it is next year, though?

JJA: Yes.

EN: Cool. By the way, music is so important, and sound is so important on that show. I love the player piano playing nineties alternative stuff and hard rock to set the scene. If you know the music cue is happening, you know something else is going to happen in the story. Brilliant.

JJA: I'm glad you liked it. That's Jonah Nolan and Lisa Joy, and they are just killing it.

EN: Final question: because you've done so many franchises like *Star Trek* and *Star Wars*, they all have collectible lines and figures and things like that. When's the J. J. figure coming out? When's the Funko Pop?
JJA: You know, there's such a huge demand.

EN: I want one. I would have had it here if that was the case.
JJA: Oh, my God. Well, I hope "never" is the answer.

EN: Of all your influence—you can make all these major projects happen with billions of dollars invested. You can't get a toy. You have not succeeded in this business.
JJA: There is no justice.

EN: J. J., thank you so much.
JJA: Thank you.

EN: I'd love to talk to you again next time you're around, hopefully, for *Westworld*, and congratulations.
JJA: Thank you so much.

Index

Abrams, Gerald, 12

Abrams, J. J.: on 3D, 126, 147, 157–58; on appeal of imagination and mystery, 32, 65, 105–6, 138, 143; on Apple products, 32, 34; on approaching sequels/reboots, 15, 19, 41, 48, 51–53, 59, 124, 126–27, 129, 160, 177; on Bad Robot, 89; on being a director, 4, 37, 54; on collaboration, 73–74, 139–41, 150, 152, 156; on creative problem solving, 34–35, 94–95; on family, 29, 39, 65, 82, 103, 157; on the influence of his grandfather, 30–31; on his childhood, 61, 81, 87–88, 100, 103, 115, 138; on his filmmaking approach, 48, 71, 86, 90–91, 96, 101–2, 151, 158, 174; on his inspirations, 12–13, 27–28, 32, 38, 62, 72, 74–75, 78, 88, 101, 103–14, 126, 135, 139; on his role as producer, 120, 134–35, 148, 164; on lens flares, 90; on making films as a child, ix, 4, 31, 39, 61–62, 76, 84, 93–94, 98, 101; on marketing his films, 77, 79–80, 84–85, 97, 109–10, 165; on mistakes, 10, 123, 147; on multitasking, 73, 142; on set, 8, 47; on spending time on the Paramount lot as a child, 12, 39, 103; on success, 29; on technology, 63–64; on visiting Universal Studios as a child, ix, 115

Works: *10 Cloverfield Lane*, 163–66, 176; *Alcatraz*, 81, 120, 122; *Alias*, 7, 10, 20, 22–23, 25, 27, 45, 63, 74, 111, 121, 138; *The Attic*, 94–95; *Believe*, 148; *Cannibal Airlines*, 163–64; *Cloverfield*, 40, 70, 135, 163, 177; *The Cloverfield Paradox* (formerly *God Particle*), 163; *Felicity*, 9, 18, 23, 27, 71, 74; *Flyby*, 6–7, 77, 97, 109; *Fringe*, 36–37, 40, 70, 73–75, 138; *High Voltage*, x; *Little Nothings*, 4; *Lost*, 8–13, 23, 30, 32, 34, 37–38, 40, 50, 62–63, 66, 74, 90–91, 101, 111, 120–21; *Mission: Impossible III*, 15–29, 34, 48, 57, 62–64, 70, 111, 150; *Mission: Impossible—Ghost Protocol*, 81, 123; *Nightbeast*, x; *Person of Interest*, 81, 120–22; *The Play That Went Wrong* (play), 167; *Regarding Henry*, 71, 100; *S.*, 131–44, 146; *Star Trek*, 37–39, 41–67, 70, 73–74, 97, 111, 129; *Star Trek: Into Darkness*, 81, 122, 124, 147; *Star Wars: The Force Awakens*, 130, 145–47, 150–62; *Star Wars: The Last Jedi*, 173; *Super 8*, 76–81, 87–90, 93, 95–99, 107–9, 112–16, 122; *Undercovers*, 73–74, 123; *Westworld* (TV), 177–78

Affleck, Casey, 20

Alien (1979), 9, 33

Aliens (1986), 25

Allen, Woody, 110